Concerning Laws, and Their Several Kinds in General

Concerning Laws, and Their Several Kinds in General

Richard Hooker

An Annotated Paraphrase
Edited, with an Introduction

by

Ret Miles

Pilos Press
Rogers, Arkansas, MMXXVI

Concerning Laws, and Their Several Kinds in General

An Annotated Paraphrase, Edited, with an Introduction

Pilos Press

Rogers, Arkansas

ISBN: 979-8-234-06749-4

Library of Congress Control Number: 2026932822

Cover design by Ret Miles

Cover portrait of Richard Hooker is a detail from an engraving by Wenceslas Hollar (1607–1677), part of the University of Toronto Wenceslaus Hollar Digital Collection. Scanned by the University of Toronto from the Thomas Fisher Rare Books Library.

This edition is a modern paraphrase, commentary, and compilation of Richard Hooker's *Of the Laws of Ecclesiastical Polity, Book I* (William Stansbye, London, 1622), first published in 1593.

First Edition

Printed in the United States of America

For my godson, Nick.

True law is right reason in agreement with nature, it is of universal application, unchanging and everlasting; it summons to duty by its commands, and averts from wrongdoing by its prohibitions. And it does not lay its commands or prohibitions upon good men in vain, though neither have any effect on the wicked. It is a sin to try to alter this law, nor is it allowable to attempt to repeal any part of it, and it is impossible to abolish it entirely. We cannot be freed from its obligations by senate or people, and we need not look outside ourselves for an expounder or interpreter of it. And there will not be different laws at Rome and at Athens, or different laws now and in the future, but one eternal and unchangeable law will be valid for all nations and all times, and there will be one master and ruler, that is, God, over us all, for he is the author of this law, its promulgator, and its enforcing judge. Whoever is disobedient is fleeing from himself and denying his human nature, and by reason of this very fact he will suffer the worst penalties, even if he escapes what is commonly considered punishment.

—MARCUS TULLIUS CICERO, *On the Republic*, in CICERO, *De Re Publica, De Legibus*, translated by Clinton Walker Keyes (William Heinemann, London, 1928)

Contents in This Book

Preface to This Edition

The Relevance of Richard Hooker's *Concerning Laws, and Their Several Kinds in General*

IN 1593 RICHARD HOOKER published the first four books of his magnum opus, *Of the Laws of Ecclesiastical Polity*[1] (originally spelled, *Of the Lawes of Ecclesiasticall Politie*) with a fifth book published in 1595. From a historical perspective, *Of the Laws of Ecclesiastical Polity* is considered to be the first major systematic *ecclesiastical* work originally written in English,[2] the first major *philosophical* work originally written in English, and the first major statement of the principles of the English constitution. From the perspective of the Church of England, *Of the Laws of Ecclesiastical Polity* provides a foundation for much of Anglican theology, as well as systematic justification for the Act of Supremacy, the law which vests the governorship of that Church in the English monarch—thus joining church and state—and in the episcopacy, the centralized, hierarchical government of the church by bishops instead of autonomous governance by pastor, other presbyters, or other local council of elders.

To argue against Presbyterians and Puritans who wanted to end the centralized governance by bishops and eliminate practices which seemed too Roman Catholic, Hooker systematically addressed and

---

[1] C. J. SISSON (Charles Jasper Sisson), *The Judicious Marriage of Mr. Hooker and the Birth of* The Laws of Ecclesiastical Polity (Cambridge University Press, Cambridge, 1940).

[2] Previously, English scholars wrote their major works in Latin.

countered their arguments.[3] To do so, he needed to discuss church laws and rules. And to do *that*, he first defined and explained what laws are, their nature, and their purpose in *Concerning Laws, and Their Several Kinds in General*, which is Book I of that larger work.

The relevance of this first book, beyond an importance to the Church of England, is that, while written at a time when the mediæval concept of natural law was under attack, it provides the most eloquent overview of natural law, and has directly or indirectly shaped the development of liberal democracies. It was written only fifteen years before the Dutch wonderkind lawyer, Hugo Grotius, first published *Mare Liberum* ("*The Free Sea*" or "*The Freedom of the Seas*", depending on the translation), the treatise which demonstrated the existence of natural *rights*, changing the liberal focus from natural *law*, and also directly or indirectly shaping the development of liberal democracies.

---

[3] C. S. Lewis said that this more-strategic approach "marks a revolution in the art of controversy", as cited in W. BRADFORD LITTLEJOHN, "The Founders' Founder", *The University Bookman*, April 21, 2014 (The Russell Kirk Center, Mecosta, Michigan, 2014), which, in turn, was quoting from the following:

> [T]he *Polity* marks a revolution in the art of controversy. Hitherto, in England, that art had involved only tactics, Hooker added strategy. Long before the close fighting in Book III begins, the puritan position has been rendered desperate by the great flanking movements in Books I and II. Hooker has already asked and answered questions which Cartwright and Travers had never considered and which are fatal to their narrow scripturalism. He has also provided a model for all who in any age have to answer similar ready-made recipes for setting the world right in five weeks. (Travers is dead, the type is perennial.) …

Walter Travers' attitude toward anything Roman Catholic was one of vehement, uncompromising hostility, and referred to that church as the "Seat of the antichrist". Continuing with the quote:

> … And all this, though excellent strategy, never strikes us as merely strategical. Truths unfold themselves, quietly and in due order, as if Hooker were developing—nay, we are sure that he is developing—his own philosophy for its own sake, because 'the mind of man' is 'by nature speculative and delighted with contemplation…for mere knowledge and understanding's sake' (i vm 5). Thus the refutation of the enemy comes in the end to seem a very small thing, a by-product. There had been nothing like this in English polemics before.
>
> — C. S. LEWIS (CLIVE STAPLES LEWIS), *English Literature in the Sixteenth Century, Excluding Drama* (The Completion of The Clark Lectures, Trinity College, Cambridge, 1944) (Clarendon Press, Oxford, England, 1954), Book III ("Golden"), Chapter II ("Prose in the 'Golden' Period"), part III, page 459.

One of the later thought leaders influenced by both Hooker and Grotius was John Locke, whose *Two Treatises of Government* synthesized Hooker's focus on natural law with Grotius' focus on natural rights. While Hooker provided the idea that reason discovers an objective, divine law serving as a moral compass toward our duties, Grotius provided the idea of the legal machinery of rights and property. Locke argued that we possess natural *rights* so that we may fulfill the duties of natural *law*. All three of these men greatly influenced the founding fathers of the United States of America.[4] Not only has Hooker's *Concerning Laws, and Their Several Kinds in General* influenced liberal democracies, it has special importance for the development of the United States of America, as it is the only nation to ever have been founded upon a philosophy. Hooker's first book is one of the sources of that philosophy, too-often overlooked in these times.

Later, during the Revolutionary Era, Edmund Burke was profoundly influenced by Hooker. In English-speaking countries, Hooker, through Locke, has influenced generations of classical liberals, and, through Burke, Hooker has influenced generations of conservatives.

In the period after World War II, American political conservatism was shaped by writers such as the political philosopher, historian, and critic, Russell Kirk, who in turn was influenced by Richard Hooker, Edmund Burke, Orestes Brownson, and Herbert Butterfield.[5]

The Reason for This Paraphrase

It is tempting to think of the King James Authorized Version of the Bible (KJV) as being representative of the English language of Hooker's era. Published in 1611, the KJV was written only a few years after Richard Hooker's death, except for portions written by William

[4] Despite the influence of Hooker's book, which was written, in part, to help justify the English monarch's governorship of the Church of England, the United States is a society with a strong tradition of a separation of church and state, a tradition in many, modern, liberal democracies.

[5] Michael Federici, "Reassessing Russell Kirk: Three Critical Views", *The Imaginative Conservative*, April 27, 2014 (The Free Enterprise Institute, Houston, 2008).

Tyndale well before Hooker was born. However, the translators of the KJV intentionally used language which was already considered archaic in an effort to give the translation more grandeur.[6] That being said, it should also be noted that most of that archaic language is relatively easy for an English reader to understand.

While the English of Richard Hooker's time had some differences with the English of our time, when printed with a modern typeface the English of the late Sixteenth Century is mostly comprehensible to a modern reader, especially if the reader has experience reading the KJV or the works of Shakespeare. Even so, when not writing sermons Hooker wrote long, complicated sentences for elite scholars. His text is notoriously dense, convoluted, and, despite its elegance, challenging for most readers today, with seemingly endless paragraphs.

In this edition an effort has been made to transpose Book I to more current English spelling and usage, and to paraphrase when that would be helpful, with Greek quotes rendered in English as translated by Hooker, also somewhat transposed or paraphrased. It is hoped that this, along with notes and an introduction providing background and insights, as well as other aids, will help make this influential book more accessible to general readers, and even helpful for more specialized readers.

A final observation: this edition's title for Book I, *Concerning Laws, and Their Several Kinds in General*, is a title sometimes used by scholars, but it is not a title given by Hooker himself. His original title was simply, *Book I.*

RET MILES
February, 2026

[6] Ironically, the King James Authorized Version, along with the works of Shakespeare, helped mold English as it is spoken and written, today (less some of the archaic language, of course), including during the expansion of the American frontier.

EDITOR'S INTRODUCTION

THE EARLY PROTESTANT CHURCH IN ENGLAND

LESS THAN HALF a century after Columbus first voyaged to the New World the English Parliament passed the 1534 Act of Supremacy, separating the English church from the Roman Catholic church. This was done in part to facilitate the divorce of the English king, Henry VIII, from a wife who was not giving birth to a male heir.[7] Despite the schism, the theology, liturgy, and practices of the English church differed little from the Roman Catholic Church. However, during the reign of Henry's

---

[7] Henry had received permission from the Pope to marry his deceased brother's widow, Catharine of Aragon; but, after no surviving son was produced by this union, Henry was convinced that they were being punished for incest, since marriage to a brother's widow is Biblically forbidden:

> He that weddith the wijf of his brother, doith an vnleueful thing; he schewide the filthe of his brother, he schal be without fre children. ["He that weds the wife of his brother, does an unlawful thing; he has shown the filth of his brother, he shall be without free children."]
>
> —*Leviticus* 20:21 (Wycliffe Bible). (Wycliffe followed a literal reading of the Latin text from which he was translating, with the Latin, "liberis", meaning, "free ones", referring to children who are not slaves. In context, it means, "legitimate children", or simply, "children".)

However, the Pope refused to annul the marriage. In part because of Henry's concern that he was being punished by God, as foretold in the Bible, and in part because of his infatuation with the woman who was to become his next wife, Anne Boleyn, Parliament gave English courts independence from Papal influence, and Henry was granted an annulment under English law. His new marriage to Anne was declared valid by the Archbishop of Canterbury, Thomas Cranmer, and in response the Pope excommunicated Henry and Cranmer. These and other actions, followed by the Act of Supremacy, split the English church from the Roman Catholic church.

son, Edward VI, the English church adopted a Reformed Protestant theology—more closely aligned with the teachings of Martin Luther in German-speaking regions and John Calvin in French-speaking regions—and Parliament passed the 1549 Act of Uniformity requiring the *Book of Common Prayer* to be used throughout England as the only authorized form of worship, and establishing the precedent of Parliament authorizing doctrine and liturgy for the English church instead of the monarch. Roman Catholics opposed the *Book of Common Prayer* while some Reformed Christians opposed it as being too Roman Catholic. The resulting tensions were high, and in 1549 over 5,500 people died in the Prayer Book Rebellion in Devon and Cornwall.

After the death of Edward, his Protestant first cousin, once removed, Lady Jane Grey, was Queen for nine days before she was deposed by Edward's Roman Catholic half-sister, Mary I. Mary spent her five-year reign attempting to reverse the Protestant Reformation in England, often brutally, for which later commentators named her, "Bloody Mary". Mary's harsh attempts to stop Protestantism ended with her death from influenza in 1558, when Edward's and Mary's half-sister, Elizabeth I, succeeded as monarch. Parliament passed the 1558 Act of Supremacy establishing an English Protestant church, with the monarch as supreme governor, and separate from the Roman Catholic church. This reestablished church became the Church of England.

THE ELIZABETHAN SETTLEMENT

The 1558 Act of Supremacy was the first of the laws which are collectively referred to as the "Elizabethan Settlement". Parliament also passed the 1558 Act of Uniformity, re-introducing the *Book of Common Prayer*, another key part of the Elizabethan Settlement, as well as compromises between different factions. This was accompanied in 1559 by fifty-seven Royal Injunctions which instructed how the settlement should be implemented, such as requiring preachers to be licensed and banning certain Catholic practices like pilgrimages. In 1571 the English Protestant bishops adopted the *Thirty-Nine Articles* stating the beliefs of the English church, and a *Book of Homilies* was issued detailing the church's reformed theology. These are also considered to be part of the Elizabethan Settlement. The settlement brought stability to the kingdom, averting a civil war for the time being by being a compromise via media.[8] Still, Roman Catholics opposed the settlement as it made some of their practices illegal. The Pope excommunicated Elizabeth.

Puritans and other radical Protestants also opposed the settlement, but they did so because they saw the settlement as still too Roman Catholic.[9] In 1572 Puritans submitted a manifesto, *An admonition to the Parliament,*[10] demanding that Elizabeth restore the "purity" of New Testament worship in the Church of England and eliminate remaining Roman Catholic practices from the Church of England. The "admonition" advocated greater direct reliance on the authority of the Scriptures to adopt church oversight by ministers and elders instead of a hierarchy of bishops. Elizabeth opposed this document. Despite opposition from the extremes, the Settlement ensured that the English church survived.

Finally, it should be noted that Puritans wanted civil laws and government to be based upon the laws of the Bible. Some Twentieth-Century historians, as well as C. S. Lewis, called this system a *bibliocracy*, and people who advocate or participate in that, *bibliocrats*.

RICHARD HOOKER'S LIFE

Influential English scholar, teacher, priest, theologian, and philosopher, Richard Hooker (1554–1600), sometimes called, "the judicious Hooker", was born in the Spring of 1554 in Heavitree, a village then just outside the city walls of Exeter in the English county of Devon, to a good family of moderate means. From 1562 to 1569 he attended Exeter Grammar School. In 1568 he enrolled in the Corpus Christi College at Oxford University as a *commoner* under the patronage of Bishop John Jewel, where he was a student and then also a tutor. In

---

[8] i.e., "middle way".

[9] As trivial as this seems, a major bone of contention was the matter of priestly vestments.

[10] So assured of their rightness, the Puritans admonished Parliament, not petitioned.

1573 he was elevated to a *scholar* of the college foundation.[11] In 1574 he earned his B.A. and his M.A. in 1577, becoming a *fellow*[12] in the same year and deputy professor of Hebrew in 1579. During the period from 1579 to 1581 he was ordained as a *deacon* in the Church of England and then as a *priest.*[13]

---

[11] The college *foundation* was established by the *founder* of the college, the Bishop of Winchester, Richard Foxe, and was an endowment to provide funding for a core body of students, scholars, fellows, and priests, typically covering tuition, lodging, and meals.

[12] A *fellow* was, and in many cases still is, a member of the teaching and self-governing body of a college, responsible for managing the affairs of the college and upholding its statutes.

[13] There were three ranks in the Church of England clerical hierarchy. Ordination into these was sequential, requiring the lower orders before the higher.

deacon: a cleric who assisted the priest during a service, read the Gospel, and could baptize in an emergency, but was not permitted to consecrate the Eucharist (Communion) or pronounce the absolution of sins. This was often a probationary step lasting one year before being ordained as a priest.

priest: a cleric who had the authority to celebrate the Eucharist, pronounce absolution, and preach. Also called a *presbyter*, although this terminology was controversial in Hooker's time. Both words, "priest" and "presbyter", are derived from the Ancient Greek adjective, πρεσβύτερος ("prezbýteros"), meaning, "older", "elder", or "very old or aged", and derived from the adjective, πρέσβυς ("prézbys"), meaning, "elderly" or "aged". Puritans disliked the word, "priest", because it reminded them of clerics who performed ritual sacrifices, and so they preferred, "presbyter", an "elder" who teaches and shepherds a church congregation. Hooker defended the use of the word, "priest".

bishop: the highest order, a bishop was a chief pastor who oversaw a *diocese*, a geographic region of several local church parishes. Only a bishop could ordain new deacons and priests and perform confirmations.

An *archbishop* was a bishop with authority over a *province*, a group of dioceses, and considered a "first among equals" in relation to other bishops. In the Church of England there were only two archbishops: the Archbishop of Canterbury and the Archbishop of York.

A priest would usually be appointed to a parish *living*, which would be one of the following parochial *offices* (i.e., duties).

rector: a priest who was the governor of the property of a parish, and who received all tithes paid by parishioners (usually 10% of what their farms produced). This was typically a better paid position. Tithes consisted of *great tithes*, paid from the proceeds of major crops like wheat and barley (called, *corn*), and *small tithes*, paid from the proceeds of livestock, eggs, and garden produce. The *parish* was the fundamental unit of church and local governance, an area served by a local church where all inhabitants were expected to attend services (enforced with fines specified by the Elizabethan Settlement).

In 1581 Hooker regularly preached outdoor sermons at a prestigious public venue, Paul's Cross, London, with the sermons typically printed later for distribution.[14] From 1584 to 1585 Hooker was *rector* at St. Mary's Church in Drayton Beauchamp, Buckinghamshire (the first rector after an extensive rebuilding of the church), but likely did not live in the parish. In 1585 Elizabeth I appointed him *master*[15] of Temple Church in London. On February 13th, in 1588, he married Ioan[16] Churchman, the daughter of a wealthy merchant. From 1591 to 1595 Hooker was subdean of Salisbury Cathedral and rector at a small church in Boscombe, in Wiltshire, and *prebendary*[17] of Netheravon, Wiltshire. Finally, on November 3, 1595 he was appointed by Elizabeth I as *vicar* of St. Mary's church in Bishopsbourne, Kent, where he served until his death, there, in 1600 (from complications of a cold).

---

vicar: a priest receiving only the small tithes and a stipend, while great tithes went to a monastery, college, or layman. The rectorship was technically held by that monastery, college, or layman. In terms of spiritual duties, a vicar and rector were equal, with the differences being primarily financial and historical.

canon: a member of a *chapter*, a governing body of a cathedral or collegiate church, who helped administer the cathedral's or college's estates and finances, and was obliged to attend morning and evening prayer services. This was a prestigious office, which often came with a house and a steady income.

master: the head of a foundation. The duties varied. A master was also the term for any clergyman who had earned an M.A. degree. Having an M.A., Hooker would have been addressed as, "*Master* Hooker", while a priest without an M.A. would be called, "*Sir*".

[14] Paul's Cross was an outdoor pulpit in the churchyard of Saint Paul's Cathedral, London. The free-standing, eight-sided structure was gazebo-like, with an lead-covered ogee dome roof upon which was set a large finial in the shape of the cross. This functioned as a *preaching cross*, an outdoor, standing cross where sermons are given.

(An *ogee dome roof* is S-shaped—convex near the bottom and edge of the roof, and concave near the top—culminating in a point in the center. Although not continuously rounded or having any symbolic function, an ogee dome is otherwise similar to the onion-shaped domes associated with Russian Orthodox churches.)

[15] i.e., senior pastor.

[16] An old spelling of, "Joan".

[17] In Hooker's time, a *prebendary* was a clergyman in the Church of England who served in absentia as an administrator of a cathedral or large collegiate church while serving as priest elsewhere, and who received an income from the cathedral or church's properties and estates.

EVENTS LEADING TO HOOKER WRITING *OF THE LAWS OF ECCLESIASTICAL POLITY*

As a notable preacher and lecturer, Hooker's controversial 1581 Paul's Cross sermons challenged the Puritans' strict, Calvinist views on predestination, and thrust him into the debate between the mainstream of the Church of England and the Puritans, those who wanted to purify the Church of England of all Roman Catholic liturgy and practices and eliminate the oversight and administration of churches by bishops. As master of the Temple Church[18] he was brought even more attention by another controversial sermon:

> In 1585 Richard Hooker, then newly appointed Master of the Temple, had seemed to the puritans to confirm their darkest suspicions by his sermon, *Of Justification,* in which he said of our popish ancestors, "God, I doubt not, was merciful to save thousands of them." He had bidden his hearers, "Beware lest we make too many ways of denying Christ". As if this were not scandal enough, he had gone on to say that even a contemporary Papist, "yea, a cardinal or pope", truly penitent, and erroneous only on the doctrine of "merit", will not be rejected by "a merciful God ready to make the best of that little which we hold well"...
>
> — C. S. LEWIS (CLIVE STAPLES LEWIS), *English Literature in the Sixteenth Century, Excluding Drama* (Clarendon Press, Oxford, England, 1954), Book III, "Golden", Chapter II, "Prose in the 'Golden' Period", part III, page 451

This sermon, *A Learned Discourse of Justification,* was part of the famous "Battle of the Pulpit". Over a series of Sundays, from 1585 to 1586, Hooker preached in the morning, representing the established Church of England. His sister's husband's brother, Walter Travers, the *reader*[19] at the church, preached a strictly Calvinist or Puritan sermon in the afternoon, often specifically arguing positions opposed to what

[18] The Temple Church served and serves the Inner Temple and Middle Temple, two of London's Inns of Court (collegial affiliations for lawyers). The congregation consisted of highly educated lawyers, judges, and politicians—an important and attentive audience.

[19] The *reader* was responsible for afternoon sermons.

Hooker had preached that morning, despite that the two men were personally on good terms and respected each other. They disagreed, of course, on the question as to whether church polity[20] should be the *presbyterian* model—with presbyters instead of priests, and more independence for local congregations—or the *episcopal* model—with bishops and a more-centralized church government.

The more fractious disagreement was over the doctrine of justification, the subject of Hooker's most famous sermon. He argued that, although the Roman Catholic church was in error, it was still part of the true Church. Travers attacked this as heresy and argued that, because Rome falsely taught that justification is accomplished by works plus faith, Roman Catholics did not have a "saving faith" and could not, therefore, be truly saved. For Travers, Hooker's moderation betrayed the Protestant Reformation.

After the battle of sermons had continued several Sundays, the Archbishop of Canterbury forbade Travers to preach. Travers then continued to debate in writing, and appealed to Queen Elizabeth's Privy Council.[21]

WRITING AND PUBLISHING *OF THE LAWS OF ECCLESIASTICAL POLITY*

Hooker decided to write a thorough defense of his position. Realizing that a simple sermon would not be enough, in 1591 Hooker resigned his position at the Temple Church in order to focus on his writing. He was made rector of a small country church in the village of Boscombe, Wiltshire, serving from 1591 to 1595, although he lived mainly in London. He also spent time in Salisbury, Wiltshire, where he was *subdean*[22] of Salisbury Cathedral and utilized the cathedral's library. The income from his position as rector supported him while writing.

The controversies which motivated Hooker to write *Of the Laws of Ecclesiastical Polity* were not between Reformed theology and

[20] While the word, *polity*, can refer to an organized, governed society, in this case it refers to the governance of a society.

[21] i.e., her advisers.

[22] i.e., an assistant to the dean of a large cathedral

Arminian theology. Arminius[23] was developing his ideas around the time of Hooker's death, and the *Remonstrance* of Dutch Arminians was not even issued until a year after Arminius' death, which was ten years after Hooker's death. Instead, the controversies were intramural, between factions of the Reformed Protestants. Some Reformed Protestants, the Puritans,[24] wanted to cleanse the church of Roman Catholic practices. To them, the Protestant Reformation had not gone far enough. More moderate or conservative Reformed Protestants, such as Hooker, opposed what they saw as the more extreme agenda and doctrine of the Puritans.

In 1593 John Windet published a volume with Books I–IV of Hooker's monumental critique of some key Puritan principles, *Of the Laws of Ecclesiastical Polity*, with the title page stating that the complete work would be eight books. In 1597 Windet published Hooker's much longer Book V. Hooker was working on the remaining books when he died.

After his death in 1600, Hooker's draft manuscripts were entrusted to his friends, such as Bishop Lancelot Andrewes, and those papers were eventually acquired by Bishop James Ussher, a renowned collector of books, manuscripts, and documents. In 1604, Windet published a second edition of Books I–IV, containing a new preface,

---

[23] Jakob Hermanszoon (Dutch for "Jacob, Herman's son") or Jacobus Arminius (Latinized)—also known as Jakob Herman, and in England known as Jacob Arminius or James Arminius—was a Dutch Reformed minister who from 1603 was professor in theology at the University of Leiden. He came to disagree with the principle of predestination associated with Calvinism, and, although the concepts he argued predated him, especially with Anabaptists, his name became associated with Arminianism. Down through the years, Arminianism has influenced Anabaptists, Free Will Baptists, Mennonites, Amish, Methodists, Nazarenes, Pentecostals, Seventh-day Adventists, and the Salvation Army. But, although Anabaptists and even non-Calvinist Puritans existed during Hooker's time, the main controversies Hooker addressed in *Of the Laws of Ecclesiastical Polity* dealt with church practices and the authority of bishops. Tensions between Calvinism and Arminianism came after Hooker's death.

[24] Puritans were not a monolithic movement. Instead, there were English church Puritans, presbyterian Puritans, congregationalist Puritans, and Separatists who wanted to establish a new polity. (Of this last group, some, known today as the Pilgrim Fathers, migrated to the Americas several years after Hooker's death and founded Plymouth Colony.) All were part of the Protestant Reformation, as were those Episcopalians, Presbyterians, and Congregationalists who were not Puritans. Eventually, some Puritans held Arminian beliefs.

"To the Reader", by John Spenser (who would later serve as president of Corpus Christi College). In his preface, Spenser stated that "some evil disposed minds" had taken "the perfect copies of [Hooker's] three last books", leaving only "unperfect and mangled draughts".[25]

In 1611, well after Hooker's death, and in 1617, 1622, and 1632, William Stansbye, the prolific printer and heir of his former master, John Windet, was the first to publish an edition of the first five books of *Polity* as a single-volume edition, with a title page engraving by William Hole. The remaining three books were too controversial to publish at that time. In 1618, Stansbye's 1617 edition was combined with minor tracts and sermons by Hooker, and printed for bookseller, Henri Featherstone.

In 1638 or 1639, Richard Bishop, who had purchased Stansbye's entire printing business, published a single-volume edition of *Polity*, along with tracts and sermons by Hooker. This was the seventh edition of Books I–IV, the sixth edition of Book V, and the second edition of the overall collection.

From 1639 to 1653 the tensions between the Puritan Protestants, other Protestants, and Roman Catholics led to the Wars of the Three Kingdoms which were fought between and within England, Scotland, and Ireland. These conflicts included the Bishops' Wars, the English Civil Wars, the Irish Confederate Wars, and the Anglo-Scottish War. In 1649 King Charles I was executed, and from 1649 to 1653 the Kingdom of England was replaced by the Commonwealth of England. From 1653 to 1660 it was the Commonwealth of England, Scotland, and Ireland. During the years of the Commonwealth strict adherence to Puritan laws was required and the episcopacy was eliminated for the Church of England.

Puritans valued scholarship and Biblical knowledge, including that of the respected intellectual, Bishop Ussher. Therefore, in 1657, after Bishop Ussher's death the year before, his collection was bought by the military council under Henry Cromwell, son of Oliver Cromwell and

---

[25] i.e., drafts. In Spenser's preface, "To the Reader", the phrase, "perfect copies", means the finalized manuscript, ready for the printer, without any further editing remaining to be done. The phrase, "unperfect and mangled draughts", refers to rough drafts, notes, and fragments left behind, and not finalized for publication. Spenser was saying that the last three books had been stolen.

commander of the New Model Army,[26] and gifted to Trinity College in Dublin in order to keep Ussher's collection from being dispersed by foreign buyers, and to strengthen the prestige of the Protestant school. Among the papers were drafts of Books VII and VIII of Richard Hooker's *Of the Laws of Ecclesiastical Polity* and his notes for Book VI. The purchase was made by the army instead of the government because it was more feasible after the dissolution of Parliament. The New Model Army in Ireland had financial means and autonomy due to its collection of local taxes and confiscation of royalist and Roman Catholic lands, while the English government was short on funds. Additionally, some of Hooker's papers, the Fairhurst Papers, were in the safekeeping of John Selden during the English Civil War.

The eventual discovery of all of these documents enabled future, more-authoritative editions of the last three books of *Polity* to be edited and published. Although the manuscripts of Books VII and VIII were essentially complete, with only minor editing remaining to be done, the manuscript of Book VI was incomplete.

All of this resulted in the late publication, by Richard Bishop, of Books VI and VIII in 1648, long after Hooker's death, with Book VI being carefully reconstructed. (It was still too risky to publish Book VII, which contained his controversial stand on the authority of the bishops.) The 1648 printing was controversial because of what was said by John Spenser in his earlier preface.

In 1660 Charles II was installed as King, restoring the monarchy and making a defense of the bishops' hierarchy more acceptable.[27] So, in 1662, the first edition including all eight books of Richard Hooker's *Of the Laws of Ecclesiastical Polity* was published by Andrew Crook. It was "unsatisfactory to high-flying episcopalians",[28] and included an incomplete and poorly researched biography of Hooker by Bishop John

---

26 Puritan military forces in Ireland.

27 The English monarch was and is the head of the Church of England.

28 C. S. LEWIS (CLIVE STAPLES LEWIS), *English Literature in the Sixteenth Century, Excluding Drama* (Clarendon Press, Oxford, England, 1954), Book III ("Golden"), Chapter II ("Prose in the 'Golden' Period"), part III, page 452.

Gauden, in which Hooker's character and activities were depicted as essentially in line with moderate Puritanism. In 1666 a revised edition was published by Crook, replacing the biography by Bishop Gauden with Izaak Walton's somewhat less unreliable 1665 biography of *The Life of Mr. Richard Hooker*, in which Walton discredited the last three books as not being genuinely Hooker's. Despite the likely exaggerations of Hooker's marital difficulties by Walton, who could be a gossip, this biography was the standard biography of Richard Hooker until reassessments of Walton's biography of Hooker began with C. J. Sisson's 1938 Sandars Lectures in Bibliography, given at Cambridge University, followed by the publication of C. J. SISSON, *The Judicious Marriage of Mr. Hooker, and the Birth of* The Laws of Ecclesiastical Polity (The University Press, Cambridge, England, 1940).

In 1836 John Keble edited an important four-volume edition (or three volumes, depending on the bookseller's binding) published by Clarendon Press, which included previously unpublished notes by Hooker. This Keble-edited work was again published in 1841 (2nd edition), 1845 (3rd edition), 1863 and 1865 (4th edition, printed both years), 1865 and 1874 (5th edition, printed both years), and 1874 (6th edition). In 1888 a three-volume seventh edition was published of Keble's Hooker, itself edited by R. W. Church and F. Paget. This 1888 Keble edition was the standard, definitive edition until the publication of the comprehensive eight-volume *Folger Library Edition of The Works of Richard Hooker*, edited by W. Speed Hill (Belknap Press), published from 1977 to 1998.

Over time the authenticity of Books VI, VII, and VIII has been vindicated by researchers examining Hooker's papers and using the tools of literary criticism, culminating in the commentaries and textual introductions of the 1982 fourth volume of the Folger Library Edition. As of that edition, and still today, experts consider that the last three books are authentic but incomplete. Book VI is considered to be more incomplete, and possibly having a different structure than what Hooker intended (although its content is certainly Hooker's), while Books VII and VIII are considered to be mostly complete, with the manuscript of Book VII having been in near readiness for the printer.

The following paraphrase of this edition is derived from Stansbye's 1622 edition, supplemented by paraphrased or summarized notes from that and Keble's 1836 edition, with other clarifying notes added.

AN OVERVIEW OF *OF THE LAWS OF ECCLESIASTICAL POLITY*

In Richard Hooker's time Puritans argued that if a church practice or liturgy was not commanded by the Bible it was forbidden, and criticized the Church of England for engaging in what they viewed as Roman Catholic forms of worship and church governance. Having been pastor to lawyers at the Temple, Hooker's eight books comprising *Of the Laws of Ecclesiastical Polity* were primarily intended as a *legal defense* of the Church of England against her *prosecutorial* Puritan critics.

Hooker argues that the Bible's purpose is to tell us of the Way of salvation; it is not a rulebook for everything in life, science, politics, etc. He rejects the Puritan claim that Scripture is the only authority.

Hooker also argues that where the Bible is silent (such as in what symbolic clothing a pastor might wear, the architecture of a church building, exact rituals, etc.), God grants the Church the authority to use reason to create laws for the sake of order and decency.

Hooker further argues that, while the doctrines of salvation are eternal and unchangeable, laws of church polity (i.e., governance) are changeable, with different contexts requiring different rules.

Finally, arguing that church and state are a united "body-politic", Hooker defends the position of the English monarch as governor of the church against both the presbyterian system and the Pope.

OVERVIEW OF BOOK I: *CONCERNING LAWS, AND THEIR SEVERAL KINDS IN GENERAL*

While most of the books of *Polity* are concerned with differences between the Episcopal Puritans and the more traditional Episcopalians regarding church liturgy, ceremonies, and governance, the first book is focused on providing a common ground for understanding based on the universal principles of reason and natural law, and a shared awareness of these principles. Book I begins with *eternal law* (i.e., God's nature), then God's natural law governing natural agents (what we now typically call, the *inviolable laws of nature*—i.e., the laws of physics which cannot be violated), and then God's *law of reason* which guides humans (what we now typically call, the *violable natural law*—i.e., laws of moral right and wrong which can be violated, although there are consequences).

Even in this first book, though, Hooker takes a stand opposed by Puritans: human reason has a role in establishing order when the Bible offers no guidance. This understanding was contrary to the Puritans' extreme Biblicism, which was driven by the Puritan rejection of perceived Roman Catholic influence.

Hooker relates three characteristics of the law of reason (natural law):

1. People who obey this law reflect the works of nature.
2. The law of reason (natural law) can be understood without the aid of the Bible or other divine revelation.[29]
3. Generally, humans have always recognized the existence and justice of the law of reason (natural law).[30]

Hooker recognizes a hierarchy whenever there is a perceived conflict between these authorities: 1. scripture; 2. reason; 3. church tradition.

Hooker's ultimate purpose for this first book was to provide a foundation for his later arguments against extremist Puritans, specifically relating to two types of laws created by a human government:

1. *Mixed law* has provisions complying with the law of reason (natural law), binding people in a society to what has already been bound by their individual consciences. These are

[29] There is support for this in a Biblical letter written by the apostle, Paul of Tarsus:

> For the wrath of God appears from heaven, against all ungodliness and unrighteousness of men, which withhold the truth in unrighteousness. For that that may be known of God, is manifest among them, because God has shown it unto them. For his invisible things, being understood by his works, through the creation of the world, are seen, that is, both his eternal power and godhead: So that they are without excuse.
>
> —*Romans* 1:18–20, Bishops' Bible, updated to more modern English by Ret Miles

[30] Supported by the previously cited passage by Paul of Tarsus (*Romans* 1:18–20).

universal moral laws which consist of binding duties known by reason, not just through Biblical scriptures.

2. *Positive law* (whether *posited* by God or humans, including ecclesiastical law) is binding as long as it does not, itself, violate or contradict the law of reason or divine law. It deals with any matter which reason teaches to be proper and convenient, and which, if violated, does not result in a transgression of the law of reason (natural law). An example is the inheritance distribution of land to heirs.

Hooker perceives the law of reason (violable natural law) as requiring government, but not any specific *form* of government (an understanding shared 250 years later by the political economist, Frédéric Bastiat[31]). Once a political authority is created by a society of people it is perpetual—the laws of a society in the past bind the people living in the same society in the present, "because corporations are immortal".[32]

At this point an observation regarding Hooker's theology might be helpful. He is often seen as a via media between Catholic theology and Protestant theology, but this is problematic, as is the view that he argued for Anglicanism and against Reformed theology. In fact, Hooker was essentially a Calvinist. The term, "Anglican", was not even in use until over twenty-five years after Hooker's death, and the

---

[31] In *The Law*, FREDERIC BASTIAT stated:

> Law is the organization of the natural right of lawful defence. It is the substitution of the collective force for individual forces, for the purpose of acting in the sphere in which they have a general right to act, of doing what they have a right to do, to secure persons, liberties, and properties, and to maintain each in its right, so as to cause justice to reign over all. ... If a people were constituted on this basis, it seems to me that order would prevail among them, both in fact and in idea. It seems to me that such a people would have the most simple, the most economical, the least heavy, the least felt, the most just, and consequently the most solid Government which could be imagined, whatever were its political form.
>
> —*Essays on Political Economy*, translated by Patrick James Stirling (Provost & Co., London, 1874). *The Law* was originally published in French in 1850.

[32] RICHARD HOOKER, *Concerning Laws, and Their Several Kinds in General*, Chapter 10.

Church of England did not dramatically move toward a more Arminian doctrine until a third of a century after Hooker's death.[33]

In Hooker's time the key disagreements were both over whether the liturgical and ceremonial practices of the Church of England were too much like those of the Roman Catholic church, and over whether bishops should have authority and power, with some insisting that the Church of England should not operate in a Roman Catholic manner, and should instead operate according to sola scriptura.[34] Hooker, and others who took *Romans* I to heart, disagreed.

LEGACY OF RICHARD HOOKER AND *OF THE LAWS OF ECCLESIASTICAL POLITY*

Richard Hooker's magnum opus, *Of the Laws of Ecclesiastical Polity*, including Book I, *Concerning Laws, and Their Several Kinds in General*, pleased Queen **Elizabeth I**, and influenced several notables who came after Hooker, including **James I** and **Charles I**, who both commended Hooker to their children as a foundational text for understanding their authority and the Church of England. James I especially admired Hooker's work.

Hooker and **Edmund Spenser** were contemporaries, each living entirely within the latter-Sixteenth Century and working in similar circles. Spenser was secretary to the Bishop of Rochester, John Young, a close associate of the Archbishop of York, Edwin Sandys, while Sandys patronized Hooker and sent his son to be tutored by him. In

---

[33] Hooker had never heard of a religion called Anglicanism. He would never have dreamed of trying to "convert" any foreigner to the Church of England. It was to him obvious that a German or Italian would not belong to the Church of England, just as an Ephesian or Galatian would not have belonged to the Church of Corinth. Hooker is never seeking for "the true Church"... For him no such problem existed. If by "the church" you mean the mystical church (which is partly in Heaven) then, of course, no man can identify her. But if you mean the visible Church, then we all know her. She is "a sensibly known company" of all those throughout the world who profess one Lord, one Faith, one Baptism (III.i.3)

— C. S. LEWIS (CLIVE STAPLES LEWIS), *English Literature in the Sixteenth Century, Excluding Drama,* Book III, Chapter I (Clarendon Press, Oxford, England, 1954)(454)

[34] i.e., "solely scripture".

a sense both Hooker and Spenser wrote the same book, but each in a different genre, with Hooker writing a legal and theological defense of the Elizabethan Settlement (*Of the Laws of Ecclesiastical Polity*), and Spenser writing a mythological and allegorical defense of the Elizabethan Settlement (*The Færie Queene*). On these two fronts they defended the Elizabethan Settlement from its critics. While Spencer does not seem to have influenced Hooker, later editions of Spenser's *The Færie Queene* and his posthumously published *Mutabilitie Cantos* have parts which were possibly influenced by Hooker.

Whether or not **William Shakespeare** and Hooker influenced each other (a debated subject) they moved in the same circles, with Hooker's congregation of lawyers and students at the Temple Church overlapping Shakespeare's primary audiences. Both argued that if you remove the hierarchy of authority the universe dissolves into chaos.

While known for his poetry, **John Donne** was a contemporary clergyman who shared Hooker's pious style, and whose sermons often echo Hooker's arguments about the via media and church ceremonies. Although Donne lived a little later (his life overlapped the lives of Hooker and Spenser), Donne and Hooker were part of the same circle of families. Donne is often viewed as the emotive voice of Hooker's and Spenser's defense of the Elizabethan Settlement, with Donne internalizing the defense in his book of private devotions, *Holy Sonnets*, published two years after his death and thirty-three years after Hooker's death. Together, these three Anglican pillars form a trivium[35] of methods of defense:

Hooker:	legal, theological	reason	logos	head	The Church is *true.*
Spenser:	artistic, visionary	imagination	mythos	eye	The Church is *glorious.*
Donne:	psychological, demonstrative	emotion	pathos	heart	The Church is *alive.*

[35] The "trivium" is the name of a classification of three of the seven traditional liberal arts (rhetoric, grammar, and logic), while the "quadrivium" consists of the remaining four (astronomy, arithmetic, geometry, and music). The examples of Hooker, Spenser and Donne provide a kind of trivium:

Hooker: logic
Spenser: grammar of symbolism
Donne: rhetoric

In *A Christian Directory* **Richard Baxter**, a leading Puritan, wrote of Hooker's *Polity*:

> In a word, there is no man that hath written better of these things...

Most notably, Hooker influenced the philosopher and political theorist, **John Locke**, who refers to him several times in his 1689 *Second Treatise of Government* as the "Judicious Hooker" whenever he wants to make an unassailable, foundational point. For example, in Chapter II, "Of the State of Nature", section 5, he establishes his concept of a state of nature, the law of nature, and natural equality upon Hooker's authority:

> This equality of men by Nature, the judicious Hooker looks upon as so evident in itself, and beyond all question, that he makes it the foundation of that obligation to mutual love amongst men on which he builds the duties they owe one another, and from whence he derives the great maxims of justice and charity. His words are:
>
>> The like natural inducement hath brought men to know that it is no less their duty to love others than themselves, for seeing those things which are equal, must needs all have one measure; if I cannot but wish to receive good, even as much at every man's hands, as any man can wish unto his own soul, how should I look to have any part of my desire herein satisfied, unless myself be careful to satisfy the like desire, which is undoubtedly in other men weak, being of one and the same nature: to have anything offered them repugnant to this desire must needs, in all respects, grieve them as much as me; so that if I do harm, I must look to suffer, there being no reason that others should show greater measure of love to me than they have by me showed unto them; my desire, therefore, to be loved of my equals in Nature, as much as possible may be, imposeth upon me a natural duty of bearing to themward fully the like affection. From which relation of equality between ourselves and them that are as ourselves, what several rules and canons natural reason hath drawn for direction of life no man is ignorant.[36]

In Chapter II, section 15, Locke quotes Hooker to confirm the existence of a state of nature, and to confirm that all governments are in a state of nature as they relate to each other.

> To those that say, there were never any men in the state of nature, I will not only oppose the authority of the judicious Hooker...
>
>> ...The laws which have been hitherto mentioned... do bind men absolutely, even as they are men, although they have never any settled fellowship, never any solemn agreement amongst themselves what to do, or not to do: but forasmuch as we are not by ourselves sufficient

[36] *Of the Laws of Ecclesiastical Polity*, Book I, Chapter 8, as quoted by Locke.

> to furnish ourselves with competent store of things needful for such a life as our nature doth desire, a life fit for the dignity of man; therefore to supply those defects and imperfections which are in us, as living singly and solely by ourselves, we are naturally induced to seek communion and fellowship with others. This was the cause of men's uniting themselves at the first in politic societies.[37]

In Chapter VII, "Of Political or Civil Society", section 74, Locke uses the same passage from Hooker to argue that men are naturally inclined to be pragmatically "driven" into society to avoid the "inconveniences" of the state of nature, and that, therefore, legitimate political power is derived from the consent of the governed, not directly from God as had been argued by Robert Filmer, whom Locke was refuting.

In Chapter VII, sections 90 and 91, Locke argues that an absolute monarchy is not a civil society, because the monarch remains in a state of nature with his subjects. In support, he quotes Hooker in a footnote:

> To take away all such mutual grievances, injuries, and wrongs, i.e. such as attend men in the state of nature, there was no way but only by growing into composition and agreement amongst themselves, by ordaining some kind of government public, and by yielding themselves subject thereunto.[38]

In Chapter XI, "Of the Extent of the Legislative Power", section 135, Locke argues that a legislature must govern with "promulgated, standing laws" instead of arbitrary decrees. He cites Hooker in two footnotes.

> The lawful power of making laws to command whole politic societies of men, belonging so properly unto the same entire societies, that for any prince or potentate of what kind soever upon earth, to exercise the same of himself, and not either by express commission immediately and personally received from God, or else by authority derived at the first from their consent upon whose persons they impose laws, it is no better than mere tyranny.[39]

...and...

> Human laws are measures in respect of men whose actions they must direct, howbeit such measures they are as have also their higher rules to be measured by, which rules are two, the law of God, and the law of nature; so that laws human must be made according to the general laws of nature, and without contradiction to any positive law of Scripture, otherwise they are ill made.[40]

---

37 *Of the Laws of Ecclesiastical Polity*, Book I, Chapter 10, as quoted by Locke.

38 Ibid.

39 Ibid.

40 Ibid.

American political philosopher and historian, Joseph Knippenberg, has said,

> John Locke—whose language of rights and free and equal individuality rolls trippingly off the tongues of my students—cannot fully be understood without also coming to grips with the position against which he defines himself: the Christianized Aristotelianism of Richard Hooker.
>
> —JOSEPH M. KNIPPENBERG, "C. S. Lewis in a Secular Core: The Abolition of Man and a More Natural Science", *Public Discourse,* August 5, 2018 (Witherspoon Institute, Princeton, 2018)

Locke was also influenced by the then-relatively new tradition of modern, natural rights theory of Hugo Grotius and others. His *Two Treatises of Government,* in which he synthesizes Hooker and Grotius, serves as a blueprint for modern liberal democracy, and inspired the founders of the United States of America. The *Second Treatise* was quoted in their battle flags, writings, speeches, debates, and *Declaration of Independence.*

In *Discourses Concerning Government* (1698), **Algernon Sidney**, a major influence on the American founding fathers, cites Hooker to argue that government is based on the consent of the governed, turning Hooker's conservative arguments into republican ones.

In *A Tale of a Tub*, **Jonathan Swift** satirizes religious extremism with three brothers representing major branches of Western Christianity.

Peter:	Roman Catholicism
Martin:	the via media of Lutheranism, Anglicanism, and Richard Hooker
Jack:	Calvinism and the "Dissenters"[41]

Swift revered Hooker as a model of sanity as opposed to zealotry.

---

[41] "Dissenters", another name for the Separatists, left the Church of England for their own churches. Many emigrated to Amsterdam, Leiden, or the eastern coast of North America. One faction were the Brownists, calling themselves, the "Saints". Some Brownists, the "Pilgrims" or "Pilgrim Fathers" of American lore, founded Plymouth Colony. Historically these are the Brownist Emigration. Indeed, in 1620 they were the majority of Dissenters or Separatists aboard the *Mayflower*. After the American Revolution, thousands of Loyalists, including a few Brownists and other Dissenters, moved to what remained of British North America (areas which would eventually become Canada).

Brownist groups were eventually absorbed by the Mennonites and Baptists.

To England's premier man of letters, the author, moralist, sermonizer, critic, and lexicographer, **Samuel Johnson**, Richard Hooker was one of the primary influences on his thinking and on the English language. Johnson saw himself as doing battle with many of the same forces besieging the Church of England. While in Hooker's time the challenge was from the Puritans and Dissenters, Johnson saw the challenge as coming from Whigs[42] and Dissenters, whom he believed were undermining the authority of the Church of England and the King.

Adopting Hooker's method, Johnson's sermons avoid emotional enthusiasm, using Reason to prove that God's laws are rational and necessary for our happiness. James Boswell, in his *Life of Johnson*, lists Hooker as one of the "giants" upon whom Johnson formed his style, and Johnson's friends, as well as subsequent scholars, recognized that Johnson's style of long rhythmic sentences was modeled on Hooker's style.

When Johnson compiled his famous 1755 *Dictionary of the English Language* he selected a small group of authors to serve as the ultimate authorities for how English words should be used. For words related to religion, law, and philosophy he chose Hooker as his primary authority, citing Hooker thousands of times in the *Dictionary*. For abstract concepts like law, faith, reason, and nature, the definition is frequently a direct block quote from Hooker's *Of the Laws of Ecclesiastical Polity*. And in his "Preface" to the *Dictionary* Johnson quotes Hooker to justify his own conservatism regarding change in language:

> Change, says *Hooker*, is not made without inconvenience, even from worse to better.

By placing thousands of his sentences into the *Dictionary* Johnson essentially codified Hooker, ensuring that his definitions became the standard for the English-speaking world for the next 150 years.

Founder of Methodism, **John Wesley**, was grounded in Hooker's theology. His understanding of the via media and his insistence on the fourfold authority of Scripture, reason, tradition, and experience[43] is derived from Hooker's threefold formulation of Scripture, reason, and tradition.

---

[42] Whigs were a political party who opposed absolute monarchy and Roman Catholic emancipation, and supported constitutional monarchism and parliamentary government.
[43] Together these four authorities are called, the "Wesleyan Quadrilateral".

James Wilson was the first professor of law at the University of Pennsylvania, key architect of the executive branch of the U.S. government, the electoral college, and the Constitutional Compromise of 1787, and the only individual to have done all of the following: sign the *Declaration of Independence*, sign the 1787 *Constitution*, and serve in the first U. S. Supreme Court. Wilson, profoundly influenced by Hooker (and Cicero, Grotius, and Locke), said in a published lecture, "Let us listen to the judicious and excellent Hooker: what he says always conveys instruction."[44]

By way of Locke's treatises, Hooker's early concepts of a social contract influenced **Jean-Jacques Rousseau**. Rosseau's philosophy is often associated with the French Revolution; however, that revolution was less influenced by any of Hooker's philosophy and more influenced by Rousseau's idea of, "General Will",[45] resulting in the Revolution's more radical, violent phases and the Reign of Terror. The American Revolution, being conservative in its goals and more influenced by Hooker, avoided much of the excesses of the more radical French Revolution.

William Blackstone, the primary successor to Hooker in writings on the law, and whose 1765 *Commentaries on the Laws of England* were widely read by the American founders, effectively copied Hooker's theories of the law of nature and divine law from Book I of Hooker's *Polity*, paraphrasing these into his own *Commentaries*.

---

[44] JAMES WILSON, *Collected Works of James Wilson*, Volume I, Part 2, "Lectures on Law", Part I, Chapter II, "Of the General Principles of Law and Obligation", edited by Mark David Hall and Kermit L. Hall (Liberty Fund, Indianapolis, 2007).

Wilson frequently cited Cicero, Hooker, Grotius, and Locke in his lectures and writings.

[45] i.e., the collective power.

> If then we discard from the social compact what is not of its essence, we shall find that it reduces itself to the following terms—
>
> > Each of us puts his person and all his power in common under the supreme direction of the general will, and, in our corporate capacity, we receive each member as an indivisible part of the whole.
>
> ... In order then that the social compact may not be an empty formula, it tacitly includes the undertaking, which alone can give force to the rest, that whoever refuses to obey the general will shall be compelled to do so by the whole body.
>
> ...the general will, the source and supplement of all laws...
>
> —JEAN-JACQUES ROUSSEAU, *The Social Contract and Discourses*, Translated with Introduction by G. D. H. Cole (J. M. Dent & Sons Ltd., London, 1913)

Because of the importance of Blackstone's *Commentaries*, this effectively cemented Hooker's vision into modern English law, and becoming part of the default setting for American law.

In his pamphlet, *The Farmer Refuted* (1775), **Alexander Hamilton** quotes Hooker to argue that the King has no right to rule without consent:

> The judicious Hooker...affirms that "The lawful power of making laws to command whole politic societies of men, belongeth so properly unto the same entire societies..."

Theologically, **John Adams** was Unitarian[46] and would have disagreed with Hooker's Trinitarianism; however, he respected Hooker's historical grasp of law, owned his works, and was intimately familiar with them.

With his educational background and mastery of religious liberty arguments, **James Madison** would have been familiar with, and influenced by, the writings of Richard Hooker, even though he rarely cited Hooker, preferring more-contemporary writers and the authority of reason.

Edmund Burke and Richard Hooker are often viewed as the two primary pillars of the Anglo-American conservatism, with Burke being Hooker's spiritual heir. Burke quotes Hooker in his *Appeal from the New to the Old Whigs* (1791), referring to him as, "that great man", and using Hooker to support his arguments about the organic nature of society and the dangers of rapid, abstract political innovations. Hooker argued in Book IV, Chapter 14, of *Polity* that while laws can be changed, the "burden of proof" lies with the innovators, not those supporting the established order. Burke argued that, without overwhelming necessity, the French Revolution should not discard long-standing institutions—the church, the monarchy, and the aristocracy—for abstract theories.

Burke shared with Hooker a skepticism of perfectionism in politics. As Hooker argued against the Puritans who wanted a perfect church modeled strictly on Scripture, ignoring history and custom, Burke argued against Jacobins who wanted a perfect state modeled on abstract rights, likewise ignoring history and custom.

---

[46] Unitarianism is a liberal theology which emphasizes the oneness of God, rejects belief in the Trinity, and prioritizes human reason, personal spiritual experience, and social justice.

In the preface to his landmark 1828 *An American Dictionary of the English Language* (which eventually became the modern *Merriam-Webster's Dictionary*), lexicographer, spelling reformer, textbook author, and political writer, **Noah Webster**, cites Hooker as a standard for grammar and usage.

The Romantic Era poet and philosopher, **Samuel Taylor Coleridge**, was notably influenced by Richard Hooker during his later years. He viewed Hooker's *Of the Laws of Ecclesiastical Polity* as the ideal model for the relationship between church and state. In *On the Constitution of the Church and State* (1830), Coleridge uses Hooker's ideas to argue that the church and state are not two separate corporations, but are two aspects of a single organic Christian commonwealth. Coleridge also saw Hooker as the champion of *reason* (a higher, intuitive spiritual faculty) against the Puritans' mere *understanding* (an empirical calculation).

The **Oxford Movement** for reinstatement of older traditions, often associated with Roman Catholicism, into Anglican liturgy and theology was influenced by Hooker and his via media and threefold authority: Scripture, tradition, and reason, which they referred to as, the "threefold cord". However, they tended to distort Hooker's theological stance as being more Roman Catholic than it was.

Nineteenth-Century Anglican priest, **John Keble**, a founder of the Oxford Movement and the namesake of Keble College at Oxford University, was influenced by Hooker not engaging in the kind of rationalism which undermines faith, and by Hooker's avoidance of the errors of Calvinism. Keble observed that Hooker's work influenced key later Anglican theologians, helping to keep the Church of England from becoming a sect aligned with the Calvinism associated with Geneva. Keble was the editor of *The Works of that Learned and Judicious Divine, Mr. Richard Hooker*, which was for many years the definitive edition of Hooker's works.

The liberal British politician, statesman, Chancellor of the Exchequer, Prime Minister, and evangelical Anglican, **William Ewart Gladstone**, said of Hooker's writings:

> [I]n the spring and summer of 1828 I set to work on Hooker's Ecclesiastical Polity and read it straight through. Intercourse with my saintly elder sister Anne had increased my mental interest in

> religion and she though generally of Evangelical sentiments had an opinion that the standard divines of the English Church were of great value. Hooker's exposition of the claims of the Church of England came to me as a mere abstraction: but I think that I found the doctrine of baptismal regeneration, theretofore abhorred, impossible to reject and the way was thus opened for further changes.
>
> —WILLIAM EWART GLADSTONE, "Early Religious Opinions, 1828–41" (July 26, 1894), *The Prime Minister's Papers: W. E. Gladstone*. I: *Autobiographica*, Edited by John Brooke and Mary Sorensen (Her Majesty's Stationery Office, London, 1971)

Charles H. Spurgeon occasionally quoted Richard Hooker's eloquent proverbs in his sermons, but did not seem to be directly influenced by his theology of church organization.

In the Twentieth Century Hooker was **C. S. Lewis**' favorite Sixteenth-Century author—an exception in a century of mediocre prose—and one of Lewis' favorite authors in general. Lewis referred to Hooker's sentences as, "music". Hooker also profoundly influenced Lewis' thinking. For example, in Lewis' *The Abolition of Man*, a defense of universal natural law—which Lewis refers to as, "Tao"[47]—he argues that moral axioms are self-evident and cannot, themselves, be proven because they are the basis for all proof. This is a restatement of Hooker's positions in chapter eight that...

> ...signs and tokens which, always accompanying goodness, argue that, where they are found, there, also, is goodness...

...and that...

> ...there are in the law of reason some things which stand as universally agreed-upon principles, and that, out of those principles, which are in themselves evident [i.e., 'self-evident'], the greatest, moral duties we owe towards God or man may be understood...

When he argues that the "first principles" of the Tao are known to all men, Lewis is restating Hooker's famous chapter eight assertion that

> [T]he main principles of reason are, in themselves, apparent. For to make nothing evident of itself [i.e., again, 'self-evident'] to man's understanding is to take away all possibility of knowing anything.

---

[47] In East Asian religions and philosophies, the Tao (or Dao), meaning "way", "path", or "road", is the incomprehensible, eternal, formless, unmoving, unchanging, omnipresent, self-existing, principle and source of the universe, of all existence. C. S. Lewis used this term as his name for natural law, in order to emphasize its universality and objective value.

Finally, in *The Abolition of Man*, Lewis sees the universe as a hierarchy with related but distinct physical and moral laws. This is similar to Hooker's cascading hierarchy of laws in chapters two through five.

first, eternal law God sets for himself

↓

second, physical, inviolable, eternal law governing natural agents
(rocks falling, trees growing, for every action there is an equal and opposite reaction, etc.)

↓

third, violable, eternal law governing angels

↓

fourth, moral, violable law directing humans so that they imitate God

And it is similar to the description of law in the ending of Hooker's chapter sixteen:

> [O]f law it can be no less acknowledged than that her seat is the bosom of God, her voice the harmony of the world, all things in Heaven and Earth do her homage, the very least as feeling her care, and the greatest as not exempted from her power; both angels and men and creatures of whatever condition, though each in different way and manner, yet all with uniform consent, admiring her as the mother of their peace and joy.

In the sixth chapter of the *Problem of Pain*, and in his *Reflections on the Psalms*, to answer the question as to whether something is good because God commands it, or whether God commands it because it is good,[48] Lewis uses a theological argument central to Hooker's dispute with the Puritans, and concludes that God commands the good because it is good. The converse cannot be true, because if something is good only because God commands it, then that would make God an arbitrary tyrant. To assert that something is good only because God commands it is a denial of His intrinsic goodness. For Christians, God is good *and* commands the good—there is no conflict. So, Lewis agrees with Hooker that God's law is not decided by His arbitrary will. Instead, God's law is a manifestation of His own nature: God commands the good because He

---

[48] This is the "Euthyphro Dilemma". Plato relates Socrates saying the following to Euthyphro.

> The point which I should first wish to understand is whether the pious or holy is beloved by the gods because it is holy, or holy because it is beloved of the gods.
>
> —Plato, "Euthyphro", in *The Dialogues of Plato*, translated by Benjamin Jowett, Third Edition, Volume I (Clarendon Press, Oxford, England, 1892)

is good. Morality is not the arbitrary whim of a tyrant—a key theme in Hooker's rejection of the Puritan view of a "God of Will".

Hooker states the following in the second chapter.

> [A]ll things work in a manner according to law. All other things are according to a law, of which some Superior to whom they are subject is Author. Only both the works and operations of God have Him as their Worker, and for the law by which they are wrought.
>
> The Being of God is a kind of law to His working. For that Perfection, which God is, gives perfection to what He does. …

Elsewhere, Lewis states…

> God neither obeys nor creates the moral law. The good is uncreated;… it has in it no shadow of contingency… God is not merely good, but goodness; goodness is not merely divine, but God.
>
> —C. S. LEWIS, "The Poison of Subjectivism", in *Christian Reflections* (Wm. B. Eerdmans Publishing Co., Grand Rapids, 1967)

In *The Discarded Image: An Introduction to Medieval and Renaissance Literature* (Cambridge University Press, Cambridge, England, 1964) Lewis uses the Argument from Desire, the argument that the desire for joy or God exhibited by all of nature, including humans, is evidence of the existence of God. This argument can be traced back to Richard Hooker, Thomas Aquinas, and Aristotle. In the eleventh chapter of *Concerning Laws, and Their Several Kinds in General,* Hooker states…

> It is an axiom of nature that natural desire cannot be utterly frustrated.

Just as hunger demonstrates the existence of food, our innate desire for a joy which this world cannot satisfy demonstrates the existence of supernatural fulfillment.

In his private letters Lewis indicated that he saw Hooker not just as a philosopher, but as an important theologian who was a modern tie to the mediæval Schoolmen[49] and Thomas Aquinas, and a theological model for the English Church as simply part of Christianity, not a sect.

---

[49] The Schoolmen were intellectually rigorous teachers in mediæval and Renaissance monasteries and universities. Also called, "Scholastics", the most famous and influential is Thomas Aquinas. Others include Anselm of Canterbury (the "Father of Scholasticism"), Peter Abelard, Duns Scotus, William of Ockham (or Occam), and Francisco de Vitoria (founder of the influential School of Salamanca, and an indirect influence on the American Founding Fathers through his influence on Hugo Grotius).

After converting to Anglicanism **T. S. Eliot** saw Hooker as a model of the "English mind". In his essays Eliot commended Hooker's style and intellect, seeing him as the perfect synthesis of Renaissance humanism and Christian theology.

Eric Voegelin, a Twentieth-Century political philosopher and author of *The New Science of Politics*, was influenced by Hooker's analysis of the Puritans, and used Hooker's critique of the Puritan "inner light" to formulate his own theory of "Gnosticism" in modern politics, the idea that toxic ideologies, like Marxism or Nazism, are secularized versions of the ancient heresy which claims to have "secret knowledge" which can perfect the world. Voegelin considered Hooker the first great analyst of the mind of modern revolutionaries.

British conservative philosopher, **Michael Oakeshott**, admired Hooker's understanding of law as a tool for peace instead of perfection. He saw Hooker as a predecessor in his skepticism about political rationalism.

Martin Luther King, Jr., a student of natural law, argued that an "unjust law is no law at all", usually citing Augustine or Aquinas. Still, Richard Hooker was the primary transmitter of this idea into the English language. When King argued that human laws must square with moral law, he was speaking in the intellectual tradition of Hooker, even if he cited Aquinas.

Hooker surprisingly impressed or influenced not only Anglican and Reformed Christian notables, but Roman Catholic notables as well. Upon reading parts of Hooker's *Polity* which had been translated into Latin for him, Pope **Clement VIII** admired Hooker's profound grasp of the connection between the finite and the infinite.

Ironically, **James II** found Hooker's fifth book of *Polity* so convincing that he concluded the only church which possessed indications of authority was the Roman Catholic Church, not the Church of England. He *claimed* that reading Richard Hooker's defense of the Church of England actually led him to convert to Roman

Catholicism. Although the Roman Catholic James II became King with the support of a coalition of Protestants and Catholics, his policies and the possibility of his being succeeded by a Roman Catholic heir resulted in his being deposed during the Glorious Revolution, and replaced by the Protestant, William of Orange, and his Protestant wife, Mary, who was the daughter of James.

Richard Hooker's cosmology[50] and style influenced **Alexander Pope**, who respected Hooker as a philosopher of *order* and as a literary master. Pope's philosophical poem, *An Essay on Man*, is essentially a poetic expression of Hooker's cosmology in Book I of *Polity*. Both argue that the universe is a divinely structured hierarchy with a specific place and duty for each inhabitant, with Hooker stating:

> ...of law it can be no less acknowledged than that her seat is the bosom of God, her voice the harmony of the world...

And Pope stating:

> Order is Heaven's first law.

Hooker argues that human misery comes from trying to violate the law of nature so as to rise above our station—like the Puritans trying to be as perfect as Scripture. Likewise, Pope argues that human misery comes from pride—like trying to break the "Great Chain of Being" so as to be like angels or God.

Despite their different religious affiliations, Pope's defense of good sense and nature is an Eighteenth-Century continuation of Hooker's Sixteenth-Century defense of reason and law. Pope shared a common opponent with Hooker: enthusiasm.[51] While Hooker argued against the Puritans, whom he saw as chaotic destroyers of tradition, Pope opposed those whom he saw as chaotic destroyers of culture (called, the "Dunces", in his satirical poem, *The Dunciad*).

In his last years, Pope planned an English dictionary (which Samuel Johnson would later complete). He made a short list of authors

---

[50] i.e., the study of the origin and development of the universe.

[51] i.e., fanaticism.

whose works could serve as a standard for grammar and style. For theology and ecclesiastical history Pope listed Richard Hooker as the primary model.

Author, philosopher, journalist, editor, and Christian apologist, **G. K. Chesterton**, who converted from Anglicanism to Roman Catholicism later in life, appreciated how Hooker's rational approach avoided the extremes of both Catholicism and Puritanism.

In 1932 **Alessandro Passerin d'Entrèves**, the prominent Italian Roman Catholic legal philosopher and historian, wrote *Riccardo Hooker: Contributo alla teoria e alla storia del diritto naturale* ("*Richard Hooker: A Contribution to the Theory and History of Natural Law*"). He was responsible for reviving the continental European study of Richard Hooker's work, and argued that Hooker was the vital bridge which carried Aquinas' mediæval concept of law into the modern world, and is, therefore, a writer of European significance, not just a parochial English writer.

Most notably for late-Twentieth Century American conservatives, Hooker's influence on the political philosopher, critic, and Roman Catholic convert, **Russell Kirk**, was primarily through ideas which provided a theological foundation for Kirk's conservative political theory. He viewed Hooker as the primary conduit through which the mediæval natural law tradition of the Schoolmen and Thomas Aquinas was transmitted to the American founding fathers. Kirk often argued that Hooker's influence on the American order was greater than that of John Locke.

Kirk admired Hooker for navigating a via media between the extremes of Roman Catholic absolute authority and Puritan radical individualism. He saw this balanced and prudent approach, which was wary of ideological zealotry, as the model for conservatism.

In his book, *The Roots of American Order*, Kirk traces the ideas underlying the United States of America to five cities:[52]

Ancient Jerusalem:	moral and religious foundations, and "a purposeful moral existence under God".
Ancient Athens:	"philosophical and political self-awareness", and origins of Western thought, including democratic ideals and rational political thinking.
Ancient Rome:	"law and social order", and a constitutional framework.
London:	"liberty under law", duty, common law, representative government, economic foundation, moral restraints on government, self-reliance, and via media, as well as the *Magna Carta* and the *Bill of Rights*.
Philadelphia:	where these ideas culminated in a conservative maintenance of an established order while appealing to natural law, as seen in the 1776 *Declaration of Independence* (a conservative document which speaks of changing the government, not the state[53]), and in the complementary written *Constitution* of 1787.

When discussing the influences of London, Kirk prominently mentions Hooker as the architect of the via media. Kirk also relies on Hooker's concept of order, quoting Hooker from Book VIII, Chapter 2, *Of the Laws of Ecclesiastical Polity*:

> Without order, there is no living in public society, because the want thereof is the mother of confusion.

For Kirk, this is an essential argument that social order is divinely ordained and necessary for liberty. Kirk also recognizes that Hooker kept

---

[52] Quotes taken from RUSSELL KIRK, *The Roots of American Order* (Open Court Publishing Company, La Salle, Illinois, 1974).

[53] A state is a governed, geopolitical society with an established, civil, social order.

the concept of "natural law" alive in English common law, teaching England and, consequently, America that human law is not merely the will of the state. When just, human law is a reflection of divine reason, the "voice of God". This was the basis of Kirk's critiques of legal positivism[54] and totalitarianism.

In his most famous work, *The Conservative Mind* (1953), Kirk presents Hooker as a predecessor of Edmund Burke (Kirk's primary hero), and an intellectual source of Burke's conservatism. Kirk also uses Hooker to validate the principle of *prescription*, the concept that established customs and laws have a presumption of validity because they embody the wisdom of generations. To support a conservative preference for tradition over radical innovations, Kirk cites Hooker's view that...

> ...the general and perpetual voice of men is as the sentence of God himself...

Kirk acknowledged that Burke revered Hooker. By studying Hooker, Kirk was able to demonstrate that Burke's ideas were not new, but that a long tradition of classical and mediæval thought was part of the roots of modern, Burkean conservatism.

In *Enemies of the Permanent Things* (1969), Kirk challenges the dominant opinion that Locke was the primary philosophical source of the American Revolution. He argues that Richard Hooker has more to do with the principles of the American founding fathers than Locke does, and that, when the founders spoke of "natural rights", they were thinking in terms of Hooker's sense of rights bound up with duties and divine law, not abstract, autonomous rights.

In *The Roots of American Order* and *The Conservative Mind* Kirk adopted Hooker's and Burke's view that society is not a social contract broken at will, but is a spiritual corporation of the dead, the living, and the yet unborn. In *The Conservative Mind* Kirk described this as a "sacramental view of society".

---

[54] Legal positivism is the view that the validity of a law comes from authorities accepted by a society, like legislation or judicial rulings (positive law—i.e., law which has been posited), or social customs. Put another way, it is the view that the validity of a law comes from its existence (what the law *is*), not from the law's morality (what the law *ought to be*).

Above all, when seen from a practical perspective, Hooker influenced Kirk's view that change, when necessary, must be gradual and organic. It should be growth, not construction. This outlook was central to Kirk's arguments against revolution and social engineering.

In turn, Kirk influenced a generation of political and social commentators and politicians, from William F. Buckley to Ronald Reagan, serving, along with the continuing influence of Edmund Burke, as a conservative counterbalance to the more libertarian influences of Frédéric Bastiat, Ludwig von Mises, F. A. Hayek, Rose-Wilder Lane, Isabel Paterson, Ayn Rand, Leonard Read, Milton Friedman, and Thomas Sowell.

Finally, Hooker influenced the Russian Orthodox priest, theologian, and historian, **Georges Florovsky**, one of the most significant Russian Orthodox theologians of the Twentieth Century. Florovsky admired Hooker as the one Western theologian who avoided errors associated with both Scholastics and Reformed Christians. He frequently cited Hooker in ecumenical dialogues, suggesting that Hooker's theology was the closest the Western church has come to the Patristic spirit of Eastern Orthodoxy.

Hooker's and Related Terms

ecclesiastical:	relating to a church or its clergy.
polity:	a governed, organized society or its governance.
reason:	the human faculty by which we infer principles of nature. This word usage follows a tradition associated with Aristotle and Thomas Aquinas. Reason helps us both *know* (reason's primary function is to proceed from self-evident truths to consistent conclusions—we must identify what is true before we can conclude what is good) and *do* (reason's ultimate purpose is to guide our actions—once we know what is good, we know what we should do).
rational:	according to reason.
natural agents:	all rational or irrational entities and phenomena in the universe.
law:	a principle of inevitable or preferred behavior.
eternal law:	God's plan, or His own will for Himself.
law of nature:	eternal law as it applies to God's creation—i.e., universal principles of how natural agents operate. Hooker's use of the term includes both of the modern ideas of inviolable laws of nature (i.e., principles of physics, scientific constants, etc.—i.e., inevitable behavior) and violable natural laws (i.e., universal principles of morality—i.e. proper behavior).

law of reason:	(also called, "law rational" or "the law of man's nature") a part of the law of nature which applies to rational agents (humans). It consists of rules of inference and thought, and general principles of good and evil which human reason can logically infer, without supernatural revelation, by using reason informed by what is observed in nature. The law of reason (i.e., the modern idea of violable natural law, universal principles of morality) is derived from the nature of humans, and is binding upon them. Briefly, the law of nature is the entire set of God's principles for the universe, and the law of reason is a subset of those principles which is written in human hearts, making it the governing law for voluntary human action.
non-rational agents:	solids, liquids, gases, plasmas, atoms, chemicals, metal, wood, sand, minerals, rocks, beasts, fish, insects, plants, fungi, clouds, rain, snow, rivers, seas, islands, mountains, deserts, wind, planets, stars, fire, lightning, light, heat, etc. These natural agents *must* follow the law of nature. They have no choice. Examples: a rock thrown into the air must eventually fall; heated air from a fire must rise; cold air must settle.
rational agents:	humans, natural agents who must follow some laws of nature (e.g., if one trips when walking, one must stumble or fall), but are free to violate the law of reason (although not without consequences).
voluntary obedience:	The law of reason specifies a proper operation which humans *should* perform. This law is binding upon humans, yet they can disobey it (although there are consequences). This equates to the more modern idea of the "violable", in "violable natural laws".
human law:	laws humans make for governing their societies.
ecclesiastical law:	human law which governs a church or its clergy. Hooker also calls this, "human positive law".

positive law:	human or divine laws which are binding only because they were enacted, and are not inherently binding by nature or reason, alone. Examples are traffic laws, church ceremonies, etc.
mixed law:	human laws which enforce provisions already binding by the law of reason—i.e., laws confirming moral duties known by reason, such as laws against fraud, theft, assault, kidnapping, murder, etc.
divine law:	laws stated by God, often in Biblical scriptures.
power:	the ability to act.
tradition:	the wisdom of the early Church, which can be a guide to scriptural truth, or the wisdom of any predecessors.
body-politic:	a governed, organized society.
Scripture:	The Bible.
mutable:	changeable.
mutability:	ability to change.
immutability:	the quality of being unchangeable.
heresy:	a false doctrine or teaching—i.e., contrary to orthodox religious doctrine.
First Cause:	that agent upon which the being of all things originally depends. In Christian beliefs, this is God.
Stoicism:	an Ancient Greek and Roman philosophy which held that the highest good is virtue based upon knowledge of the divine reason governing nature.
Stoic:	according to the principles of Stoicism. Or one who lives according to those principles and is indifferent to both pleasure and pain.
Reformation:	a Sixteenth Century, European, religious movement which advocated reform of the Roman Catholic Church, and, failing that, the establishment of Protestant churches. Key principles included a return to the sole authority of Scripture in matters of salvation and the rejection of papal authority.

Lutheranism:	theology associated with Martin Luther, emphasizing the sovereignty of God and the supreme authority of Scripture, as well as single predestination. (Lutherans usually prefer to say they emphasize "universal grace", but affirm "election".)
single predestination:	the doctrine that God elects people to salvation through Christ, and that condemnation to Hell comes only from rejecting salvation.

Reformed theology:	Christian doctrines emphasizing the sovereignty of God, the Bible's supreme authority in matters of faith, and salvation by grace, alone. Hooker and his Puritan opponents held to the precepts of Reformed theology, with disagreements mainly related to matters of church governance, liturgy, practices, whether to use the *Book of Common Prayer* or to engage in more extemporaneous, spirit-led prayer, and whether the Bible was the sole authority in these matters.

Calvinism:	theology associated with John Calvin, emphasizing the sovereignty of God and the supreme authority of Scripture, as well as double predestination.
double predestination:	the doctrine that God elects people either to salvation through Christ or to damnation.

presbyterian:	local church governance by elders (called, "presbyters") and a minister, emphasizing the independence of local congregations or regional assemblies rather than submitting to the authority of a hierarchy of bishops.
Presbyterian:	referring to the churches in a Christian denomination with, "Presbyterian", in its name, or in a related denomination, and having doctrinal similarities with the Church of Scotland, as well as a presbyterian governance of local churches.
Church of Scotland:	Calvinistic Presbyterian churches founded by John Knox in 1560. It is the national church of Scotland, also known as, "the Kirk o' Scotland", or "the Kirk".

episcopal:	church governance by an episcopacy.
Episcopal:	referring to the churches in a Christian denomination with "Episcopal" in the denomination's name, and which can often trace their operational and theological roots to the Church of England.
Anglican:	referring to churches in a Christian denomination which is affiliated with the Church of England.
ἐπίσκοπος ("episcopos"):	an Ancient Greek compound word literally meaning, "watcher upon", and more generally meaning, "watcher", "overseer", "guardian", "lookout", or "scout". It was imported into Ancient Latin as, "episcopus", meaning, "watcher", "supervisor", or "bishop" (derived from the Greek, ἐπίσκοπος). The σκοπός ("scopós") part of the compound word is the origin of the English word, "scope".
bishop:	an overseer of a diocese.
diocese:	a geographical district with multiple churches which are overseen by a bishop.
episcopacy:	a hierarchy of bishops who have authority over dioceses and clergy.
via media:	Latin phrase meaning, "middle way", usually referring to any theological or political position which seeks middle ground between extremes. In the context of the Church of England, "via media" often refers to Anglicanism being a middle, "Goldilocks" position between other Protestant denominations and Roman Catholicism.

justification: being righteous in God's eyes. Roman Catholicism of the Sixteenth Century held that justification is accomplished by faith plus works, whereas Sixteenth Century Lutheran and Reformed theology held that justification is accomplished solely by faith in Christ Jesus, with good works being fruits and evidence of faith, and part of the process of sanctification.

Arminianism:	theology associated with the Dutch Reformed theologian, Jacobus Arminius, emphasizing that God's prevenient grace is universal and resistible. Over the course of the Seventeenth Century, following Richard Hooker's death, the Church of England became more Arminian in its theology.
prevenient grace:	God's grace in an individual's life which prepares that individual for—and precedes—conversion, regeneration, and ongoing sanctification.
conversion:	in the context of prevenient grace, "conversion" is believing that the Christ Jesus is the only begotten Son of God, and accepting His gift of salvation.
regeneration:	rebirth to a new relationship with God.
sanctification:	the process of being made holy and set apart.
universal:	in the context of Arminianism, "universal" refers to Christ's atoning sacrifice being made for everyone.
resistible:	in the context of Arminianism, "resistible" means that anyone has "free will" to refuse the gift.

Roman Catholicism: the Christian church governed by an episcopacy led by the Bishop of Rome (the Pope). In the Sixteenth Century the Roman Catholic church held to the authority of both Scripture and Church tradition, the necessity of the priesthood and sacraments for salvation, and the doctrine that justification is a process involving faith as well as merit earned from good works.

office: a duty, obligation, or hierarchical position vested with that duty or obligation.

Chapter One

The Reasons for This Book

He that goes about to persuade a multitude that they are not so well governed as they ought to be shall never lack for attentive and favorable hearers, because they know the many and varied defects to which every kind of government is subject. But the secret obstacles and difficulties, which in public proceedings are innumerable and inevitable, they typically do not have the judgement to consider. And because those who openly condemn supposed disorders of state are taken for principal friends of the common benefit of all, and are also taken for men who think for themselves, under this fair and plausible posture whatever they utter passes for good and current wisdom. That which is lacking in the weight of their speech is supplied by the aptness of men's minds to accept and believe it. While, on the other hand, if we maintain things which are established, we not only have to deal with a number of heavy prejudices deeply rooted in the hearts of men who think that we are opportunists speaking in favor of the status quo, because by that we either have or seek preferential treatment, we also have to deal with minds so hostile before-hand that they usually take offense at that which they are loath to accept.

Therefore, although perhaps much of what we are to speak in this present case may seem tedious to some, and maybe even obscure, dark, and intricate—for many talk of the truth who never found the depth from which it springs, and, therefore, when they are led to it they are soon weary, as men drawn from those beaten paths on which they have been injured—yet this may not prevail so far as to cut off that which the matter itself requires, regardless of whether it pleases the refined sensibilities of some.

They to whom we shall seem tedious are in nowise injured by us, because it is in their own hands to spare that labor which they are not willing to endure.

And if any complain of obscurity, they must consider that in these matters it is no different than in various works of both art and nature, where that which has greatest force in the very things we see is, nevertheless, itself often not seen. The stateliness of houses and the goodliness of trees delight the eye when we behold them. But that foundation which bears up the one, that root which ministers nourishment and life to the other, is concealed in the bosom of the Earth. And if at any time there is occasion to search into it, such labor is then more necessary than pleasant, both to them who undertake it and for the onlookers.

In like manner, all who live under good laws may use, benefit, and enjoy them with delight and comfort, although the grounds and first original causes from which they have sprung are unknown—as to the greatest part of men they are.

But, when they who withdraw their obedience pretend that the laws which they should obey are corrupt and vicious, for better examination of their quality it is necessary to discover the very foundation and root, the highest wellspring and fountain of them—which, because we are not often accustomed to do so, when we undertake to discover the grounds and causes for the laws a great deal of the time the pains we take are more necessary than acceptable, and the matters which we handle seem dark, intricate, and unfamiliar because of their newness, until the mind grows better acquainted with them. For as much help as is possible in this case, I have endeavored throughout the body of this whole discourse that every early part might give strength to all of which follows, and every later part bring some light to all of which was before, so that, as touching upon these first, more general, meditations, if the judgements of men are suspended until they have perused the rest which follows, that which may seem obscure at first will later be found plainer, even as I have no doubt that the later, particular decisions will appear stronger when the others have been read before.

The laws of the Church—by which together we have been guided in the exercise of Christian religion and the service of the true God for so many ages—our rites, customs, and orders of ecclesiastical government are all called into question. We are accused of being men who will not have Christ Jesus to rule over them but have willfully cast His statutes behind their backs, hating to be reformed and made subject to the scepter of His discipline. Behold, therefore, we offer the laws by which we live to the general trial and judgement of the whole world, heartily beseeching Almighty God, whom we desire to serve according to His own will, that both we and others (all kind of partiality being laid clean aside) may have eyes to see, and hearts to embrace, the things which in His sight are most acceptable.

And because the point about which we strive is the quality of our laws, our first entrance into this cannot be better made than with consideration of the nature of law, in general, and of that law which gives life to all of the rest which are commendable, just, and good—namely the law by which the Eternal, Himself, works. Proceeding from this—first to the law of nature, then the law of Scripture—we shall have easier access to those things which come afterwards to be debated concerning the particular cause and question which we have in hand.

Chapter Two

The First Eternal Law, Which God Sets for Himself

All things which exist have some operation which is not violent or casual. Neither does anything ever begin to exercise that operation without some preconceived end for which it works. And the end for which it works is not obtained unless by work which is also fit to obtain that end. For every operation will not serve every end.

We call a *law*...

> that which assigns to each thing its kind,
>
> that which moderates the force and power of work,
>
> and that which appoints the form and measure of work,

...so that no certain end can ever be attained unless the actions by which it is attained are *regular*—that is to say, made suitable, fit, and corresponding to its end by some canon, rule, or law—which first takes place even in the works of God, Himself. Therefore, all things work in a manner according to law. All things other than the works and operations of God are according to a law of which some superior to whom they are subject is author. Only both the works and operations of God have Him as their Worker, and for the law by which they are wrought.

The Being of God is a kind of law to His working. For that Perfection, which God is, gives perfection to what He does. Those natural, necessary, and internal operations of God—the generation of the

Son, the preceding of the Spirit—are outside the purpose of my book, which is to touch upon only such operations as have their beginning and being by a voluntary purpose, with which God has eternally decreed when and how they should be. Such an eternal decree is what we call an *eternal law*.

It is dangerous for the feeble brain of man to wade far into the doings of the Highest—although it is life to know Him, and joy to say His name. Yet, our fondest knowledge is to know that we neither know Him as, indeed, He is, nor *can* we know Him. And our safest eloquence concerning Him is our silence when we confess, without confession, that His glory is inexplicable, His greatness above our capacity and reach. He is above and we are upon the earth. Therefore, it is proper that our words be wary and few.

Our God is one, or, rather, very *oneness* and mere Unity, having nothing but Itself in Itself, and not consisting of many things—as all things do besides God. In this *essential* Unity of God a *personal* Trinity nevertheless exists after a manner far exceeding the possibility of man's conception. The works which outwardly are of God are in such a manner of Him being one that each Person of the Trinity has in them[55] something which is peculiar and proper. For being three, and They all existing in the essence of one Deity, all things are *from* the Father, *by* the Son, *through* the Spirit. That which the Son hears of the Father, and that which the Spirit receives of the Father and the Son, the same we have at the hands of the Spirit as being the Last and, therefore, the nearest to us in order, although in power the same with the Second and the First.

The wise and learned among the very Heathens, themselves, have all acknowledged some First Cause, upon which the being of all things originally depends. Neither have they spoken of that Cause other than as an Agent, which knowing *what* and *why* It works, observe in Its work a most exact *order* or *law*.

---

[55] i.e., in the works.

Thus, much is signified by that which Homer mentions:

> Jupiter's counsel was accomplished.
>
> —HOMER, *The Iliad*, Book I[56]

Thus, much is acknowledged by Mercurius Trismegistus:[57]

> The Creator made the whole world, not with hands, but by reason.
>
> —HERMES TRISMEGISTUS, *Corpus Hermeticum* IV, I

Thus, much is confessed by Anaxagoras and Plato, describing the maker of the world as an *intellectual* Worker.[58]

Finally, the Stoics, although imagining the first cause of all things to be fire, nevertheless held that the same fire, having art, did *proceed by a certain and set way in the making of the world.*

Therefore, they all confess that, in the work of that First Cause, counsel is used, reason followed, a Way observed—which is to say, constant order and law is kept, of which Itself necessarily must be the Author of Itself. Otherwise, it would have something worthier and higher to direct it, and, so, could not, itself, be the first. Being the

---

56 In his translation, Hooker uses the Romans' Latin name of the god, "Jupiter" (derived from, "Djeus pater", meaning, "father God"), instead of the Greek names, "Dios", "Djeus", or "Zeus". This preference for the Roman names of Classical Era gods was common during Hooker's era, and not uncommon as late as the mid-Twentieth Century.

57 Again, Hooker uses the Latin name, "Mercurius" (i.e., "Mercury"), instead of the Greek, "Hermes". Called, "Trismegistus" ("Thrice-Majestic" or "Thrice-Great"), Hermes was associated by the Greeks with the Egyptian God, Thoth, an amalgam of various figures, including the deified historical person, Imhotep.

It is likely that there was no single author named, Hermes Trismegistus or Mercurius Trismegistus, and the work was written by multiple anonymous authors over the years.

58 Anaxagoras stated this in the opening to his now largely lost treatise, *On Nature*, which was quoted by Diogenes Laërtius.

> All things were together; then came Mind and set them in order.
>
> —DIOGENES LAËRTIUS, "Anaxagoras", *The Lives and Opinions of Eminent Philosophers*, translated by R. D. Hicks (G. P. Putman's Sons, New York, 1925), Volume I, Book II, Chapter 3

According to the tenth paragraph of PLATO, "Timæus", *The Dialogues of Plato, Translated into English, with Analyses and Introductions*, Volume II, by Benjamin Jowett (Charles Scribner's Sons, New York, 1897), the Maker of the world is declared to be intelligent and working rationally in His choice of fair and intelligible patterns.

First, It can have no other than the making of Itself to be the Author of that law by which It willingly works. God, therefore, is a law both unto Himself, and unto all other things, besides.

Unto Himself, He is a law in all those things of which our Savior speaks, saying:

> My Father works as yet, so I.
>
> —paraphrase of *John* 5:17

God works nothing without cause. All those things which are done by Him have some end for which they are done. And the end for which they are done is a reason of His will to do them. His will would not have inclined to create woman except that He saw that it could not be well if she were not created.

> It is not good that man should be alone. Therefore, let us make a helper for him.
>
> —paraphrase of *Genesis* 2:18

That and nothing else is done by God which to leave undone would not be so good. Therefore, if we ask why it is that with God, although having power and infinite ability, the effects of that power are all so limited as we see they are, the reason for this is the end which He has proposed. And the law—by which His wisdom has stinted the effects of His power in such a way that it does not work infinitely—correspondingly works to that end for which it works well, even all things in most decent and comely sort, all things in measure, number, and weight.[59]

The general end of God's external working is the exercise of His most glorious and most abundant virtue—which abundance shows itself in variety, and for that cause this variety is often expressed in Scripture by the name of, "riches".[60]

> The Lord has made all things for his own sake.
>
> —*Proverbs* 16:4, Great Bible, spelling updated

---

[59] *Wisdom of Solomon* 8:1 and 11:17.

[60] *Ephesians* 1:7, *Philemon* 4:19, *Colossians* 2:3.

Not that anything is made to be beneficial to him, but all things for him to show beneficence and grace in them. We are not able to discern the particular drift of every act proceeding externally from God, and, therefore, cannot always give the proper and certain reason of His works. Undoubtedly, however, there is a proper and certain reason of every finite work of God, in as much as there is a law imposed upon it—which, if there were not, it should be as infinite as the Worker, Himself. They err, therefore, who think that, of the will of God to do this or that, there is no reason besides His will.[61] Many times there is no reason known to us. But that there is no reason at all I judge it most unreasonable to imagine, in as much as He works all things not only according to His own will, but "the counsel of His own will".[62] And whatever is done with counsel or wise resolution necessarily has some reason why it should be done, although that reason is to us in some things so secret that it then forces the wit of man to stand amazed, as does the blessed apostle, Saint Paul, himself.

> O the depth of the riches, both of the wisdom, and knowledge of God! how unsearchable are His judgements! ...
>
> —*Romans* 11:33, a slight misquoting of the Bishops Bible

How should either men or angels be able to perfectly behold that eternal law which God, Himself, has made unto Himself, and thus works all things of which He is the Cause and Author?

> That law in the admirable frame of which shines with most perfect beauty the countenance of that Wisdom which has testified concerning Herself.
>
> > The Lord possessed me in the beginning of his way, even before his works of old I was set up...
> >
> > —paraphrase of *Proverbs* 8:23

---

61 As the theologians of the doctrine of divine will say...who believe there is no reason...but only the will of God revealed to us... However, the truth is that all precepts of the law have a cause and are directed towards some end and use.

—Moses Maimonides, *Guide for the Perplexed*, Part III, Chapter 26, paraphrased by Ret Miles

62 *Ephesians* 1:11, Hooker translating from the Ancient Greek.

That law which has been the pattern to make, and is the chart[63] by which to guide the World.

That law which has been of God, and everlastingly with God.

That law the Author and Observer of which is only one God to be blest forever.

The book of this law we are neither able nor worthy to open and look into. Therefore, that little which we darkly comprehend we admire. The rest we humbly and meekly adore with religious ignorance. Therefore, seeing that "of whom, through whom, and for whom are all things"[64] according to this law which He works—although there seems to us that there are confusion and disorder in the affairs of this present world—"Let no man doubt but that everything is well done, because the world is ruled by so good a Guide" as transgresses not His own law, that nothing can be more absolute, perfect, and just.[65]

The law by which He works is eternal and, therefore, can have no show or color of changeability—for which cause a part of that law being opened in the promises which God has made, because His promises are nothing else but declarations of what God will do for the good of men. Touching upon those promises the apostle, Saint Paul, has testified that God might as well deny himself and not be God as fail to perform them.[66] And concerning the counsel of God Saint Paul likewise calls it an "unchangeable" thing[67]—the counsel of God and that law of God, of which we now speak, being one. Nor is the freedom of the will of God a whit abated, thwarted, or hindered by means

[63] Hooker's word is, "card", likely referring to a map chart. The words, "card" and "chart" are etymologically related. He is likely not referring to a compass card, as can be seen in the word usage of his contemporary, EDMUND SPENSER, who, in Book II, Canto VII of *The Faerie Queene,* referred to the chart and compass separately: "Upon his card and compass firms his eye..."

[64] Paraphrase of *Romans* 11:36.

[65] Hooker is paraphrasing BŒTHIUS, *On the Consolation of Philosophy* (523 A.D.), Book IV, Prose V.

[66] *II Timothy* 2:13.

[67] *Hebrews* 6:17.

of this—because the imposition of this law upon Himself is His own free and voluntary act. This law, therefore, we may name, *eternal*, being "that order which, before all ages, God has set down with Himself, for Himself by which to do all things".[68]

---

[68] This law by which God works all things is the *first eternal law* in Hooker's philosophy. Writing three and a half centuries later, C. S. Lewis said:

> [T]he medieval conception of Natural Law…reached its fullest and most beautiful expression when the tide of history had turned against it. In the first book of Hooker we find that God Himself, though the author, is also the voluntary subject, of law. "They err who think that of the will of God to do this or that there is no reason besides his will" (I 1 5). God does nothing except in pursuance of that "constant Order and Law" of goodness which He has appointed to Himself. Nowhere outside the minds of devils and bad men is there a *sic volo sic jubeo* ["Thus I wish, thus I command"]. The universe itself is a constitutional monarchy.
>
> — C. S. LEWIS (CLIVE STAPLES LEWIS), *English Literature in the Sixteenth Century, Excluding Drama,* Book III, Chapter I (Clarendon Press, Oxford, England, 1954)(49)

Chapter Three

The Second Eternal Law, Governing Natural Agents

I AM NOT ignorant that, by *eternal law* the learned, for the most part, do not understand it to be the order by which God has eternally purposed Himself in all his works to observe, but, instead, that which with himself he has set down as expedient to be kept by all of his creatures, according to the several conditions with which he has invested them. Thus, they, who are accustomed to speak, apply the name of, *law*, only to that rule of working which Superior Authority imposes; whereas we, enlarging somewhat more the sense of it, call any kind of rule or canon by which actions are framed, a law.

Now, that law, which, as it is laid up in the bosom of God, is called, *eternal*, accordingly receives the different kinds of things which are subject unto it, having different and sundry kinds of names.

> That part of it which orders natural agents we usually call, *nature's law*.[69]
>
> That which angels clearly behold, and without any deviation observe, is a *celestial and heavenly law*.

---

[69] Hooker is referring to what can be called, the *inviolable laws of nature*, such as constants in nature (speed of light, Planck's constant, etc.) and the laws of physics. Being *inviolable*, these laws *cannot be violated* except by God or his agent performing a supernatural miracle.

> That which binds reasonable creatures in this world, and with which, by reason, they may most plainly perceive themselves bound, is the *law of reason*.[70]
>
> That which binds them, and is not known except by special revelation from God, is *divine law*.[71]
>
> That which, out of either the law of reason or of God, men probably gathering to be expedient, they make it a law, is *human law*.[72]

Therefore, all things which are as they ought to be are conformed to *this second, eternal law*,[73] and even those things which are not conformable to this eternal law are, notwithstanding, in some manner ordered by *the first, eternal law*. For whatever good or evil there is under the sun, whatever action correspondent or repugnant to the law which God has imposed upon His creatures, in or upon it God works according to the law which He, Himself has eternally purposed to keep—that is to say, *the first, eternal law*. So that a two-fold, eternal law being thus made, it is not hard to conceive how they both take place in all things.[74]

---

[70] Hooker is referring to what can be called, the *violable natural laws*, which can be logically deduced—as opposed to those violable natural laws revealed to us in Scripture—and which are considered to be part of human nature. Being *violable*, these laws *can be violated*, even if there might be a temporal or eternal consequence to so doing.

[71] Hooker is referring to the violable natural laws revealed to us in Scripture.

[72] Hooker is referring to manmade law ("lex humana"), sometimes misleadingly called, "positive law" ("lex posita"). Positive law, divine law, and manmade law overlap: *positive* law is called that because it is *posited* (i.e., *positioned, (im)posed*, placed, or put forth) by some person, whether divine or human, and requires enforcement in order to be practical (as opposed to inviolable laws of nature which cannot be broken except by a divine miracle, and so need not be enforced); divine law is a subset of positive law and is posited by God; manmade law is a subset of positive law and is posited by one or more humans or their agent institutions (such as government).

To emphasize the meaning of, "positive law", perhaps we should pronounce it in such a way as to emphasize its etymology: "pósitive law."

[73] In Hooker's philosophy, the *second eternal law* is the law which God imposes upon Creation.

[74]
> ...all actions and movements of the whole of nature are subject to the eternal law.
>
> —THOMAS AQUINAS, 1st Part of the 2nd Part, Question 93, Art. 5, *The Summa Theologica*, translated by the Fathers of the English Dominican Province. 22 vols. (R. & T. Washbourne, London, 1911 – 1925). The specific translator was Fr. Laurence Shapcote, O.P.

So, to come to the law of nature—although, by this term, we sometimes mean that manner of working which God has set for each created thing to keep. Yet, for as much as those things are most properly called, "*natural* agents", which keep the law of their kind unwittingly, as do the heavens and elements of the world, and which cannot do otherwise, and for as much as we give intellectual natures the name of, "*voluntary* agents", so that we may distinguish them from the other, it will be expedient that we sever the law of nature, observed by the one, from that to which the other is tied. Touching upon the former, their strict keeping of one tenure, statute, and law is spoken of by all, but has in it more than men have as yet attained to know or perhaps ever shall attain. Seeing that the travail of wading into this matter is given of God to the sons of men, and perceiving how much the least thing in the world has in it more than the wisest are able to understand, they may by this means learn humility.

In a footnote, Hooker quotes this passage in Latin from an older edition, and essentially summarizes this point as being made by Articles 4, 5, and 6. He then proceeds to provide other quotes with his insights (the below translated by Ret Miles from Hooker's Latin quotes and commentary).

> In no manner is anything withdrawn from the laws and ordering of the supreme creator, by whom the peace of the universe is administered.
>
> —AUGUSTINE OF HIPPO, *On the City of God against the Pagans*, Book XIX, Chapter 12

Indeed, even sin, insofar as it is justly permitted by God, falls under the eternal law. Even sin is subject to the eternal law, inasmuch as a voluntary transgression of the law introduces a certain penal disadvantage to the soul, according to that saying of Augustine:

> You decreed, Lord, and so it is, that every disordered soul receives its own punishment.
>
> —AUGUSTINE OF HIPPO, *Confessions*, Book 1, chapter 12

Nor is it badly said by the Scholastics:

> Just as we see that, by the very fact that they swerve from their particular end and from the eternal law, natural things fall back into the same eternal law (insofar as they are in another resulting state established by that same eternal law in their particular case), so it is likely that men, even when they sin and depart from the commandments of eternal law, fall back into the order of the eternal law as punishment.
>
> —Cardinal Cajetan's commentary on the 1st Part of the 2nd Part, Question 93, Article 6, of *Summa Theologica*. Sixteenth Century standard editions of Aquinas' *Summa Theologica* often included Cajetan's extensive commentaries printed alongside the text. Hooker uses the plural, "Scholastics", because Cajetan's commentary was such a standard at the time, that he was often taken as representative of the tradition of the mediæval Schoolmen.

Moses, in describing the work of creation, attributes speech to God:

> God said, Let there be light... Let there be a firmament... Let the Waters under the Heaven be gathered together into one place... Let the Earth bring forth... Let there be Lights in the Firmament of Heaven...
> —summarized excerpts from *Genesis* 1

Was the intent of Moses only to signify the infinite greatness of God's power, by the ease of his accomplishing such effects, without travail, pain, or labor? Surely it seems that Moses had, besides this, a further purpose—namely:

> Firstly, to teach that God did not work as a necessary agent, but as a voluntary agent, intending beforehand and decreeing with himself that which did outwardly proceed from him;
>
> Secondly, to show that God did then institute a natural law to be observed by creatures,

Therefore, according to the manner of laws, the institution of natural law is described as being established by solemn injunction. His commanding those things to be which exist, and to exist in such sort as they are—to keep that tenure and course which they do—indicates the establishment of nature's law. This world's first creation, and the preservation since of things created—what is this execution but only a manifestation that the eternal law of God concerns natural things? And as it comes to pass in a kingdom rightly ordered that after a law is once published it presently takes effect far and wide, all States framing themselves according to its mandates, even so let us think on how it fares in the natural course of the world. Since the time in which God first proclaimed the edicts of His law upon the world, Heaven and Earth have harkened unto His voice, and their labor has been to do His will: "He made a law for the rain",[75] He gave His "decree unto the sea, that the waters should not pass His commandment".[76] Now...

> if nature should interrupt her course and altogether abandon the observation of her own laws, though it were but for a while,

---

[75] *Job* 28:26, Hooker paraphrasing.

[76] Hooker is paraphrasing *Proverbs* 8:29 and *Jeremiah* 5:22.

if those principal and mother elements of the world, by which all things in this lower world are made, should lose the qualities which they now have,

if the frame of that heavenly arch[77] erected over our heads should loosen and dissolve itself,

if celestial spheres should forget their usual motions, and by irregular articulations turn themselves any way as it might happen,

if the Prince of the lights of Heaven,[78] which now as a giant does run his unwearied course, should as it were through a languishing faintness begin to stand and to rest himself,[79]

if the Moon should wander from her beaten way,

if the times and seasons of the year blend themselves by disordered and confused mixture,

if the winds breathe out their last gasp,

if the clouds yield no rain,

if the Earth be defeated of heavenly influence,[80] the fruits of the Earth pine away as children at the withered breasts of their mother, no longer able to yield them relief,

...what would become of man, himself, whom these things now do all serve? Do we not plainly see that obedience of creatures unto the law of nature is the foundation and stability of the whole world? Nevertheless, nature sometimes comes to pass as art. Let Phidias have rude and obstinate stuff to carve.[81] Though his art does what it should, his

---

[77] i.e., the sky.

[78] Hooker, classically educated, is referring to our sun by an appellation of the Greek sun-god, Apollo.

[79] *Psalm* 19:4–6.

[80] Hooker is referring to a scenario of human society and law losing their foundation and proper functioning because of the corruption which results from human disobedience to God.

[81] Phidias was the Fifth-Century B.C. chief designer of the Parthenon's sculptures on the Acropolis in Athens, and of the large statue of Zeus at Olympia, one of the Seven Wonders of the Ancient World. The word, "rude", in this context, means, "raw", "natural", "unworked", "unformed", "unshapen", "unrefined", etc., as well as implying anything which is not a perfect medium for one's art.

work will lack that beauty which otherwise in fitter matter it might have had. He that strikes an instrument with skill, may, nevertheless, cause a very unpleasant sound if the string which he strikes happens to be incapable of harmony.[82]

As for the material of which natural things consist, a saying from Theophrastus is pertinent: Πολὺ τὸ οὐχ ὑπακουῦον οὐδὲ δεχόμενον τὸ εὖ ("Much of it is often such as will by no means yield to receive the best and most-perfect impression").[83] They among the Heathen who contemplated nature often observed deviations in the material of natural things. But, the true original cause of these deviations, divine malediction,[84] is for the sin of man laid upon these creatures which God had made for the use of man. This, being an article of that saving truth which God has revealed unto his Church, was above the reach of their merely natural capacity and understanding. But, regardless of how these defects are now and then a part of the course of nature, nevertheless, so constantly the laws of nature are obeyed by natural agents, that no man denies but those things which nature works are wrought either always or for the most part after one and the same manner.

If we ask what it is which keeps nature in obedience to her own law, we must resort to that higher law of which we have already spoken, and because all other laws do depend upon it, from that we must borrow what we need for a brief resolution in this point. We are not of opinion, therefore, as some are, that nature in working has before her certain exemplary drafts or patterns, which subsisting in the bosom of the Highest, and being there discovered, she fixes her eye upon them as sailors navigate by the North Star, and that, accordingly, she guides her hand to work by imitation. Instead, we embrace the oracle of Hippocrates that "each thing both in small and in great fulfills

---

[82] i.e., out of tune.

[83] A quote from *Metaphysics*, a book by THEOPHRASTUS OF ERESUS, Aristotle's successor as head of a school of philosophy at the temple, Lyceum.

[84] i.e., a divine curse.

the task which destiny has set down".[85] And concerning the manner of executing and fulfilling the same, "What they do, they know not; yet, it is in show and appearance as if they did know what they do, and the truth is that they do not discern the things upon which they look."[86] Nevertheless, for as much as the works of nature are no less exact than if she did both behold and study how to express some absolute shape or mirror always present before her—yes, it is such that her dexterity and skill appear as if no intellectual creature in the world had the capacity to do what nature does without capacity and knowledge—it cannot but be that nature has some Director of infinite knowledge to guide her in all her ways. Who is the Guide of nature but only the God of nature? "In Him we live, move, and are."[87]

Those things which nature is said to do are by divine art performed, using nature as an instrument. Nor is there any such divine art or knowledge working in nature, herself, but in the Guide of nature's work. Whereas, therefore, natural things—which are not in the number of voluntary agents, for only of such do we now speak, and of no other—necessarily observe their certain laws, that as long as they keep those forms[88] which give them their being they cannot possibly be apt or inclinable to do otherwise than they do. Seeing that the kinds of their operations are both constantly and exactly framed according to the several ends for which they serve, they, themselves, though doing in the meanwhile that which is fit, yet knowing neither what they do, nor why, it follows that all that they do in this sort proceeds originally from some such agent which knows, appoints, holds up, and even actually frames the same.

---

[85] Hooker mistakenly attributes this to Hippocrates. It is actually a quote of a fragment of HERACLITUS, in *Poesis Philosophica,* collected and edited by Henri Estienne, also called, Henricus Stephanus (Henri Estienne, Geneva, 1573).

[86] Ibid.

[87] Hooker paraphrases *Acts* 17:28.

[88] In a note, Hooker states, "Form in other creatures is a thing proportional [i.e., analogous] to the soul in living creatures. It is neither sensible [i.e., tangible] nor otherwise discernable, except by effects. According to the diversity of inward forms, things of the world are distinguished into their kinds."

Being far above us, we are no more able to conceive by our reason the manner of this divine efficiency[89] than unreasonable creatures by their sense are able to apprehend the manner in which we dispose and order the course of our affairs. Only this much is discerned, that the natural generation and process of all things receives order proceeding from the settled stability of divine understanding. This appoints to them their kinds of operation, the disposition of which, in the purity of God's own knowledge and will, is rightly called by the name of *providence*. The same, second, eternal law applied to the created things, themselves, here disposed by it,[90] was typically called by the ancients, *natural destiny*.[91] That law, the performance of which we behold in natural things, is, as it were, an authentic or original draft written in the bosom of God, Himself, whose spirit being to execute that law, uses every particular nature, every mere natural agent, only as an instrument created at the beginning, and used ever since the beginning to work His own will and pleasure, as well.

Nature, therefore, is nothing else but God's instrument: in the course of which Dionysius[92], perceiving some sudden disturbance, is said to have cried out,

> Either the God of nature is suffering, or the fabric of the world is being dissolved!
>
> —*Breviarium Romanum*, 1568, the standard Roman Catholic breviary in Hooker's time

---

[89] i.e., divine power.

[90] i.e., positioned, put into place, ordered, or arranged by the second eternal law. The verb, "disposed", in this context, does not mean to "get rid of". It is related to the words, "posited", "positioned", "posed", "imposed", "deposed", "proposed", "propositioned", "supposed", and "positive". To better understand this usage of "disposed", remember Thomas à Kempis' rhyming quote from his early-Fifteenth Century book, *An Imitation of Christ*: "Homo proponit, sed Deus disponit", ("Man proposes, but God disposes", a paraphrase of *Proverbs* 19:21).

[91] Hooker uses the Latin phrase, "naturali destinie"—i.e., the natural order, the natural process of cause-and-effect, seen by some ancient thinkers as the fulfilling of one's destiny, one's fate, one's doom, one's predestination.

[92] i.e., Dionysius the Areopagite, as quoted in PSEUDO-DIONYSIUS, *Corpus Areopagiticum*, written in the late-Fifth Century or early-Sixth Century. Dionysius was an areopagite, a judge who met with other judges on Athen's Areopagus ("Mars Hill"), and who converted to Christianity after hearing the apostle, Paul, give his sermon to those judges. The ancient Christian tradition, related in *Corpus Areopagiticum* (which was credited as being written by Dionysius, although he lived long before it was written), holds that Dionysius was startled by the darkening of the sun in Athens

Either God suffers impediment and is hindered by a greater one than Himself, or, if that is impossible, then He has determined to make a present dissolution of the world, the execution of that law—without which the world cannot stand—beginning now to stand still.

This Workman,[93] whose servant is nature, being in truth but only one, the Heathens imagining Him to be more, gave Him in the sky the name of, *Jupiter*; in the air, the name of, *Juno*; in the water, the name of, *Neptune*; in the earth, the name of, *Vesta*, and sometimes of, *Ceres*; in the Sun, the name of, *Apollo*; in the Moon, the name of, *Diana*; in the winds, the name of, *Æolus*, and diverse others; and, to conclude, even so many guides of nature they dreamed of, according to the kinds of natural things which they saw in the world. These they honored, as having power to work or cease according as men deserved of them. But, for us, there is only one Guide of all natural agents, and He both the Creator and the Worker of all in all, alone to be blessed, adored, and forever honored by all.

So far, that of which has been spoken[94] concerns natural agents considered in themselves. But, we must also further remember (and a brief reminder shall suffice) that, as in this respect, natural agents have their law, which law directs them in the means by which they tend to their own betterment. So, likewise, another law applies to those who are sociable parts united into one body—a law which binds each of them to serve others well, and to always prefer the good of the whole before their own particular good, as is reasonably plain if we imagine a scenario in which natural things forget their nature, and we imagine a heavy object, which naturally stays on the surface of the Earth as it seeks the Earth's center, rising upwards of its own accord, instead, and forsaking the gravity of the Earth—not naturally staying on the Earth's surface—so as to relieve some common, present distress of nature, almost as if it had heard itself commanded to abandon its proper nature.[95]

---

on the day when Christ Jesus was crucified, and exclaimed the words quoted. Then, years later, he heard Paul's Mars Hill sermon and converted.

[93] i.e., God.

[94] i.e., the second eternal law.

[95] Hooker has distinguished two aspects of the second eternal law:

1. the second eternal law as it applies to each natural agent in and of itself;

2. the sociable law, which is the second eternal law as it applies to interactions among individuals in a society.

His metaphor of the rising object, written in terms of Aristotelian physics decades before the formulation of Newtonian physics, is a metaphor of a principle which he applies to geopolitical societies (and the church, in later books). That principle is the core of his entire argument against the Puritans insistent on purifying the English church in only their way: the common good always takes priority over the private good.

CHAPTER FOUR

The Third Eternal Law, Governing the Angels

BUT NOW THAT we may lift up our eyes, as it were, from the footstool to the throne of God, and, turning from these natural agents, consider the state of heavenly and divine creatures a little, touching upon angels which are immaterial and intellectual spirits,[96] the glorious inhabitants of those sacred palaces where there is nothing but light and blessed immortality, no shadow of an occasion for tears, discontentments, griefs, and uncomfortable passions to work upon, but all joy, tranquility, and peace, even forever and ever do dwell. In number and order they are huge, mighty, and royal armies.[97] So like armies they

---

96 …he maketh his angels spirits…
—*Psalm* 104:4 and *Hebrews* 1:7, Bishops' Bible

97 …a thousand thousands ministered unto him, and ten thousand thousands stood before him…
—*Daniel* 7:10, Bishops' Bible, spelling updated

Thinkest thou that I cannot now pray to my father, and he shall give me more than twelve legions of angels?
—*Matthew* 26:53, Bishops' Bible, spelling updated

…there was with the angel, a multitude of heavenly soldiers…
—*Luke* 2:13, Bishops' Bible, spelling updated

But ye are come unto ye mount Sion, and to the city of the living God, the celestial Jerusalem, and to an innumerable company of angels…
—*Hebrews* 12:22, Bishops' Bible, spelling updated

BASIL OF CÆSAREA (also called, SAINT BASIL THE GREAT), in his *De Spiritu Sancto* ("*On the Holy Spirit*"), Chapter XVI, explains that the angels have a hierarchy where some command and others obey, with perfect peace with no envy.

are in complete obedience to that law which the Highest—whom they adore, love, and imitate—has imposed on them. So observant they are of this that our Savior, Himself, Who set down the perfect *idea* of that which we are to pray and wish for on Earth, did not teach us to pray or wish for more than only that here it might be with us as it is with them in Heaven.[98] God, Who moves mere natural agents as only an efficient cause, does otherwise move intellectual creatures, and especially His holy angels. For, beholding the face of God[99] in admiration of so great excellence, they all adore Him. And being rapt with the love of His beauty they inseparably cleave to Him, forever. Desire to resemble Him in goodness makes them unwearying, and even insatiable, in their longing to do by all means all manner of good unto all of the creatures of God,[100] but especially unto the children of men[101] in the countenance of whose nature looking downward they

---

98 Thy will be done, as well in earth, as it is in heaven.
—*Matthew* 6:10, Bishops' Bible, spelling updated

99 Take heed that ye despise not one of these little ones: For I say unto you, that in heaven their angels do always behold the face of my father, which is in heaven.
—*Matthew* 18:10, Bishops' Bible, spelling updated

100 How oft do they, their silver bowers leave,
To come to succour us, that succour want?
How oft do they with golden pinions, cleave
The flitting skies, like flying Pursuivant,*
Against foul fiends to aid us militant?
They for us fight, they watch and duly ward,
And their bright Squadrons round about us plant,
And all for love, and nothing for reward:
O why should heavenly God to man have such regard?

—EDMUND SPENSER, *Færie Queene* (1590), Book II, Canto viii, Stanza 2, in Alexander B. Grosart, Editor, *The Complete Works in Verse and Prose of Edmund Spenser* (Grosart, London, 1882), spelling updated

* A *pursuivant* is a junior herald.

101 For he will give his angels charge over thee: to keep thee in all thy ways
They will bear thee in their hands: that thou hurt not thy foot against a stone
—*Psalm* 91:11–12, Bishops' Bible, spelling updated

I saw in the visions of my head upon my bed, and behold a watcher and a holy one came down from heaven
—*Daniel* 4:13, Bishops' Bible, spelling updated

At the beginning of thy supplications, the commandment came forth, and I am come to show thee, for thou art greatly beloved: therefore understand the matter and consider the vision
—*Daniel* 9:23, Bishops' Bible, spelling updated

behold themselves beneath themselves, even as upward in God, beneath Whom they, themselves, are, they see that character which resembles nothing else but themselves and us.

This far even the Pagan philosophers have approached. This far they have seen into the doings of the angels of God. Orpheus confessed that the fiery throne of God is attended by those most industrious angels which are careful as to how all things are performed among men.[102] And the mirror of human wisdom plainly teaches that God moves angels, even as things stir man's heart which are presented to it as something desirable.[103]

> Take heed that ye despise not one of these little ones: For I say unto you, that in heaven their angels do always behold the face of my father, which is in heaven.
>
> —*Matthew* 18:10, Bishops' Bible, spelling updated
>
> I say unto you, that likewise joy shall be in heaven over one sinner that repenteth...
>
> —*Luke* 15:7, Bishops' Bible, spelling updated
>
> The same saw by a vision evidently, about the ninth hour of the day, an angel of God coming in to him, and saying unto him...
>
> —*Acts* 10:3, Bishops' Bible, spelling updated
>
> Are they not all ministering spirits, sent forth into ministry for their sakes which shall be heirs of salvation?
>
> —*Hebrews* 1:14, Bishops' Bible, spelling updated

[102] And near Thy Fiery Throne stand the most-industrious of the angels, to whom it is a care that all things be completed for men.

—attributed to the likely-mythical ORPHEUS, and quoted in TITUS FLAVIUS CLEMENS (CLEMENT OF ALEXANDRIA), Στρώματα ("*Stromata*", literally, "*Patchwork Quilt*", and figuratively, "*Miscellanies*"), Book V, Chapter XIV. Excerpt translated by Ret Miles.

See also, CLEMENT OF ALEXANDRIA, *The Miscellanies; or Stromata*, translated by William Wilson, Book V, Chapter XIV, "Greek Plagiarisms from the Hebrews", in *Ante-Nicene Christian Library: Translations of the Writings of the Fathers down to A.D. 325*, edited by Alexander Roberts and James Donaldson, Volume IV, "Clement of Alexandria, Vol. I (*Exhortation to the Heathen, The Instructor, Miscellanies*)" (T. & T. Clark, Edinburgh, 1867).

[103] It moves as the loved; and by the movement, others are moved.

—translated by Ret Miles from Hooker's quote of Thomas Aquinas' Latin paraphrase ("Movet ut amatum: moto vero, alia moventur.") of a principle described by ARISTOTLE in *Metaphysics*, Book XII, Chapter 7, 1072β. See, ST. THOMAS AQUINAS, "Commentary on the Metaphysics of Aristotle", translated by John P. Rowan, *Library of Living Catholic Thought*, Volume I (Henry Regnery Company, Chicago, 1961), Book XII, Lecture 7.

Therefore, angelic actions may be summarized as three general kinds:

> first, most delectable *love*, arising from the visible comprehension of the purity, glory, and beauty of God, only visible to Spirits which are pure;[104]
>
> secondly, *adoration*, grounded on the evidence of the greatness of God, on Whom they see how all things depend;[105]
>
> thirdly, *imitation*, bred by the presence of His exemplary goodness, Who daily before them ceases not to fill Heaven and Earth with the rich treasures of most free and undeserved grace.[106]

Of angels we are not only to consider what they are and do in regard of their own being, but also that which concerns them as they

---

[104] Where wast thou when the morning stars praised me together, and all the children of God rejoiced triumphantly

—*Job* 38:7, Bishops' Bible, spelling updated

Take heed that ye despise not one of these little ones: For I say unto you, that in heaven their angels do always behold the face of my father, which is in heaven.

—*Matthew* 18:10, Bishops' Bible, spelling updated

[105] Praise him all ye his angels: praise him all ye his host

—*Psalm* 148:2, Bishops' Bible, spelling updated

And let all the angels of God worship him.

—*Hebrews* 1:6, Bishops' Bible, spelling updated

In the year that king Oziah died, I saw also the Lord sitting upon an high and glorious seat, and his train filled the temple

And about him stood Seraphims, whereof [each] one had six wings, with twain* each covered his face, with twain his feet, and with twain did he fly

They cried also each one to another on this manner, "Holy, holy, holy is the Lord of hosts: the whole earth is full of his glory"

—*Isaiah* 6:1–3, Bishops' Bible, annotated and spelling updated

* The word, "twain", means, "two".

[106] Implied wherever we find angels called, "the sons of God" or "the children of God".

And upon a day when the children of God came and stood before the lord, Satan came also among them…

—*Job* 1:6, Bishops' Bible, spelling updated

Where wast thou when the morning stars praised me together, and all the children of God rejoiced triumphantly…

— *Job* 38:7, Bishops' Bible, spelling updated

are linked in a kind of corporation among themselves and of society or fellowship with men. Consider angels separately—each of them in himself—and their law is that which the Prophet David mentions: "All ye his angels praise him."[107] Consider the angels of God as a group, and their law is that which arrays them as an army, one in order and degree above another.[108] Finally, consider the angels as having with us that communion which the apostle to the Hebrews notes, and in regard of which angels have not disdained to profess themselves our fellow-servants. From here there springs up a third law which binds them to works of ministerial employment,[109] of which each of their several functions are performed by them with joy.

Nevertheless, we know that a part of the angels of God have fallen,[110] and that their fall has been through the voluntary breach of that law which did require at their hands continuation in the exercise of their high and admirable virtue. It was impossible that their will should ever change or incline to omit any part of their duty without

---

107 *Psalm* 148:2.

108 Thinkest thou that I cannot now pray to my father, and he shall give me more than twelve legions of angels?

—*Matthew* 26:53, Bishops' Bible, spelling updated

And straightway, there was with the angel, a multitude of heavenly soldiers, praising God,

—*Luke* 2:13, Bishops' Bible, spelling updated

109 But ye are come unto ye mount Sion,* and to the city of the living God, the celestial Jerusalem, and to an innumerable company of angels…

—*Hebrews* 12:22, Bishops' Bible, spelling updated

* "Sion" is an alternate form of, "Zion".

I John saw these things, and heard them: And when I had heard and seen, I fell down to worship before the feet of the angel, which showed me these things.
And he said unto me: see thou do it not, for I am thy fellow servant, and the fellow servant of thy brethren the prophets, and of them which keep the sayings of this book: But worship God.

—*Apocalypse* (i.e., *Revelation*) 22:9–9, Bishops' Bible, spelling updated

110 …God spared not the angels that sinned, but cast them down into hell, and delivered them into chains of darkness, to be kept unto judgement…

—*II Peter* 2:4, Bishops' Bible, spelling updated

The angels also which kept not their first estate, but left their own habitation, he hath reserved in everlasting chains under darkness, unto the judgement of the great day.

—*Jude* 1:6, Bishops' Bible, spelling updated

some object which had the power to divert their focus from God and to draw it another way—and all of that before they attained that high perfection of bliss in which now the elect angels are without possibility of falling,[111] or could not possibly prefer anything over God, because they comprehend that anything apart from God is only something which is dependent upon Him—because God must necessarily seem infinitely better than anything which they could so apprehend. Things beneath them could not in such sort be presented to their eyes, except that, in doing so, they had to always see how those things depended upon God. Therefore, it seems that there was no other way for angels to sin except by thinking about themselves. When, in the grip of an admiration of their own sublimity and honor, the memory of their subordination to God and their dependence upon Him was submerged in this conceit, their adoration, love, and imitation of God could only be also interrupted.

The fall of angels, therefore, was pride.[112] Since their fall, their practices have entirely been the contrary to those mentioned before.[113] For

---

[111] I testify before God, and the Lord Jesus Christ, and the elect angels…
—*I Timothy* 5:21, Bishops' Bible, spelling updated

[112] But pride, impatient of long resting peace,
Did puff them up with greedy bold ambition,
That they gan cast their state how to increase*
Above the fortune of their first condition,
And sit in God's own seat without commission:
The brightest angel, even the child of light,
Drew millions more against their God to fight.

—EDMUND SPENSER, *Hymn on Heavenly Love,* lines 78–84, published 1596. See "Fowre Hymnes: An Hymne of Heavenly Love", in *The Poetical Works of Edmund Spenser in Three Volumes,* Volume I, *Spenser's Minor Poems,* edited by Ernest de Sélincourt (Clarendon Press, Oxford, England, 1910).

* Even in Spenser's time, the word, "gan", which means, "began to", was archaic. He used it for poetic effect and to maintain the meter. The word, "state", meant, "status". The line, "That they gan cast their state how to increase", means, "That they began to plan or scheme how to increase their status".

[113] …the serpent beguiled me…
—*Genesis* 3:13, Bishops' Bible, spelling updated

And Satan stood up against Israel
—*I Chronicles* 21:1, Bishops' Bible, spelling updated

And the Lord said to Satan, Whence comest thou? Satan answered the Lord and said: From compassing the earth to and fro, and from walking through it
—*Job* 1:7, Bishops' Bible, spelling updated

some being dispersed in the air, some on the earth, some in the water, and some among the minerals, dens, and caves which are under the earth, they have by all means labored to effect a universal rebellion against the laws, and, as far as in them lies, utter destruction of the works of God. These wicked spirits the Heathens honored instead of gods, both generally under the name of, dij inferi ("infernal gods"), and particularly—some in oracles, some in idols, some as household gods, some as nymphs. In a word, there was no soul and wicked spirit which was not in one way or the other honored by men as God, until such time as light appeared in the world, and dissolved the works of the devil.

This much, therefore, may suffice for our discourse on angels, the next unto whom, in degree, are men.

And the Lord said unto Satan, From whence comest thou? Satan answered the Lord and said: I have gone about the land, walked through it

—*Job* 2:2, Bishops' Bible, spelling updated

Howbeit, they understood not that he spoke to them of his father.

—*John* 8:27, Bishops' Bible, spelling updated

Ye are of your father the devil, and the lusts of your father will ye do. He was a murderer from the beginning, and abode not in the truth: because there is no truth in him. When he speaketh a lie, he speaketh of his own: For he is a liar, and the father of the same thing.

—*John* 8:44, Bishops' Bible, spelling updated

...how is it, that Satan hath filled thine heart, that thou shouldest lie...

—*Acts* 5:3, Bishops' Bible, spelling updated

...your adversary the devil, as a roaring Lion walketh about seeking who he may devour:

—*I Peter* 5:8, Bishops' Bible, spelling updated

And they had a king over them, which is the angel of the bottomless pit,

—*Apocalypse* (*Revelation*) 9:11, Bishops' Bible, spelling updated

And when the thousand years are expired, Satan shall be loosed out of his prison.
And shall go out to deceive the people which are in the four quarters of the earth, whose name in the Hebrew tongue is Abadon, but in ye Greek tongue Apollyon, [that is to say, a destroyer.]

—*Apocalypse* (*Revelation*) 20:7–8, Bishops' Bible, spelling updated

Chapter Five

The Law Which Directs Man So That His Actions Imitate God

EXCEPT ONLY GOD—Who actually and eternally is whatever He may be, and cannot ever be what He is not now—all things which are not yet actually in existence are to some extent possible. Because of this, there is in all things an appetite or desire by which they tend toward something which they may be. And when they are it, they shall be better off than they are, now. All of these betterments are included under the general name of *goodness*. And, because there is not anything in the world by which another thing may not in some manner be the means of its betterment, all things which are, are good.

Again, since there can be no desired goodness which does not proceed from God, Himself, as from the Supreme Cause of all things, and since every effect does in some manner contain—or at least resemble—the cause from which it proceeds, all things in the world are said to seek the Highest in some manner, and more or less to desire the participation of God, Himself.[114] Yet nowhere does this appear so much as it does in man, because there are so many kinds of betterments which man seeks.

---

[114] In a note, Hooker quotes Aristotle: Πάντα γοὲρ ἑχείνε ὀρέζεταυ ("For all reach toward [or seek] that", with "that" referring to the good). He cites ARISTOTLE, *Of the Soul*, Book II, Chapter 4, but the incorrectly transcribed quote is actually, πάντα γὰρ ἐκείνου ὀρέγεται ("for all reach toward [or seek] that"), similar to the idea expressed in the first sentence of ARISTOTLE, *Nicomachean Ethics*, Book I, Chapter 1:

The first degree of goodness is that general betterment which all things seek in desiring the continuance of their being. Therefore, all things wanting, as much as may be, to be eternal like God, that which cannot yet personally succeed in that seeks to continue itself another way—that is, by offspring and propagation.

The next degree of goodness is that which each thing wants by being more like God in the constancy and excellency of those operations which belong to their kind.[115] They strive toward the changelessness of God by working—either always or for the most part—after one and the same manner. They imitate His perfection by attempting the best for their particular kind. Hence have risen a number of axioms in philosophy showing how "The works of nature always aim at what is best."[116]

These two kinds of goodness, which have been described, are so nearly united to the things, themselves, which desire them, that we scarcely perceive the urge towards them. But the desire of those outward improvements is more apparent—especially those not expressly desired unless they are first known, or those desired for the sake of knowledge, itself. Among the creatures of this inferior world, man, by proceeding in this kind of knowledge of truth, and by growing in the exercise of virtue, aspires to the greatest conformity with God. This is not only known to

---

> Every art and every investigation, and likewise every practical pursuit or undertaking, seems to aim at some good: hence it has been well said that the Good is That at which all things aim.
>
> —H. RACKHAM, editor and translator, *Aristotle in 23 Volumes*, Volume 19 (Harvard University Press, Cambridge, Massachusetts, 1934). The word, "art", in this case, means, "technique" or "method".

[115] i.e., the functions and behaviors according to their species, form, purpose, or design.

[116] A paraphrase of Aristotle. In a note, Hooker concatenates two quotes: Ἐν τοιξ φύσει δει῀τὸ βέλτιον, ἐὰν ἐνδέχηται, ὑπάρχειν μαλλον...ἡ φύσις ἀεὶ ποιει῀τωῦ ἐνδεχομένων τὸ βέλτιστον. ("In nature, it is binding [i.e., compelling, necessary, inexorable] that the better be more, if possible… nature always makes the best of possibilities.") Although he credits both parts to ARISTOTLE, *On the Heavens*, Book II, Chapter 5, only the second part is in that text. The first part quotes an abridgement of a passage in ARISTOTLE, *Physics* (ca. 350–23 B.C.), Book VIII, Chapter 6: ἐν γὰρ τοῖς φύσει δεῖ τὸ πεπερασμένον καὶ τὸ βέλτιον, ἂν ἐνδέχηται, ὑπάρχειν μᾶλλον ("for in nature, it is binding that the [intended] end, and the better, be more, if possible").

us, whom He, Himself, has so instructed,[117] but even those acknowledge this fact who among men are not judged the nearest unto God. With Plato, is there anything more usual than to excite men unto the love of wisdom by showing how much it is that wise men are, therefore, exalted above men, how knowledge raises them up into Heaven, how it makes them, though not gods, yet as gods: high, admirable, and divine?[118] And

---

[117] Hooker cites *Matthew* 5:48 and the apocryphal *Book of Wisdom* (also called, *Wisdom of Solomon*) 7:27.

[118] In Plato's dialogs, *The Republic* and *Phædrus*, men are elevated by their increased knowledge and wisdom. Much of Plato's writings related to the concept of *forms*.

In Book VII of *The Republic*, Plato's dialog has Socrates telling the Allegory of the Cave to Glaucon, Plato's brother. Inside the cave, prisoners who have been chained their entire lives are constrained so that they can only see a cave wall illuminated by a fire above and behind them, and the shadows it casts of people and carried objects passing between the firelight and the wall of the cave (but behind and above the prisoners). They only hear the echoes of the voices of the hidden people. Seeing only the shadows, hearing only the echoes, and having been chained there since their childhood, they mistake the shadows as reality, and the echoes as coming from the shadows, not having ever experienced the world outside of the cave. They also confer honors among themselves for having certain insights about what they've seen and heard, and being able to predict what will be seen next. These prisoners represent the majority of humans, for whom the shadows are their "truth".

When they are released, and are allowed to turn around and see the actual firelight, it hurts their eyes, and they are confused. One of the prisoners, representing philosophers, ascends out of the cave, and sees the sunlit world, which is difficult and painful to see at first in the bright light, but eventually he can, and then he sees the sun. This ascent is both a physical and spiritual journey toward a higher, divine reality. Now seeing the form of the good, the source of all truth and knowledge, he no longer cares for the irrelevant honors bestowed by the less-enlightened, below, in the cave. And if he were put back in the darkness of the cave, after having experienced the brighter world above the cave, all would look dark to him, and what he would say to those still in the cave would sound nonsensical, even dangerous. If he tries to lead anyone else out of the cave to the higher world, he would be at risk of being killed as a dangerous subversive.

Socrates then explains the allegory.

> [T]he prison-house [i.e., the cave dungeon] is the world of sight, the light of the fire is the sun, and the journey upwards [is] the ascent of the soul into the intellectual world... [I]n the world of knowledge the idea of good appears last of all, and is seen only with an effort; and, when seen, is also inferred to be the universal author of all things beautiful and right, parent of light and of the lord of light in this visible world, and the immediate source of reason and truth in the intellectual [world]; and that this is the power upon which he who would act rationally either in public or private life must have his eye fixed. ... [T]hose who attain to this beatific vision are unwilling to descend to human affairs; for their souls are ever hastening into the upper world where they desire to dwell; which desire of theirs

Mercurius Trismegistus, speaking of the virtues of a righteous soul, says, "Such spirits are never cloyed with praising and speaking well of all men, with doing good unto everyone by word and deed, because they study to frame themselves according to *THE PATTERN* of the Father of spirits."[119]

> is very natural… [O]ne who passes from divine contemplations to the evil state of men…while his eyes are blinking and before he has become accustomed to the surrounding darkness…is compelled to fight in courts of law, or in other places, about the images or the shadows of images of justice, and endeavoring to meet the conceptions of those who have never yet seen absolute justice?
>
> —Benjamin Jowett, translator, *The Republic of Plato: An Ideal Commonwealth* (The Colonial Press, New York, 1901), Book VII

In Plato's dialog, *Phædrus*, Socrates speaks to the title character figuratively of the soul as a charioteer with two horses, one noble and one ignoble, trying to steer a course toward a divine realm. While the "chariots of the gods" each have two noble horses, the mortal charioteer's struggle to control the mixed horses, and ascend to contemplate the forms, is figuratively how reason elevates humans toward the divine. During the ascent, the charioteers—the souls—with the best-behaved horses are able to look upon the divine heaven and its forms. See BENJAMIN JOWETT, *The Dialogues of Plato, Translated into English, with Analyses and Introductions*, Third Edition (Oxford University Press, London, 1892).

Hooker alludes to Platonic forms, part of a major theme in many of Plato's works (not just the two cited, here) that intellectual and moral excellence lifts human nature and brings one closer to the divine source of truth. This idea was a usual reference which would have been well-known to Hooker's typically more-educated contemporaries.

[119] The quote is a paraphrase of:

> But such a psychè [i.e., the soul], hymning [singing of or to God] and speaking well of all people, and by words and by works doing good to all, mimicking its father, never has satisfaction [i.e., never has enough].
>
> —HERMES TRISMEGISTUS, *Corpus Hermeticum*, Chapter X, Section 21

See note 57.

Chapter Six

The Beginning of Humanity's Understanding of the Law

IN THE MATTER of knowledge, there is between the angels of God and the children of men this difference: angels already have full and complete knowledge in the highest degree which can be imparted unto them; men, if we view them in the springtime of their years, are at the first without any understanding or knowledge. Nevertheless, from this utter mental vacancy they grow by degrees, until they come at length to be even as the angels are, themselves.[120] That which is with the one, now, the other shall acquire in the end—they are not so far separated and severed but that they come at length to meet. Therefore, the soul of man being at the first as a book wherein nothing is written and yet

---

[120] In a note, Hooker cites *Isaiah* 7:16, likely intending only the first part of that verse, "For or ever [i.e., For before] the child shall know to refuse the evil, and choose the good..." (Bishops Bible).

The context of the quote is the full paragraph which prophesies the birth of the Messiah, preceded by the fall of the Kingdoms of Judah and Israel:

> And he [Isaiah] said, "Hear ye now, O house of David; Is it a small thing for you to weary men, but will ye weary my God also? Therefore, the Lord himself shall give you a sign; Behold, a virgin shall conceive, and bear a son, and shall call his name Immanuel. Butter and honey shall he eat, that he may know to refuse the evil, and choose the good. For or ever the child shall know to refuse the evil, and choose the good, the land that thou abhorrest shall be forsaken of both her kings."
>
> —*Isaiah* 7:13–16, Bishops Bible, spelling and punctuation updated

all things may be imprinted,[121] we are to search by what steps and degrees the book rises unto perfection of knowledge.

To what has been said about natural agents, this we must add: although within that category we have included living creatures, if they be in degree of nature beneath men, as well as anything void of life. Nevertheless, a difference we must observe between those natural agents which work altogether unwittingly and those which have some understanding, although weak, of what they do,[122] as fishes, fowls, and beasts have. The senses of beasts are as developed as even are the

---

[121] This concept is frequently referred to as, "tabula rasa", a Latin phrase used by the Islamic Golden Age philosopher, Avicenna, and others, literally meaning, "razed table", "scraped (wax) tablet", or "erased table"), and, by extension, meaning, "blank tablet", "blank slate" (its most frequent English translation), "unscribed tablet" (Aristotle's metaphor), or "white paper" (John Locke's metaphor). The term, "tabula rasa" or "blank slate", refers to the theorized state of a newborn child who is completely ignorant (i.e., his or her mind is essentially a "blank slate") until knowledge is gained by experiences and perceptions, with this knowledge being written upon the slate, tablet, or book which is the mind's memory. The metaphor of an unscribed tablet was first introduced by ARISTOTLE, in his lecture, *De Anima* ("*Of the Soul*"), and developed by Stoic philosophers, then Avicenna, Abubacer, and Thomas Aquinas, and then, writing after Hooker's time, René Descartes, John Locke (with whom the theory is most famously associated), and Sigmund Freud.

The concept of tabula rasa or blank slate is essentially the "nurture" side of the "nature versus nurture" debate over whether a person's genetics ("nature") or their environment and experiences ("nurture") have more influence on his or her development.

The word, "tabula", is a source of such English words as, "table", "tablet", "tabulate", "tabular", "tab", "tablature", "tavla", "taula", and "tableau", and the word, "rasa", is derived from "rado", which is a source of such English words as "raze", "razor", and "erase", and might be related to "rodent" (but not "radical", "radish", "eradicate", "radial", "radius", or "radiate").

[122] i.e., they are sentient, they have a consciousness. Currently, scientists consider any living being with a brain and a nervous system to have some sort of sentience, of consciousness, and to be capable of feeling pain, although this is all debated for fish, crustaceans, insects, and annelids such as earthworms. Sponges, bacteria, fungi, plankton, and plants have no nervous system, and, therefore, have no sentience, no consciousness. Arachnids, shrimp, snails, clams, scallops, and mollusks have one or more clusters of nerve cells which function somewhat like a brain, but it is debated as to whether these animals are sentient, have consciousness, or feel pain (although shrimp are thought to have pain receptors). Starfish, corals, and anemones have nervous systems, but no brain, and so they are not considered to be sentient, to have consciousness. Viruses are not currently considered to be living beings, and, therefore, they have no sentience, no consciousness.

senses of men, themselves—perhaps more developed. For as stones, though in dignity of nature inferior to plants, yet the stones exceed plants in firmness of strength or durability of being. And plants, though beneath the excellency of creatures indued with sense, yet exceed them in the faculty of vegetation and of fertility. Likewise, beasts, though otherwise behind men, may, notwithstanding, in actions of sense and fancy, exceed men—because the endeavors of nature, when it has a higher perfection to seek, are in lower perfections the more remiss, not esteeming those lower perfections as much as beasts do, which have no better perfection and purpose.

The soul of man, therefore, being capable of a more divine perfection, has—besides the faculties of growing unto sensible knowledge, which man has in common with beasts—a further ability, of which in beasts there is no show at all: the ability of reaching higher than to tangible things.[123] Until we age, the soul of man only perceives inferior and more obvious things, which afterwards serve as instrumental steps to knowledge which is greater—in infancy the soul does not ascend above the reach of lesser creatures. Once the soul comprehends anything above this—such as differences in time, affirmations, negations, and contradictions in speech—we then consider it to have some use of natural reason. Afterwards, if to this knowledge there might be added the right aids of true art and learning—which aids, I must plainly confess, this age of the world, though it claims to be a learned age, neither much knows nor greatly regards—there would undoubtedly be almost as great a difference in maturity of judgement between men so endowed and that which men now are, as between what men are now and infants.

---

[123] In a note Hooker provides an Ancient Greek quote of Mercurius Trismegistus which can be translated as follows:

> ...whereas man doth mount up to heaven and measure it; he knows what things of it are high, what things are low, and learns precisely all things else besides. And greater thing than all; without e'en quitting earth, he doth ascend above.
>
> —Hermes Trismegistus, "The Key", *Corpus Hermeticum*, translated by George Robert Stowe Mead (The Theosophical Publishing Society, London, 1906)

If anyone criticizes this conclusion as being overly exaggerated, let them consider just this one thing: at first discovery, no art is so perfect as diligence may afterwards make it.

Yet, the very first man who, for whatever reason, knew the way we speak of,[124] and followed it, by that has, alone, very nearly accomplished more in all fields of natural knowledge than the whole world has since done in any single field.

Despite its inadequacy, that other, newly devised aid[125] has two, unique aspects: it is marvelously quick, and shows those who use it as almost much in three days as they would learn in sixty years the usual way. Again, because many times the curiosity of man's wit dangerously wades farther in the search of knowledge than were suitable, in consequence that curiosity is limited to such broad, obvious generalities as are everywhere apparent even to men with the weakest, bare-minimum ability to conceive. So, we find that following the rules and precepts of this newly devised aid results in a method which teaches a speedy way of communication and, at the same time, limits the intellectual understanding and wisdom of the human mind.

Education and instruction are the means—the one by use, the other by precept[126]—to make our natural faculty of reason both better and sooner able to rightly judge between truth and error, good and evil.

---

[124] Hooker is referring to Aristotelian logic.

[125] Hooker is referring to Ramistry or Ramism, a controversial, streamlined method and educational philosophy developed and advocated by Peter Ramus, a French textbook author, anti-Aristotelian, and Protestant convert who preferred that education use dialectical logic, instead of the Aristotelian logic which most scholars favored. Ramus, a Huguenot (a French Calvinist—essentially a French Puritan) was murdered during the 1572 Saint Bartholemew's Day Massacre. Ramus' educational method still had some supporters when Hooker was writing (especially among Puritans of the English church, as well as among Separatist Pilgrims), and some aspects of it had a more-lasting influence, including in curriculum mapping, textbook and instructional design, linear instruction, outlines, lesson plans, and the use of diagrams and other visual aids, and generally making education more accessible to people.

[126] The statement that *education* is the means of obtaining knowledge "by use" refers to experience and practice—learning by doing. The statement that *instruction* is the means of obtaining knowledge "by precept" refers to a more formal teaching of concepts—lecturing, reading, studying, working it out in the mind, memorizing, etc.

But when a man may be said to have sufficiently developed the use of reason so as to make him capable of obeying those laws by which he is then accountable for his actions, this is a great deal easier for common sense to discern than for any man by skill and learning to determine—even as philosophers, who best know the nature of both fire and gold, cannot teach what degree of the one will serve to purify the other as well as the artisan who by sense discerns when the fire is hot enough to purify the gold.

Chapter Seven

Human Will, the First Thing Which Laws of Action Are Made to Guide

By reason man gains the knowledge of things which can and cannot be sensed. Therefore, it remains that we search how man gains the knowledge of such things which cannot be sensed in order to know what may be done. Seeing, then, that nothing can move unless there is some end, the desire of which provokes action, how should that divine power of the soul—that "spirit of your mind", as the apostle, Saint Paul, calls it[127]—ever stir itself unto action, unless it also has such a spur?

The end for which we are moved to act is sometimes the goodness which we conceive in the very act, itself, for its own sake, and the cause which procures action is the mere desire of action, no other purpose intended by that desire. Of certain turbulent wits it is said, "To them, to have disturbed a quietness appeared a great payment."[128] They thought the very disturbance of things established a wage sufficient to set them to work. Sometimes an act which we do is done for another purpose, without which we would not desire to do the act at all, as in the actions of men giving alms in order to purchase the praise of men.[129]

---

127 *Ephesians* 4:23.
128 Sallust, *Conspiracy of Catiline*, chapter 21.
129 *Matthew* 6:1–4.

Man in perfection of nature being made according to the likeness of his Maker, resembles Him also in the manner of working, so that whatever we work as men, the same work we wittingly and freely do. Neither are we in any way so bound in the manner of natural agents but that it is in our power to leave the things we do undone. Whether good comes from an action, or the action, itself, is good, does not cause us to act. We only act if we comprehend, like, and desire the good. Whatever we do toward such an end, we choose and prefer to not leave it undone. There is no choice, unless the task be so much in our power that we might have refused and left it. If fire consumes the stubble, it does not choose to do so, because its nature is such that it has no choice. To choose is to will one thing before another. And to will is to bend our souls to the having or doing of that which to the soul appears good. Goodness is seen with the eye of understanding, and the light of that eye is reason.

So, there are two principal fountains of human action, *knowledge* and *will*. And the will, in things tending towards any end, is called, *choice*.[130] Concerning *knowledge*, "Behold," says Moses, "I have set before you this day good and evil, life and death."[131] Concerning *will*, Moses immediately adds, "*choose* life"—that is to say, choose the things which tend toward life.

But we must pay special attention to one thing as being a matter of no small importance, and that is how the *will*, strictly speaking—as it is of things intended for an end which man desires—differs greatly from that inferior natural desire which we call, *appetite*. The object of appetite is whatever good sensation may be wished for. The object of will is that good which reason leads us to seek. Emotions, such as joy and grief, fear and anger, and so on, being, as it were, the different fashions and forms of appetite, can neither arise at the perception of something which is irrelevant, nor yet choose but arise at the sight of some things.

---

130 ARISTOTLE, *Nicomachean Ethics*, Book III, Chapters 2 and 3, and Book VI, Chapter 2.

131 The passage quoted here, is as follows (quoting in this note from the Bishops Bible).

> I call heaven and earth to record this day against you, that I have set before you life and death, blessing and cursing: therefore choose life, that both thou and thy seed may live…
>
> —*Deuteronomy* 30:19

For it is not altogether in our power whether we will be stirred with emotions or not, whereas actions which issue from the disposition of the will are in the power of the will to be performed or not.

Finally, appetite is the will's solicitor, while the will is appetite's controller—what we covet according to the one, by the other we often reject.[132] Neither is any other desire properly called, *will*, but that where reason and understanding, or the show of reason, prescribes the thing desired. Therefore, it may be a question as to whether those operations of men are to be counted voluntary in which that good sensation provokes appetite—and appetite causes action, reason never being called to counsel—as when we eat or drink, or betake ourselves unto rest, and so on. The truth is, human actions are voluntary when they result from the use of reason. For as the authority of higher powers has force even in those things which are done without their conscious awareness, and are so insignificant that there is no need to acquaint them with that, we likewise also say that we voluntarily do that which the will, if it chose, might hinder from being done. Although in doing it we do not expressly use our reason or understanding, we still will the act. Therefore, in such cases, the will, with a kind of silence, yields her assent, as it were, by not dissenting. In this respect, the force of the will is not as apparent as it is in express mandates or prohibitions, especially if these mandates and prohibitions are preceded by advice and consultation.

Therefore, where understanding is needed, reason is the director of man's will by discovering what is good in an action. For the laws of moral right and wrong are the dictates of right reason. Children who have not yet reached the age when they can reason, innocents who cannot reason because of natural impairment, and the insane who, for the present, cannot possibly have the use of right reason to guide themselves—all are guided by the reason which guides those who are their guardians. In the rest there is that light of reason by which good may be known from evil, and which, distinguishing what is good, is properly judged to be right.

---

[132] In this context, *solicitor* means, "prompter", "prod(der)", "goad(er)", "inciter", "urger", "tempter", or "proposer", while *controller* means, "governor", "limiter", "restrictor", "manager", "supervisor", "director", or "master".

However, the will is not inclined to have or do what reason teaches to be good unless reason also teaches it to be possible. For though the appetite, being more general, may desire anything which seems good, no matter how impossible,[133] the reasonable will of man never seeks impossible things. Let reason teach that something is impossible, and the will of man lets it go. The will does not attempt anything obviously impossible. The will is naturally free to take or refuse any particular object presented to it.[134]

---

133 "O, that great Jove would give me once again my vanished years!"

—VIRGIL, *The Æneid*, Book VIII, lines 562–563 [line 580 in some translations]. See *The Æneid of Virgil*, translated by Theodore C. Williams (Houghton Mifflin Co., Boston, 1910).

134 In *A Christian Letter*, a 1599 letter from some Puritans to Hooker, they stated [spelling and grammar here updated]:

> Here we ask for your help to teach us how *will* is apt (as you say) to freely take or refuse any particular object, whatever, and that, by diligence, *reason* is able to find out any good concerning us: if it is true that the Church of England professes that without the preventing [i.e., preparing] and helping grace of God, we can will and do nothing pleasing to God.

In response to their suggestion that his arguments about the will are contrary to the doctrine of the Church of England, Hooker's note for a planned response is included in the 1622 edition of his first five books of *Polity* [spelling and grammar here updated]:

> There are certain words, as nature, reason, will, and such like, which, wherever you find them used, you immediately suspect them as bugs words [i.e., bugbears or hobgoblins, causing obsessive apprehension or confusion], because you do not comprehend what they mean, as you should. You have heard that man's nature is corrupt, his reason blind, his will perverse. As a result, in the appearance of condemning *corrupt* nature, you condemn *nature*, and so in the rest.

Hooker is saying that they are so fixated on the corrupted version of nature, reason, will, and so on, that they have come to obsessively fear the concepts of nature, reason, and will, themselves, forgetting their original purposes as given to us by God. He cites the following:

> Hilary of Poitiers, *De Trinitate* ("*On the Trinity*"), Book 12 (Basel edition, 1570, p. 822).
>
> Philo of Alexandria, *Legum Allegoriæ* ("*Allegorical Interpretation*"), Book 1 (Paris edition, 1552, p. 33).
>
> Dionysius the Areopagite, *De Divinis Nominibus* ("*The Divine Names*"), Chapter 4 (Paris edition, 1562, p. 338).

Hooker goes on to explain [here translated from Latin]:

> The will of man by its nature is not bound, but by the force of viciousness [i.e., vice] which has been added to its nature.
>
> "Apt," originally, "apta" ("able"): Reason, instructed by divine help, can find every necessary good. Left to itself, it can find none. Even so, every good inherently has enough by which it can prove itself to a man who is diligently and carefully attentive. Yet our laziness turns us away, elsewhere, until the Holy Spirit

Therefore, it follows that there is no particular object so good but that it may exhibit some difficulty or unpleasant quality—in respect of which the will may shrink and decline it. Conversely—for so things are blended—there is no particular evil which does not have some appearance of goodness by which to insinuate itself. For evil as evil cannot be desired.[135] If evil is desired, the cause is the goodness which is, or seems to be, joined with it. Goodness does not move by being, but by being apparent; therefore, many of the most precious things are neglected only because the value of them is hidden. Goodness of sensation is most apparent, near, and present, which causes the appetite, therefore, to be strongly provoked. Now, in the will, pursuit and refusal follow—*pursuit* being the affirmation of goodness, *refusal* the negation of goodness—which the understanding comprehends,[136] grounding itself upon sensation unless some higher reason happens to teach the contrary. And if reason has rightly taught that something is good, yet did not teach it so clearly that the mind is convinced of that

---

excites the zeal for virtue (see CYPRIAN OF CARTHAGE, on his conversion, in *Ad Donatum* ["*To Donatus*"], in *Opera* ["*Works*"], page 3, edited by John Fell).

Also, the things that wisdom professes about herself in the book of *Proverbs* and elsewhere: so, human reason is lazy on account of the great difficulty of investigating good things. The light of divine grace removes that difficulty. By this we are made eager; otherwise, we are prone to vice from labor. Virtue has more and stronger things than vice to attract a man, but these things are hidden from most men. Why? Because reason, which is the eye of the mind, lies lazily buried in a deep sleep within us. Yet, when it is awakened and enlightened by the power of the Holy Spirit, it judges all things, and what was formerly unknown and a source of disgust is now, when perceived, decreed to be embraced in every way.

135 In a note, Hooker provides the following quotes [here translated from Greek].

> If someone is driven by evil, he will not initially be driven towards evil as evil, itself, but towards something good.

And a little later in his cited source's text:

> For it is impossible to be driven towards evil while desiring it—either with the hope of something good or with the fear of a greater evil.
>
> —ALCINOUS, Ἐπιτομὴ τῶν Πλάτωνος δογμάτων ("*Epitomè tôn Plátōnos Dogmátōn*", or "*Abridgement of the Dogmas of Plato*" or "*Summary of the Doctrines of Plato*") or Διδασκαλικὸς τῶν Πλάτωνος δογμάτων ("*Didascalicòs tôn Plátōnos Dogmátōn*", or "*For the Teaching of the Doctrines of Plato*", *Didaskalikos*, or "*The Handbook of Platonism*") (Oxford Edition, 1667)

136 In a note, Hooker provides the following quote [here translated from Ancient Greek].

> What in thought is affirmation and negation, in desire is pursuit and flight.
>
> —ARISTOTLE, *Nicomachean Ethics*, Book VI, Chapter2

goodness, then there is still room for the will to take or leave it. Therefore, while among so many things to be done there are so few of which reason discovers or easily can discover the goodness in some way, we should not be surprised by the choice of evil, even when the contrary good is probably known. So it happens that the mind being accustomed by long practice, and so leaving there a tangible impression, prevails more than reasonable persuasion ever could. Reason, therefore, may rightly discern the thing which is good, and yet the will of man not be inclined to that thing as often as the prejudice of tangible experience overtakes reason. Nor let anyone think that this is a just excuse of iniquity. For with every committed sin a lesser good was willfully preferred before a greater good. That cannot be done without a uniquely human violation of one's nature, and the utter disturbance of that divine order by which the highest standard is worthily judged according to the highest moral principles. There is no good which concerns us but it has enough evidence for itself, if reason were diligent to search it out. Through neglect of reason we are plagued with the appearance of what is not:

> sometimes the subtlety of Satan beguiling us, as it did Eve;[137]
>
> sometimes the impatience of our wills preventing the more considered advice of sound reason, as when the disciples of Jesus no sooner saw what they did not like but they were immediately desirous of fire from Heaven;[138]
>
> sometimes the very customariness of evil making the heart unyielding against whatever instructions to the contrary, as in those over whom our Savior spoke, weeping, "O Jerusalem,...how often..." and "...thou would not...!"[139]

Therefore, that by which we still stand blameworthy, and have absolutely no excuse, is this: in doing evil we prefer a lesser good before a greater good—the greatness of which is investigable by reason and may be known.

---

[137] *Genesis* 3:1–13, *II Corinthians* 11:3.

[138] *Luke* 9:51–56.

[139] *Matthew* 23:37–39.

The search for knowledge is a painful thing, and the painfulness of knowledge is that which makes the human will so ill-disposed to the search for it. The root of this, a divine curse by which the instruments being weakened with which the soul works—especially in reasoning—prefers rest in ignorance before wearisome labor to know. Therefore, to spur our wills to diligence, we have a natural thirst after knowledge grafted into us. But because of that original weakness in the instruments of our souls,[140] without which our minds are not able in this world by logical thought to work, the very perception of painfulness is as a bridle to stop us. For which cause the apostle, Saint Paul, who knew right well that the weariness of the flesh is a heavy clog to the will,[141] strikes mightily upon this theme: "Awake, thou that sleepest…, Cast off all which presseth down…, Watch, labor, strive to go forward and to grow in knowledge."[142]

---

140 One's body, senses, and brain are instruments (i.e., tool or implement) of one's soul.

> "For a perishable body doth burden the soul, and the earthy tent doth weigh down the mind that is busy with much. So that we can hardly tell what is good, and what is from heaven we with labour and pain do find out."
>
> —*Wisdom of Solomon*, 9:15–16, Bishops Bible

141 A clog (also called a "tie-up log" or "chog") is a short log or a heavy block or chunk of wood tied to the leg of a horse, sheep, goat, or prisoner to impede the animal or prisoner from wandering away, similar in function to a ball-and-chain used to hobble an animal or prisoner.

142 A loose amalgam of *Ephesians* 5:14, *Hebrews* 12:1 and 12, *I Corinthians* 16:13, *Proverbs* 2:4, and *Luke* 13:24, with the last part, "and to grow in knowledge", being a common New Testament theme for which Hooker did not cite a specific verse (although *II Peter* 3:18 could be considered a source).

Chapter Eight

Using the Light of Reason to Naturally Find Laws to Guide the Will toward the Good

So, to return to our former intent of discovering the natural way by which rules have been discovered concerning that goodness with which the will of man ought to be moved in human actions: as everything naturally and necessarily desires the utmost good and greatest betterment for which nature has made it capable, even so man. Therefore, our happiness being the object and accomplishment of our desire, we cannot choose but wish and covet the utmost good and greatest betterment for which nature has made *us* capable.

To all particular things which are subject to action, the will is disposed as far as reason judges them to be a benefit to us—and, consequently, the more available to our bliss. If reason errs, we fall into evil, and, to that extent, are deprived of the general betterment we seek. Therefore, seeing that, for the framing of men's actions the knowledge of good from evil is necessary, it only remains that we search how this may be had. Nor should we assume that we need one rule to know the good and another to know the evil.[143] For he who knows what is

---

[143] In a note, Hooker provides the following quote (here translated from Ancient Greek).

> We know both the straight and the curved—for a canon [i.e., rule(r)] is the critic [i.e., judge] of both.
>
> —Aristotle, *On the Soul*, Book I, chapter 3

straight, by this he also discerns what is crooked—because the absence of straightness, in bodies capable of straightness, is crookedness. Goodness in actions is like straightness, where that which is done well we call, "right". For as the straight way is most acceptable to him who travels, because by it he comes soonest to his journey's end, so, in action, that which lies the straightest between us and the end we desire necessarily must be the best for our use. Besides being best for our use, there is also beauty in integrity—as, conversely, there is ugliness in deceit. And that which is good in the actions of men not only delights as profitable, but also as amiable. In which consideration the Grecians most divinely have given to the active betterment of men a name expressing both beauty and goodness,[144] because, in ordinary speech, the name, goodness, is for the most part applied only to that which is beneficial. But, in the name of goodness, we here employ both.

And there are only these two ways to discern goodness: the one, the knowledge of the causes of goodness; the other, the observation of those signs and tokens which, always accompanying goodness, argue that where they are found there, also is goodness, although we do not know how.

The former of these is the most sure and infallible way, but so hard that all shun it and had rather stumble in the dark as men do than tread such long and intricate mazes for knowledge's sake. Therefore, as physicians are many times forced to abandon such methods of curing as they, themselves, know to be the fittest, and being over-ruled by their patients' impatience, these physicians are eager to try the best they can by applying the cure to which the patient will yield. Similarly, considering how the case stands with this present age full of tongue and weak of brain, behold, we go with the flow.[145] Into the causes of goodness we will not make any curious or deep inquiry. To touch

---

144 The Ancient Greek name is Καλοκαγαθία ("Călocăgăthíă"), meaning, "Beautiful-and-morally-good".

145 Although the scholarly satire is intended, this phrase is not intended to be sarcastic. Hooker, a gentle and caring person, was not being elitist. He was simply diagnosing the situation and charitably suggesting an easier way to present an argument to less-informed, less-disciplined, or shallower thinkers in a time when passions were high and people were being mislead by demagogues, charismatic speakers, and conflicting arguments.

upon them now and then will be sufficient when they are so near at hand that they may be easily conceived without any abstract reasoning. We are content with that easier argument which, being the worse argument, is, nevertheless, now by reason of common imbecility the more appropriate and likely to be tolerated.[146]

Signs and tokens by which to know goodness are of various kinds—some more certain and some less. The most certain token of evident goodness is whether the general persuasion of all men account it so. And, therefore, a common received error is never utterly overthrown until such times as we go from signs to causes and show some manifest root or fountain common to them all, by which it may clearly appear how it is that so many have been overseen. In which case, surmises and slight probabilities will not work, because the universal consent of men is the best and strongest argument which comprehends only the signs and tokens of goodness. Casual things vary, and that which a man happens to think well of cannot still have the same result. Although, for this reason, we do not know the cause, yet this much we may know: there is some necessary cause whenever the judgements of all men—generally or for the most part—run one and the same way, especially in matters of reasoning. For of things done according to the laws of nature, there is nothing more affirmed than this: "They have, either always or for the most part, one nature."[147]

The general and perpetual voice of men is as the statement of God, Himself.[148] For that which all men have at all times learned, nature,

---

[146] In a note, Hooker provides the following quote (here translated from Ancient Greek).

> Therefore, perhaps we must simply start from those things well-known to us.
> —ARISTOTLE, *Nicomachean Ethics*, Book I, Chapter 4

[147] ARISTOTLE, *Rhetoric*, Book I, Chapter 10.

[148] This is essentially the idea of, "Vox populi, vox Dei" ("The voice of the people is the voice of God"). A note in the originally published text states that the origin of the saying is obscure, and that it was mistaken by some in the Middle Ages as a quote or principle from the Bible. The note cites EADMER OF CANTERBURY, *Historia Novorum in Anglia* (literally, "*A History of the New Things in England*" or "*An Account of the News in England*"—i.e., recent history or current events), Book I, Chapter 42. See Geoffrey Bosanquet, translator, *Eadmer's History of Recent Events in England* (Dufour Editions, Inc., Chester Springs, Pennsylvania, 1964).

herself, most necessarily has taught. And God, being the Author of nature, her voice is but His instrument. In this way—from God through His instrument, nature—we receive whatever we learn. There are infinite duties, the goodness of which is by this rule sufficiently manifested, although we had no other warrant besides to approve them. The apostle, Saint Paul, speaking of the Heathens, said of them, "they are a law unto themselves."[149] His meaning is, that by force of the light of reason, by which God illuminates everyone who comes into the world, men, being enabled to know truth from falsehood and good from evil, by this learn in many things what the will of God is—which will, Himself not revealing by any extraordinary means to them, but men, using logic, attaining the knowledge of them, seem to be the makers of those laws which, indeed, are His, and men only the discovers.

Therefore, generally speaking a law is a rule to good behavior.

> The rule of divine outward operations is the definitive appointment of God's own wisdom set down within Himself.
>
> The rule of natural agents which work by simple necessity is the determination of the wisdom of God, known to God, Himself, their principal director, but not to those which are directed to execute that rule.
>
> The rule of natural agents which work after a sort of their own accord, as the beasts do, is driven by the judgement of common sense or fancy concerning the tangible goodness of those objects by which they are moved.[150]
>
> The rule of ghostly or immaterial natures, as spirits and angels, is their intuitive, intellectual judgement concerning the

---

Hooker is attempting to justify neither mob rule, direct democracy, the actions of crowds, nor the populist passions of the moment. Instead, in this and the following few sentences, he is arguing that, if most people believe something, and do so down through the ages, then what they believe is probably true—at least to some extent—because they have been informed by nature, one of the means by which God speaks to us, as stated by the apostle, Paul, in *Romans* 1:18–20.

[149] *Romans* 2:14.

[150] i.e., animal instinct.

> amiable beauty and high goodness of that object, which with unspeakable joy and delight sets them to work.
>
> The rule of voluntary agents on earth is the sentence which reason gives concerning the goodness of those things which they are to do. And the sentences which reason gives, are some more general, some less general, before it comes to define in particular actions what is good. The main principles of reason are, in themselves, apparent. For to make nothing evident of itself to man's understanding is to take away all possibility of knowing anything. And, in this, that saying of Theophrastus is true, "They which seek a reason for all things do utterly overthrow reason".[151]

In every kind of knowledge, there are certain fundamentals, when presented, which the mind immediately accepts without needing proof.

> These are more-general axioms or principles such as, "The greater good is to be chosen before the less."[152] Therefore, if it is asked why the will of man, which necessarily shuns harm and covets whatever is pleasant and sweet, should be commanded to count as galling the pleasures of sin, and, despite the bitter accidents about which virtuous actions are surrounded, to still rejoice and delight in virtuous actions, surely this could never be consistent with reason unless wisdom, in making these commands, grounds her laws upon an infallible rule of comparison—which is that when small difficulties are

---

151 "Seeking logos of everything, they are taking logos away."
—THEOPHRASTUS, *Metaphysics*

Arguably the most respected modern English translation is the following.

> "By seeking a rational account of all things, they destroy rational account itself."
> —William David Ross and Francis Howard Fobes, *Theophrastus: Metaphysics* (Clarendon Press, Oxford, England, 1929)

152 A key concept taught, in one way or the other, by Plato, Aristotle, Cicero, Seneca the Younger, Epictetus, Origen of Alexandria, Basil of Cæsarea, Gregory of Nyssa, Augustine of Hippo, Hierocles, Thomas Aquinas, Duns Scotus, William of Ockham, Francisco de Vitoria, Francisco Suárez, and John Jewel, Bishop of Salisbury, all of whom influenced Hooker.

exceedingly great, good is sure to ensue, and on the other side momentary benefits, when the hurt which they draw after them is unspeakable, are not at all to be heeded. This rule is the grounding upon which the wisdom of the apostle builds a law, demanding patience of himself: "The present lightness of our affliction works unto us even with abundance upon abundance an eternal weight of glory, while we look not on the things which are seen, but on the things which are not seen. For the things which are seen are temporal but the things which are not seen are eternal."[153] Therefore, whatever calamities accompanied it in the past, Christianity should be embraced. Upon the same grounding our Savior proves the law most reasonable which forbids those crimes which men, for gain's sake, fall into. For a man to win the world, if it be with the loss of his soul what benefit or good is it?[154]

Axioms less general yet so manifestly true that they need no further proof are such as these: *God to be worshipped,*[155] *parents to be honored,*[156] *others to be used by us as we ourselves would*

---

[153] Hooker is translating directly from the Ancient Greek text of *II Corinthians* 4:17–18 (spelling updated).

[154] *Matthew* 16:26.

[155] *Exodus* 20:1–6, *Exodus* 34:15, *Deuteronomy* 5:6–10, *Deuteronomy* 6:5, *Deuteronomy* 6:13, *Psalm* 29:2, *Psalm* 100:1–2, *Matthew* 4:10, *Matthew* 22:37, *Mark* 12:28–33, *Luke* 4:8, *Luke* 10:25–28, *John* 4:24, *I Chronicles* 16:29, *Hebrews* 12:28, and *Romans* 12:1. See also, HESIOD, *Works and Days*, lines 135–139, translated by Hugh G. Evelyn-White, in *The Homeric Hymns and Homerica* (Harvard University Press, Cambridge, Massachusetts, 1914).

[156] *Exodus* 20:12, *Leviticus* 19:3, *Deuteronomy* 5:16, *Deuteronomy* 27:16, *Proverbs* 23:22, *Proverbs* 30:17, *Ephesians* 6:1–3, *Colossians* 3:20. See also, PLATO, *Laws*, Book XI, 917a, translated by Robert Gregg Bury, in *Laws* (Harvard University Press, Cambridge, Massachusetts, 1926); ARISTOTLE, *Nicomachean Ethics*, Book VIII, Chapter 14, translated by Frank Hesketh Peters, in *The Nicomachean Ethics of Aristotle*, Tenth Edition (Kegan Paul, Trench, Trübner & Co., Ltd., London, 1906); MARCUS TULLIUS CICERO, *De Officiis* ("*On Moral Duties*"), Book I, Section 17, translated by Andrew Preston Peabody, in *Ethical Writings of Cicero* (Little, Brown, and Company, Boston, 1887); ANONYMOUS, *Hsiao Ching* (or *Xiaojing*, or *The Classic of Filial Duty*), Chapters I, VII, X, XI, and XVIII, translated by Ivan Chên, in *The Book of Filial Duty* (John Murray, London, 1908); MANU, *Manusmriti*, 2:145, translated by Georg Bühler (Oxford University Press, Oxford, England, 1886); *Quran* 17:23; MOSES BEN MAIMON (also called, RAMBAM or MAIMONIDES), "Rebels", *Mishneh Torah*, translated by Eliyahu Touger (Moznaim Publications, Jerusalem, ca. 1988 – ca. 2007), Chapter 5.

> *by them.*[157] Such things, as soon as they are alleged, all men acknowledge to be good—they require no proof or further reasoning to be assured of their goodness.

Nevertheless, whatever the more-or-less general principle, it was at first found out by reasoning, and drawn from out of the very bowels of Heaven and Earth. For we are to note that things in the world are discernable to us not only for the preservation of our lives, but also in a higher, two-fold respect.

> Firstly, if all of the other practical uses of knowledge were utterly taken away, yet the mind of man being, by nature, speculative and delighted with contemplation for its own sake, those more-or-less general principles would be known even for the sake of mere knowledge and understanding.
>
> Furthermore, knowledge of even the least importance in the world has in it a second distinct benefit to us, in as much as it serves to minister the rules, canons, and laws by which men direct those actions which we properly call, "human". This, the very Heathens, themselves, obscurely insinuated by making Themis—which we call, *Jus*[158] or *Right*—to be the daughter of Heaven and Earth.[159] We know things either as they are, in themselves, or as they are in mutual relation to each other.

---

[157] A version of the Golden Rule, which is often stated as, "Do unto others as you would have them do unto you." See *Leviticus* 19:18, *Tobit* 4:15, *Matthew* 7:12, *Matthew* 22:39, *Mark* 12:28–33, *Luke* 6:31, and *Luke* 10:25–28. See also *The Analects of Confucius*, translated by William Edward Soothill (William Edward Soothill, 1910), Book XV, Chapter XXIII; THE BUDDHA, ET AL, *Udânavarga* 5:18, translated by William Woodville Rockhill, in *Udânavarga: A Collection of Verses from the Buddhist Canon* (Trübner & Co., London, 1883); DIOGENES LAËRTIUS, "Thales", *Lives of the Eminent Philosophers*, translated by Robert Drew Hicks (Harvard University Press, Cambridge, Massachusetts, 1925), Book I, Chapter 5, Section 36.

[158] The word, "ius" (also spelled, "jus"), is Latin for, "law" or a "right", and is a source of such English words as "just", "justify", "justice", "judge", "judgement", "judicial", "judicious", "jurisdiction", "juridical", "jurist", "jury", "juror", "adjudicate", and "adjure". The word, "ius", is theoretically derived from a Proto-Indo-European word meaning, "straight" or "right".

[159] HESIOD, *Theogony*, translated by Richard S. Caldwell (Focus Information Group, Inc., Newburyport, Massachusetts, 1987), lines 126, 133, 134, and 135. Heaven (or Sky) is personified by the Ancient Greek primordial god Οὐρανός ("Ourănós", typically transliterated as, "Uranus"), and Earth is personified by the Ancient Greek primordial goddess, Γαῖᾰ ("Gaîă", typically transliterated as, "Gaia", "Gaea", or "Gæa").

The knowledge of that which man is (in reference to himself), and of that which other things are (in relation to man), I may justly call the *mother* of all those principles, as if they are edicts, statutes, and decrees in that law of nature by which human actions are directed.[160] Therefore, first having observed that the best things, when they are not interfered with, still produce the best operations—because when many things work together for a common purpose it is reasonable that the best are to guide the rest so that, being dominant, the work principally done by the best may have the greatest betterment—which we then come to observe in ourselves of what excellence our souls are in comparison to our bodies, and the diviner part of our souls in relation to the baser part of our souls. Seeing that all of these work together in producing human actions, they cannot work well unless the chiefest command and direct the rest.[161] The soul, then, ought to conduct the body, and the diviner spirit ought to conduct the rest of our mind's soul.[162] Therefore, this is the first law by which, in acting together, the highest power of the mind requires general obedience from all the rest working with it.

The several grand mandates being imposed by the understanding faculty of the mind, and which must be obeyed by the will of man, are discerned by the same method of discovery as to whether they indicate our duty to God or indicate our duty to man.

Touching upon the one, I may not stand here to declare by what degrees of reasoning the minds even of mere natural men have attained to know not only that there is a God, but also what power, force, wisdom, and other properties which God has, and how all things depend on Him. Therefore, this being premised from that

---

[160] i.e., violable natural law, the moral law created by God and discovered from nature by our reasoning or divine revelation.

[161] ARISTOTLE, *Politics*, Book I, Chapter 5. (This is a problematic citation, as in that chapter Aristotle attempts to justify some slavery. However, Hooker is more focused on the general principle underlying Aristotle's argument, which is that nature demonstrates that the superior naturally rules the inferior, such as the mind ruling the body.) See *Aristotle's Politics*, translated by Benjamin Jowett, Volume I (Clarendon Press, Oxford, England, 1885).

[162] *Ephesians* 4:23.

known relation which God has to us as to children[163]—and to all good things as to effects, of which He, Himself is the Principal Cause[164]—these axioms and natural laws concerning our duty have arisen:

> In all things we go about, His aid is by prayer to be craved.[165]
>
> He cannot have sufficient honor given Him, but we must try our utmost to honor Him[166]—which is, in effect, the same which we read: "Thou shalt love the Lord thy God with all thy heart with all thy soul, and with all thy mind."[167] This is the law our Savior calls the "First and the Great Commandment".[168]

Touching upon the next,[169] which as our Savior adds is like unto this[170] (he means, in amplitude and largeness, in as much as it is the root out of which all laws of duty toward men have grown, as out of the former all offices[171] of religion towards God), the same natural drive has

---

163 No god is hostile to humans.

—PLATO, *Theætetus*. See "Theaetetus", *The Dialogues of Plato*, Volume IV, translated by Benjamin Jowett (Humphrey Milford, London, 1871)

164 ...for God is thought to be among the causes of all things and to be a first principle...

—ARISTOTLE, *Metaphysics*, Book I, Chapter 2, 983ª8–9. See W. D. Ross (William David Ross), *Aristotle's Metaphysics*, English and Greek Edition (Clarendon Press, Oxford, England, 1924), Volume I

165 All men, Socrates, who have any degree of right feeling, at the beginning of every enterprise, whether small or great, always call upon God.

—PLATO, *Timæus*, Book III, Chapter 27. See T*he Dialogues of Plato translated into English with Analyses and Introductions by B. Jowett, M.A. in Five Volumes*, 3rd edition (Clarendon Press, Oxford, England, 1892)

166 This, then, is also the way in which we should associate with unequals; the man who is benefited in respect of wealth or excellence must give honour in return, repaying what he can. For friendship asks a man to do what he can, not what is proportional to the merits of the case; since that cannot always be done, e.g. in honours paid to the gods or to parents; for no one could ever return to them the equivalent of what he gets, but the man who serves them to the utmost of his power is thought to be a good man.

—ARISTOTLE, *Nicomachean Ethics*, Book VIII, Chapter 14. See "Nicomachean Ethics", translated by W. D. Ross (William David Ross), *The Works of Aristotle Translated into English*, W. D. Ross, Editor (Clarendon Press, Oxford, England, 1925)

167 *Deuteronomy* 6:5.

168 *Matthew* 22:38.

169 *Leviticus* 19:18.

170 *Matthew* 22:39.

171 i.e., duties or responsibilities.

brought men to know that it is no less their duty to love others as themselves. For seeing that those things which are equal must all have an equal standard: if I cannot but wish to receive all good, even as much at every man's hand as any man can wish unto his own soul, why should I look to have any part of my desire in this satisfied unless I am careful to satisfy the same desire which is undoubtedly in other men, we all being of one and the same nature? To have anything offered them repugnant to this desire must in all respects grieve them as much as me—so that if I do harm I must expect to suffer, there being no reason that others should show a greater standard of love to me than I have shown to them. Therefore, my desire to be loved by my natural equals, as much as may be possible, imposes upon me a natural duty of fully bearing toward them the same affection. From this equality between ourselves and them who are as ourselves there are several rules and canons which natural reason has drawn for direction of life, and of which no man is ignorant. Namely:

> Because we would take no harm we must, therefore, do none.[172]
>
> Since we would not be in anything extremely dealt with we must, ourselves, avoid all extremity in our dealings.[173]
>
> From all violence and wrong we are utterly to abstain.[174]

And so on—which further to wade through would be tedious, and to our present purpose not altogether that necessary, seeing that on these

---

[172] In a note, Hooker provides an example of this rule in Roman law, at the time of Emperor Cæsar Justinian I (Justinian the Great):

> That which in oneself one approves, in another one cannot reprove [i.e., disapprove].
>
> —a maxim appearing as a margin comment on the text of the law concerning "Inofficious Wills", in *Justinian's Code* (or *Codex Justinianus*), 3.28.1

[173] Hooker provides this example from Justinian law:

> What right anyone has established in relation to another, he must also be bound in the same way.
>
> —a maxim appearing in the law "Concerning Jurisdiction", in the *Digest of Justinian*, 2.2.1

[174] Hooker provides this example from Justinian law:

> From all injury [i.e., infringement upon another's rights] and also violence be completely abstaining.
>
> —a ruling included in the law concerning acts "By force or stealth", in the *Digest of Justinian*, 43.23.1.1

two general heads already mentioned[175] all other special cases are dependent.

Therefore, the natural standard by which to judge our doings is the judgement of reason, determining and setting down what is good to be done. Which judgement is either *mandatory*, showing what must be done, *permissive*, declaring only what may be done, or *admonitory*, declaring what is the most convenient for us to do. The first takes place when the choice is simply between doing and not doing something which in itself is absolutely good or evil, as it had been for Joseph to yield or not yield to the impotent desire of his lewd mistress[176]—the one evil, the other simply good. The second is, when of different evils, all being inevitable, we are permitted to choose one; which one saving only in case of so great an urgency were not otherwise to be taken—as in the matter of divorce among the Jews.[177] The last, when of different goods, one is principal and most eminent—as in the act of those who sold their possessions and laid their price at the apostles' feet, which possessions they might have kept to themselves without sin.[178] Again, in the apostle Saint Paul's own choice to maintain himself by his own labor,[179] while in living by the Church's maintenance, as others did, there had been no offence committed.[180] Therefore, in goodness there is a latitude or extent, by

---

[175] The two greatest commandments:

> But when the Pharisees had heard that he had put the Sadducees to silence, they came together. And one of them, which was a lawyer, asked him a question, tempting him, and saying:
>
> > Master, which is the great commandment in the law?
>
> Jesus said unto him:
>
> > Thou shalt love the Lord thy God with all thy heart, and with all thy soul, and with all thy mind. This is the first and great commandment. And the second is like unto this. Thou shalt love thy neighbor as thyself. In these two commandments, hang all the law and the prophets.
>
> —*Matthew* 22:34–40, Bishops Bible, spelling updated

[176] *Genesis* 39:9.

[177] *Mark* 10:4.

[178] *Acts* 4:32–35.

[179] *II Thessalonians* 3:8.

[180] In a note for a response to some Puritans, Hooker said [here paraphrased]:

> Did God command Paul not to marry, or not to receive his daily maintenance from the Church? He refrained from both without God's commandment, but not without God's approval. Yes, He, Himself, counsels that which He does not command, and they who followed his counsel did well, although they did it not by way of necessary obedience, but by voluntary choice.

which it happens that even of good actions some are better than others; otherwise, one man could not excel another, but all should be either absolutely good, as hitting precisely that indivisible point or center wherein goodness consists; or else milling it, they should be excluded out of the number of well-doers. Degrees of well-doing there could be none, except perhaps in the seldomness and oftenness of doing well. But the nature of goodness being thus ample, a law is properly that which reason in such sort defines to be good that it must be done. And the law of reason or human nature is that which men by natural reasoning have rightly found out themselves to be all forever bound unto in their actions.

Laws of reason have these marks to be known by.

> Such as keep them resemble most lively in their voluntary actions that very manner of working which nature herself does necessarily observe in the course of the whole world. The works of nature are all fitting, beautiful, and without superfluity or defect. Likewise, the works of men are directed in the same way if they act according to what the law of reason teaches.
>
> Secondly, those laws are investigable by reason, without the help of divine, supernatural revelation.
>
> Finally, in such sort they are investigable, that the knowledge of them is general, the world has always been acquainted with them—according to that which one in Sophocles observes, concerning a branch of this law, "It is no child of two days or yesterday's birth, but has been no man knows how long since."[181] The

[181] Hooker quotes from a passage from Sophocles' tragic, Fifth-Century B.C. play, *Antigone.* The title character explains to the king why she has violated his decree that burial rites not be performed for her brother's body, appealing to the supreme authority of what we would now consider to be violable natural law (emphasis added to the two lines which Hooker quotes):

> Yea, for these [manmade] laws were not ordained of Zeus,
> And she who sits enthroned with gods below,
> Justice [Themis], enacted not these human laws.
> Nor did I deem that thou, a mortal man,
> Could'st by a breath annul and override
> The immutable laws of Heaven.
> *They were not born today nor yesterday;*
> *They die not; and none knoweth whence they sprang.*
>
> —SOPHOCLES, *Antigone,* lines 450–457. See *Sophocles, with an English Translation by F. Storr, B.A.* (William Heinemann, London, 1912), Volume I.

> law of reason is not agreed upon by one, two, or few, but by all. This does not mean that every individual in the whole world already knows and accepts all which the law of reason contains. Instead, this law is such that, once its principles are stated, no individual can reject the law as unreasonable or unjust. Again, there is nothing in it but any man (having natural perfection of wit and ripeness of judgement) may find out by labor and travail. And to conclude, the general principles of the law of reason are such as it is not easy to find men ignorant of them. Rational law, therefore, which men commonly used to call the law of nature—meaning by this the law which human nature knows itself in reason universally bound to, which also for that cause may most fitly be called the law of reason—this law, I say, comprehends all of those things which men by the light of their natural understanding evidently know, or at least may know, to be becoming or unbecoming, virtuous or vicious,[182] good or evil for them to do.

Some have said[183] that whatever is done amiss the law of nature and reason is transgressed by that. This is true because even those offences which, by their special qualities, are breaches of supernatural laws and, therefore, generally evil, generally violate that principle of reason which universally wills to fly from evil. Yet we do not, therefore, so far extend the law of reason as to contain in it all manner of

---

[182] The word, "vicious", in this context, means, "exhibiting or having to do with vice" (i.e., immoral). It does not necessarily mean, "cruelty" or "cruel violence".

[183] Hooker provides two examples:

> [A]ll sins, as being against reason, are also against nature…
>
> —Thomas Aquinas, *Summa Theologiæ*, First Part of the Second Part (I–II), Question 94, Article 3, Reply to Objection 2. (A perhaps more literal translation is, "All sins are generally against reason and the law of nature.") See *The Summa Theologiæ of St. Thomas Aquinas, Part I–II, Literally translated by Fathers of the English Dominican Province, Second and Revised Edition* (Burns Oates & Washbourne Ltd, London, 1927), Volume VIII.

> Now every fault injures the nature, and is consequently contrary to the nature.
>
> —Aurelius Augustin, Bishop of Hippo (Saint Augustine of Hippo), *The City of God*, Book XII, Chapter 1, "That the Nature of the Angels, Both Good and Bad, is One and the Same". Here translated by Marcus Dods, in "The City of God", *A Select Library of the Nicene and Post-Nicene Fathers of the Christian Church: Series I,* edited by Philip Schaff (Christian Literature Publishing Co., Buffalo, New York, 1887), Volume II.

laws by which reasonable creatures are bound. Now, although this is all true, it has been shown that we restrain the law of reason and nature to only those duties which all men, by their natural wits, either do or might understand to be such duties as concern all men.

> Certain half-awake men—who are neither altogether asleep in folly, nor yet thoroughly awake in the light of true understanding—have thought that there is not at all anything just and righteous in itself. But look at what nations are habituated to doing—the same these half-awake men take to be right and just. Then, seeing each sort of people has a different kind of right from the others, and that that which is right of its own nature must be everywhere one and the same, their conclusion is, therefore, that in itself there is nothing right. These good folk *(he says, that I may not trouble their wits with rehearsal of too many things)* have not looked so far into the world as to perceive, that, "Do as you would be done unto", is a rule which all nations under heaven are agreed upon. This rule, as it relates to the love of God, extinguishes all heinous crimes, and as it relates to the love of your neighbor, it banishes all grievous wrongs from the world.
>
> —AUGUSTINE OF HIPPO, *On Christian Doctrine*, Book 3, Chapter 14 (paraphrased based upon Hooker's quote)[184]

Therefore, as touching upon the law of reason, it seems that this was Saint Augustine's judgement: namely, that there are in the law of reason some things which stand as universally agreed-upon principles, and that, out of those principles, which are in themselves evident,[185] the greatest, moral duties we owe towards God or man may be understood without any great difficulty.

If, then, it is here asked, by what means it should come to pass—the greatest part of the moral law being so easy for all men to know—that so many thousands of men, notwithstanding, have been ignorant even of principal moral duties, not imagining the breach of them to be sin: I deny not, but lewd and wicked custom, beginning perhaps

---

[184] See also AUGUSTINE, *De doctrina Christiana*, translated by R. P. H. Green, (Clarendon Press, Oxford, England 1995).

[185] i.e., self-evident.

at the first among few, afterwards spreading into greater multitudes, and so continuing from time to time, may be of force even in plain things to smother the light of natural understanding, because men will not bend their wits to examine, whether things with which they have been accustomed be good or evil. For example's sake, that grosser kind of Heathenish idolatry, whereby they worshipped the very works of their own hands, was an absurdity to reason so palpable that the Prophet David, comparing idols and idolaters together, makes almost no odds between them, but the one in a manner as much without wit and sense as the other, "They who make idols are like them, and so are all who trust in them."[186] That in which an idolater seems so absurd and foolish is expressed by the wise man:[187]

> He shamelessly speaks to that which is lifeless;
> He prays for health from that which is weak;
> He prays for life from that which is dead;
> He prays for help from that which has no experience;
> He prays for a good journey from that which is not able to move;
> He prays for gain, work, and success from that which has no power in any way.
> —*The Book of Wisdom* 13:17–19 (paraphrased based upon Hooker's loose translation)[188]

The cause of this senseless stupidity is afterwards attributed to custom.

> When a father mourned grievously for his son who was suddenly taken away, he made an image for him who was once dead, whom now he worshipped as a god, ordaining his servants to perform

---

[186] A paraphrase of his loose quoting of *Psalm* 115:8.

By, "like them" (the original Hebrew can mean, "as them" or "like them"), the psalmist, King David, is saying that idol worshippers become as lifeless, characterless, useless, impermanent, senseless, witless, incapable of understanding, and heartless as the idols which they worship.

[187] i.e., King Solomon (although modern scholars do not think he authored this book).

[188] See also *Book of Wisdom* 13:17–19 (Bishops Bible).

A loose paraphrase was common in Hooker's time when, in the interests of not making a long treatise unnecessarily longer, the writer was trying to give the gist of what the Bible said and move the conversation forward to points of focus. Bear in mind that his entire treatise consists of eight books.

> ceremonies and make sacrifices. Thus, by process of time, this wicked custom prevailed, and was kept as a law.
>
> —*The Book of Wisdom* 14:15–16 (paraphrased based, in turn, upon Hooker's paraphrase)[189]

The authority of rulers, the ambition of craftsmen, and such like means thrust forward the ignorant, and increase their superstition.

Unto this which the wise man has spoken, somewhat besides may be added, For whatever we have taught before, or shall teach afterwards, concerning the force of man's natural understanding, this, also, we always desire to be understood, that there is no kind of faculty or power in man or any other creature which can rightly perform the functions allotted to it without perpetual aid and concurrence of that Supreme Cause of all things. As often as we cause God in His justice to withdraw, the benefit of this understanding is lost, so that nothing can result other than that which the apostle notes: even men habituated to the light of reason still walk "in the vanity of their mind, having their thoughts darkened, and being strangers from the life of God through the ignorance which is in them, because of the hardness of their hearts."[190] And this cause is mentioned by the prophet, Isaiah, speaking of the ignorance of idolaters, who see not how the manifest law of reason condemns their gross iniquity and sin. They have not in them, he says, so much wit as to think, "Shall I bow to the stock of a tree? All knowledge and understanding is taken from them. For God has shut their eyes so that they cannot see."[191]

What we say in the case of idolatry serves for all other things in which the same kind of general blindness has prevailed against the manifest laws of reason. Within what these laws encompass we not only comprehend whatever may be easily known to belong to the duty of all men, but even whatever may possibly be known to be of that quality, so that the same be *necessarily* deduced out of clear and

---

189 See also *Book of Wisdom* 14:15–16 (Bishops Bible).

190 *Ephesians* 4:17–18. Hooker is arguing here that human reason, even if habituated to morality, is useless if God's grace is withdrawn.

191 *Isaiah* 44:18–19.

manifest principles. For if, regarding what is convenient for men, we limit ourselves to only concluding what is probable, then we are in the territory of free and arbitrary determinations—the territory of human laws, which we will later consider.

Chapter Nine

The Benefit of Keeping the Law Taught by Reason

Now the dutiful observation of this law which reason teaches us cannot but be significantly advantageous to those who conform to the law. For we see the whole world and each part of it so interdependent, that as long as each thing performs only that work which is natural to it, by this it both preserves other things and preserves itself. Conversely, let any principal thing—such as the Sun, the Moon, or any of the heavens or elements—cease, fail, or stray, and who does not easily conceive that that sequence would be ruin both to itself and to whatever depends upon it? And is it possible that man, being not only the noblest creature in the world, but even a very world in himself, his transgression of the law of his nature should not draw any harm?

Yes, "tribulation and anguish unto every soul that does evil".[192] Good happens to all things which conform to the course of their nature. Conversely, evil happens to all things which do not conform to the course of their nature.

But to natural agents there is no good which we call, *reward*, and there is no evil which we properly call, *punishment*. The reason for this is, because among creatures in this world, only man's conformance to the law of his nature is *righteousness*, only man's transgression is *sin*. And the reason for this is the difference in his manner of conforming

[192] *Romans* 2:9. For context, read *Romans* 1:18–2:16.

to or transgressing the law of his nature: man can only voluntarily do the one or the other.

We are not properly said to have done what we do *against* our wills or are constrained to do because, in those cases, the motive of doing it is not in ourselves, but carries us like the wind driving a feather in the air. We are not in the least bit contributing to an act which we are externally driven to do. In such cases, therefore, men are pitied for the evil as being, in such respect, miserable instead of culpable.

Likewise, some things are done by men neither by being externally forced and impelled nor against their wills, yet *without* their wills—as in insanity or any similar, inevitable, utter absence of wit and judgement. Because of such mental incompetence, no man has ever thought that the hurtful actions of madmen and innocents are punishable.

Furthermore, some things we do neither against our wills nor without our wills, and yet not simply and merely *with* our wills, but with our wills *moved* to the extent that, even though it is possible that we might conform to the law of our nature, nevertheless, we cannot easily do so. By this, one evil deed is made more pardonable than another.[193]

Finally, the evil someone commits is more easily pardonable in proportion to the necessity to act or how much more difficult it is to behave righteously—unless the transgressor causes that necessity or difficulty. Therefore, a drunk man who commits incest, and alleges that his wits were not his own, has no excuse in as much as he might have chosen whether his wits should, by that means, have been taken from him.

Now, rewards and punishments are not always dependent on whether something is willingly done well or ill—although, in this respect, we may sometimes receive good or harm, with good being only a benefit, and not a reward, and the harm being simply a hurt, not a punishment. From the variety of the dispositions of man's will, which is the root of all his actions, there grows a variety in the consequences of rewards and punishments which are determined by these and similar

---

[193] Hooker is alluding to overwhelming temptations, passions, or habits. While our evil deeds resulting from these influences remain sinful, we acknowledge the difficulty in choosing to behave righteously under those conditions.

rules: "Take away the will, and all acts are equal";[194] "That which we do not and would do, is commonly accepted as done."[195] By these and similar rules are men's actions judged, and a determination made as to whether they are by their own nature rewardable or punishable.

Rewards and punishments are not received but at the hands of those who, being above us, have the power to examine and judge our deeds. How men come to have this authority over each other in external actions, we shall more diligently examine later. But, for the present, everyone clearly acknowledges that, since every man's heart and conscience either approves or disapproves his good or evil act, even if secretly committed and known to none but his heart, he, accordingly, either rejoices in the hope of a reward or grieves in the fear of a punishment—neither of which, in this case, can be looked for from any other, saving only from Him Who discerns and judges the very secrets of all hearts. Therefore, God is the only Rewarder and Revenger of all such actions. And not of such actions only, but of all actions by which the law of nature is broken, of which He, Himself, is the Author. In the case of any requirements for sincerity in a man's heart—into which no human eye can see—the Roman laws called the *Twelve Tables*[196] threaten the insincere with none but divine punishment, because none but God judges the human heart.

---

[194] With free will removed, every act is equal.

—moral maxim derived from Roman Civil Law (*Corpus Juris Civilis*)

[195] Good intent is usually counted for a deed.

—Roman legal maxim ("Voluntas reputabitur pro facto") in Roman Civil Law (*Corpus Juris Civilis*)

[196] The *Lex Duodecim Tabularum* ("*Law of the Twelve Tables*", 449 B.C.), the foundation of Ancient Roman law, were placed in the Forum of the ancient city of Rome, and listed and defined the rights and duties of Roman citizens in order to limit the power of governing officials and nobility.

CHAPTER TEN

How Reason Leads Men to the Making of Laws by Which Societies are Governed[197]

THAT WHICH WE have already set down is hopefully sufficient to show the brutishness of those who imagine that religion and virtue are only a matter of men's opinion, that, if we wanted to, we could just as well value irreligion and vice without any harm to ourselves, and that religion and virtue on the one hand, and irreligion and vice on the other hand, are morally equal to each other in nature. We see, then, how nature, itself, teaches laws and statutes to live by. The laws which have already been mentioned bind men absolutely as to what to do and what not to do, even when they are individuals without a settled fellowship or any solemn agreement among themselves.[198] But as much as we cannot by ourselves sufficiently furnish ourselves with everything we need

---

[197] Hooker describes what we now call the *social contract*, giving an agent a monopoly on the right to govern a group of families not naturally subject to the agent (unlike children naturally subject to their father).

[198] In fact, there is a general idea of just and unjust in accordance with nature, as all men in a manner divine, even if there is neither communication nor agreement between them. This is what Antigone in Sophocles evidently means, when she declares that it is just, though forbidden, to bury Polynices, as being naturally just:

> For neither today nor yesterday, but from all eternity, these statutes live
> and no man knoweth whence they came.

—ARISTOTLE, *Rhetoric*, Book I, Ch. 13, quoting SOPHOCLES, *Antigone*. See ARISTOTLE, *"Art" of Rhetoric*, translated by J. H. Freese (John Henry Freese) (Harvard University Press, Cambridge, Massachusetts, 1926), Vol. 22 of Loeb Classical Library's *Aristotle (Works) in 23 Volumes.*

for such a life as our nature desires—a life fit for the dignity of man—to supply those defects and imperfections which are in us when single and living solely by ourselves we are naturally induced to seek communion and fellowship with others.[199] This was the cause of men's uniting themselves at first in geopolitical societies,[200] which societies could not exist without government, nor government without a kind of law distinct from that which has been already declared.

There are two foundations which support public societies: one is a natural inclination by which all men desire sociable life and fellowship; the other is an order openly or privately agreed upon, touching upon the manner of their union in living together. The latter is what we call the *law of a commonweal*,[201] the very soul of a geopolitical body, the parts of which are by law animated, held together, and set to work in such actions as the common good requires. Geopolitical laws, ordained for external order and government among men, are not rightly framed without presuming the will of man to be inwardly obstinate, rebellious, and averse from all obedience unto the sacred laws of his nature—in a word, even presuming that man's depravity is little better than a wild beast, they nonetheless provide laws to regulate his outward actions so that his actions will not hinder the common good for which geopolitical societies are instituted. Unless these laws do this, they are not perfect. It remains, therefore, that we consider how nature finds out which laws of government serve to direct even a depraved nature to a right end.

All men desire to lead in this world a happy life. The most happy life led is one in which all virtue is exercised without impediment or let.[202] The apostle, in exhorting men to contentment, though they have in this

---

199 This is not just a fundamental concept in social and political theory, it is also a fundamental concept in economics, getting to the need for community, collaboration, division of labor, specialization, trade, and markets.

200 The word, "geopolitical" is used in this paraphrase to convey Hooker's idea. Here Hooker's actual word is simply, "politic".

201 i.e., commonwealth or common good (the latter being what the Ancient Romans called, "salus populi", and what the Preamble to the Constitution of the United States of America calls, "the general Welfare").

202 i.e. without interference or restriction.

world no more than very bare food and raiment,[203] allows us to infer these conclusions: that even if we should be stripped of things with which we might possibly live, yet these bare necessities must remain; that destitution in these is such an impediment that, until this impediment is removed, it does not allow the mind of man to admit any other care. For this reason, God first assigned Adam maintenance of life,[204] and then appointed him a law to observe.[205] For this reason, after men began to grow to a number the first thing we read that they gave themselves to do was the tilling of the earth and the feeding of cattle.[206]

Having the means by which to live, the principal actions of their life afterward are noted by the exercise of their religion. True it is that the Kingdom of God must be the first thing in our purposes and desires.[207] But as much as righteous life is predicated on life—as much as it is impossible to live virtuously except that we live—the first impediment which we naturally endeavor to remove, therefore, is poverty and want of things without which we cannot live. For life, many implements are necessary—more, if we seek, as all men naturally do, such a life as has in it joy, comfort, delight, and pleasure. To this end we see how quickly various mechanical arts were discovered in the very prime of the world.[208] As things of greatest necessity are always first provided for, so things of greatest dignity are most accounted of by all who judge rightly. Therefore, although riches be a thing which every man wishes, yet no man of judgement can esteem it better to be rich instead of wise, virtuous, and religious. If we are both rich and of good character, or either of these, it is not because we are born so. For into the world we come as empty of riches as of good character, as naked in mind as we are in body. At first, neither of these necessities of man had other aids and supplies, except only familial. Such as that which the prophet implies: "Can a mother

---

203 *I Timothy 6:8*, written by the apostle, Paul of Tarsus.

204 *Genesis* 1:27–29, 2:8–9, 2:15–17, 3:1–2, and 9:3.

205 *Genesis* 2:17 and 3:3.

206 *Genesis* 3:23, 4:2, and 9:20.

207 *Matthew* 6:33.

208 *Genesis* 4:20–22.

forget her child?"[209] Such as that which the apostle mentions: "He that cares not for his own is worse than an Infidel."[210] Such as that which is said of Abraham: "Abraham will command his sons and his household after him, that they keep the way of the LORD."[211]

But neither that which we learn by ourselves nor that which others teach us can prevail where wickedness and malice have taken deep root. Therefore, even when there was only one family in the world, no means of instruction, human or divine, could prevent the spilling of blood.[212] After humans separated,[213] how could it be otherwise than that, when families were multiplied and increased upon Earth—each family providing for itself—inevitably envy, strife, contention, and violence grew among them? For has not nature furnished man with wit and valor, and, as it were, with armor, which may be used for extreme evil as well as good? Yes, were they not used by the rest of the world for evil, excepting only Seth, Enoch, and those few in the rest of that line? We all complain about the iniquity of our times—not unjustly, for the days are evil. But compare them with those times in which there were no civil societies, with those times in which there was as yet no manner of public government established,[214] with those times in which there were no more than eight righteous persons living upon the face of the earth,[215] and we surely have good reason to think that God has blessed us exceedingly, and has made us behold most happy days.

To take away all such mutual grievances, injuries and wrongs, there was no way but only by building upon mutual consent and agreement among themselves, by ordaining some kind of public government, and by subjecting themselves to that, that to whomever they

---

209 *Isaiah* 49:15.

210 *I Timothy* 5:8.

211 *Genesis* 18:19.

212 *Genesis* 4:8.

213 i.e., separation into different genealogical lines, geographic regions, and language groups (*Genesis* 10:1 – 11:9, and *I Chronicles* 1:1–27).

214 Hooker is referring to the anarchy (an absence of government—a "state of nature") and increasing evil of pre-Flood humanity (*Genesis* 6:5).

215 *Genesis* 7:1 and 13.

granted authority to rule and govern, by them the peace, tranquility, and happy estate of the rest might be procured. Men always knew that, when force and injury were offered, they might be defenders of themselves; however, they knew that men may seek their own interests, yet if this were done with injury to others it was not to be suffered, but by all men and by all good means to be withstood. Finally, they knew that no man might reasonably take upon himself to determine his own right, and according to his own determination proceed in maintenance of it, in as much as every man is biased towards himself and partial to those of whom he is greatly affectionate, and that, therefore, strifes and troubles would be endless unless all of them were to give their common consent to be ordered by some upon whom they would agree. Without this consent there was no reason that one man should take upon himself to be lord or judge over another—because, although there is a kind of natural right in the noble, wise, and virtuous to govern them who are of servile disposition, according to the opinion of some very great and judicious men—nevertheless, for manifestation of this, their right, and men's more peaceable contentment on both sides, the assent of them who are to be governed seems necessary.

To fathers within their private families nature has given a supreme power. For this reason we see that, throughout the world—even from the world's first foundation—all men have ever been taken as lords and lawful kings in their own houses. However, over a whole grand multitude, having no such dependency upon anyone, and consisting of so many families as every geopolitical society in the world does, it is impossible that anyone should have complete lawful power[216] except by consent of men or immediate appointment by God. That is because, lords over multitudes not having the natural superiority of fathers, their power necessarily must be either usurped, and so unlawful, or, if lawful, then either granted or consented to by those over whom they exercise that power, or else given extraordinarily from God, to whom all of the world is subject. Therefore, the arch-philosopher's opinion is probably

[216] i.e., the full and rightful power to govern.

correct that, as the chiefest person in every household was always like a king, therefore, when numbers of households joined themselves together in civil societies, kings were the first kind of governors among them.[217] Which is also—as it seems—the reason why the name of, "Father", continued still in them, who of fathers were made rulers, as it is perhaps also the reason why the ancient custom of kings such as Melchizedek exercising the office[218] of priests, which fathers did at first.

However, this is not the only kind of government which has been received in the world. The inconveniences of one kind have caused various others to be devised. So that, in a word, all public government, of whatever kind, seems evidently to have risen from deliberate advice, consultation, and formal covenant between men, judging it convenient and advantageous—there being no impossibility in nature, considered by itself, but that men might have lived without any public government. However, the corruption of our nature being a given, we may not deny but that the law of nature now necessarily requires some kind of government, so that to bring things back to their original state and to utterly take away all kind of public government in the world would apparently be to overturn the whole world.

Therefore, the case of man's nature standing as it does, the law of nature requires some kind of government. Yet, the kinds of government being many,[219] nature does not restrict us to choosing any particular one, but allows men to make an arbitrary choice. At the first, when some certain kind of government was once approved, it may be that nothing was then further thought upon for the manner of governing, but all permitted unto

---

217 ARISTOTLE, *Politics*, Book I, Chapter 2, available in *The Politics of Aristotle, trans. into English with introduction, marginal analysis, essays, notes and indices by B. Jowett* (Benjamin Jowett), Volume 1 (Clarendon Press, Oxford, 1885). See also PLATO, *Laws*, Book III, sections 680a—681d, available in *Plato in Twelve Volumes, with an English Translation*, Volume 10, translated by R. G. Bury (William Heinemann Ltd., London, 1913).

218 i.e., duty or obligation.

219 e.g., monarchical kingdom, oligarchy, direct democracy, constitutionally-limited republic, unicameral senatorial, bicameral congressional, parliamentary, chiefdom, tribal council of elders, clan, city-state, federation, feudal, communal, cooperative, theocracy, separation of church and state.

their wisdom and discretion which was to rule[220]—until by experience they found this for all parts very inconvenient, so as the thing which they had devised for a remedy did indeed but increase the sore which it should have cured. They saw that to live by one man's will became the cause of all men's misery. This constrained them to adopt laws by which all men might see their duties, beforehand, and know the penalties for transgressing them. If things be simply good or evil, and with all universally so acknowledged, there needs no new law to be made for such things.[221] Therefore, of things appointed by human laws, the first kind includes whatever is inherently good or evil by nature, yet are too obscure to be discerned by any man's present conception without some deeper reasoning and judgement. Because there is difficulty and possibility to err in many ways, many in their reasoning would be ignorant of their responsibilities who are not now, unless their responsibilities are set down by laws. And many who know what they should do, would nevertheless hide it, and pretend ignorance and simplicity in order to excuse themselves, which now they cannot.[222]

---

220 [A]s the masses in their helplessness were oppressed by the strong, they appealed for protection to some one man who was conspicuous for his virtue; and, as he shielded the weaker classes from wrong, he managed by establishing equitable conditions to hold the higher and the lower classes in an equality of right. ... [B]ut when such was not their good fortune, laws were invented...

—Marcus Tullius Cicero, *Of Offices* (i.e., duties or obligations), Book II, Chapter 12, sections 41 and 42. See *Cicero, De Officiis, with an English Translation by Walter Miller* (William Heinemann, London, 1913).

221 ...the honouring of parents, doing good to one's friends, and returning good to one's benefactors. These and similar duties are not enjoined upon mankind by written laws, but they are observed by unwritten custom and universal practice.

—Aristotle, *Rhetoric to Alexander*, Chapter 1, 1421b36–1422a1. See *De Rhetorica ad Alexandrum*, translated by E. S. Forster (Edward Seymour Forster), in *The Works of Aristotle*, translated into English under the Editorship of W. D. Ross (William David Ross), M.A., Volume XI (Clarendon Press, Oxford, England, 1924). (Scholars in Hooker's time attributed this book to Aristotle, and the 1924 Oxford edition credits Aristotle, but it is now thought to be more likely the work of Anaximenes of Lampsacus, who lived around the same time as Alexander.)

222 For so great is the influence of pleasures, that it maketh ignorance linger to take advantage of it, and bribeth knowledge to dissemble itself.

—Tertullian, *Of Spectator Games*, Chapter 1. See "Of Public Shows", in *Tertullian, Volume 1, Apologetic and Practical Treatises*, translated by the Rev. C. Dodgson, M.A., in *A Library of Fathers of the Holy Catholic Church, anterior to the Division of the East and West*, edited by E. B. Pusey, et al. (John Henry Parker, Oxford, England, 1842).

Most men prefer their own private good before anything else—even that good which is sensual before whatever is most divine. The labor of doing good, together with the pleasure arising from the contrary, makes men, for the most part, hesitant to do good and more prone to do the other, so that duty cannot sufficiently prevail with them when not prescribed by law. Therefore, as to laws which men make for the benefit of men, it has always seemed necessary to add rewards which may better allure them to do good than any unpleasantness deters them from it, and punishments which may better deter them from evil than any sweetness allures them to it. Where the generality, "Virtue is rewardable, and vice is punishable", is natural, the particular determination of the reward or punishment belongs to those who make the laws. Theft is naturally punishable, but the form of that punishment is positive, and it is lawful only if deliberative men include that punishment in the law.

In laws, that which is *natural* universally binds, and that which is *positive* does not universally bind. To skip those forms of positive laws which men impose upon themselves—by a vow to God, contract with men, or such like—it will somewhat serve our purpose a little more fully to consider what things are pertinent to the making of positive laws for the government of those who live united in public society. Laws not only teach what is good, they enjoin it. They have in them a certain constraining force. Of course, to constrain men to anything inconvenient seems unreasonable. Therefore, to devise laws which all men will be forced to obey, it is essential that none but wise men be appointed. Laws are matters of principal consequence. Men of common capacity and but ordinary judgement are not able to discern what things are fittest for each form and state of government. How could they? We cannot be ignorant of how much our obedience to laws depends upon this point. Let a man, however justly, oppose those who are disordered in their ways, and who among them commonly does not resent such a contradiction, storm at the rebuke, and hate that which would reform them? Nevertheless, even those who most resent that men should tell them of their duties, when they are told the same duty by a law they think very well and reasonably of it. Why? They presume that the law speaks objectively, that the law is impartial, that the law is like an oracle issued by wisdom and understanding.[223]

However, laws do not take their constraining force from the quality of those who devise them, but from that power which gives them the strength of laws. That which we spoke of, before, concerning the power of government, must be applied here to the power of making laws by which to govern—a power which God has over all, and by the natural law to which he has made all subject. The lawful power of making laws to command whole geopolitical societies of men belongs so properly to the whole society that it is no better than mere tyranny for any prince or potentate of any kind on the Earth to exercise the same power by himself without either express commission immediately and personally received from God, or else authority originally derived from the consent of those persons upon whom the laws are imposed.

Therefore, laws are not laws unless public approval has made them so. People give their approval by personally declaring their assent by voice, sign, or act. Their approval is also declared when others delegated by them assent in their names—as in parliaments, councils, and similar assemblies. Even if we, ourselves, are not personally present, our assent is still given by our agents acting on our behalf. And there is no reason why what we do through others should not stand as our deed, and no less effectually bind us than if we, ourselves, had done it in person.

In many things for which assent is given, they that give it do not imagine that they do so, because the manner of their assenting is not apparent. For example, when an absolute monarch commands his subjects to do what seems good in his own opinion, has his edict not the force of a law, whether they approve or dislike it? Again, that which has long since been received, and is by custom now established,

---

223 And whereas we take offence at individuals who oppose our inclinations, even though their opposition is right, we do not feel aggrieved when the law bids us do what is right.

—Aristotle, *Nicomachean Ethics*, Book X, Chapter IX, 12. See *The Nicomachean Ethics of Aristotle*, translated by F. H. Peters (Frank Hesketh Peters), M.A., 7th edition (Kegan Paul, Trench, Trübner & Co., Ltd., London, 1893).

we keep as a law which we may not transgress, yet what consent to it was ever sought or required at our hands?

Therefore, we are to note this point: since men naturally have no full and perfect power to command whole geopolitical multitudes of men utterly without our consent, we could, therefore, in some way be at no living man's commandment. But we do consent to be commanded when that society, of which we are a part, has at any prior time consented, unless we later revoke that consent by a similar, universal agreement. Just as any man's past deed is good as long as he, himself, continues, so the act of a public society of men, done five hundred years ago, stands as theirs who presently are of the same societies, because corporations are immortal. In the past we were alive in our predecessors, and in the present they live in us, their successors. Therefore, human laws, of whatever kind, are legally valid, binding, and enforceable by consent.

Even though all human laws are based upon consent, if here it is asked how it comes to pass that there should be found such a great variety, even in good laws, we must note that the reason for this is the varying particular ends, by which the varying nature of the subjects or matters for which laws are provided causes lawmakers to consider the unique circumstances when making laws. There is a law mentioned among the Greeks—of which Pittacus is reported to have been author—and by that law it was agreed that if a drunk struck any man, he should suffer double as much punishment as if he had done the same being sober. No man could ever have thought this reasonable who had intended to punish only for the injury committed, according to the seriousness of the offense. For who does not know that premeditated harm is naturally less pardonable, and, therefore, worthy of sharper punishment? But because men who were intentionally drunk were the ones who usually were the offenders—especially since it was their specific intent to drink in order to be much more freely outrageous,[224] and because the problem of this disorderly behavior was growing—it was for the public good to accordingly establish a positive law as a remedy.

224 A common, modern way to say this would be, "to drink in order to raise Hell".

Related to this are those known rules for making laws.

> Lawmakers must consider the place and men to be governed.
>
> One kind of law cannot serve for all kinds of government.
>
> Where the people rule, the laws for the preservation of that state must assign common, smaller offices[225] by lot for fear of likely strife and division, because ordinary qualities sufficing for the discharge of such offices, they could only be desired by many, and dangerously competed for, and missed out on with grudge and discontentment, while with a random lottery no one can complain about whoever receives an office.
>
> Conversely, the highest offices, of which only a few men are capable, must be determined by popular election so that the people may not envy those who have the honors, in as much as they, themselves, bestow them, and so that the highest office holders may be encouraged to exercise all parts of rare and beneficial virtue, knowing that they shall not lose their labor by growing in fame and estimation among the people.
>
> If the helm of the ship of state is in the hands of a few of the wealthiest, then laws providing for the continuance of that government must make sharp and grievous punishment for contempt and wrong offered to any of the common sort, so that that evil may be prevented by which the rich are most likely to bring upon themselves hatred from the people who are not inclined to take so great an offense when they are excluded from honors and offices and when their persons are contemptuously trodden upon.

In other forms of government, these rules are observed concerning the difference of positive laws—it is impossible and against their nature for positive laws to be the same everywhere.

---

[225] i.e., duties or obligations.

Now, as the learned in the laws of this land observe, our statutes are sometimes only the affirmation or ratification of that which by common law was previously upheld.[226] So, we should not overlook that all human laws which are made for the ordering of geopolitical societies are generally either such that they establish some duty by which all men were previously bound by the law of reason, or else such that they now make a duty where previously there was none. For the sake of distinction we may call the one sort, *mixedly* human, and the other, *merely* human.

---

[226] Hooker cites the "Preface", of *The Pleas of the Crown*, by WILLIAM STAUNFORD, the relevant passage of which may be translated as:

> I have cited not a few things from Bracton and Britton, ancient writers of the laws, with this purpose: since the laws of the crown for the greatest part consist of statutory law, the common law, which existed before those statutes were established, may be placed before the eyes of the reader. For this matter is especially conducive to correctly interpreting statutes. Understanding at once occurs as to which evil common law has reduced, and the reader completely perceives how many parts of those evils it remedies and how many it does not; and whether this kind of statute is a new law, per se, or nothing other than an affirmation of common law. (See WILLIAM STAUNFORD, "Lectori" [meaning, "(Introductory Note) To the Reader"—i.e., a preface], *Les plees del coron: divisees in plusiours titles & common lieux. Per queux home plus redement & plenaireme[n]t trovera, quelq; chose que il quira, touchant les dits plees. Composees per le tresreverend judge monsieur Guilliaulme Staunforde chivauler, derniermen[en]t corrigee avecques un table parfaicte des choses notables contenues en ycelle, et jammais per cy devant imprimee. Anno Domini. 1567* (Richardi Tottelli, London, 1567), which is the third edition.)

Although "Bracton and Britton" are references to different books, they are sometimes cited together:

> HENRY DE BRACTON was a Thirteenth Century priest and a judge on the King's Bench. Often called, "the father of English common law", his major work is *De Legibus et Consuetudinibus Angliæ* ("*On the Laws and Customs of England*"), the first systematic review of English law.
>
> *Britton* is a book written by an unknown author, sometimes mistakenly said to be a Thirteenth-Century sheriff, priest, jurist, and Bishop of Hereford, John de Breton, who died before some of the laws discussed in the book were written. It has been suggested that *Britton* is an abridgement of Bracton's book, with Britton being an alternate or erroneous spelling of his name. However, the books are arranged differently, and *Britton* has topics not included in Bracton's work. *Britton* is the first book on English law written in what is called, "Law French", instead of Latin.

That, by which plain or necessary reason binds men, for various reasons may be expedient to be ratified by human law. For example, if incestuous marriage, polygamy, or any other similarly corrupt and unreasonable custom happens to have widely prevailed and gained the upper hand over right reason with most men, so that no way is left to rectify such foul disorder without prescribing by law the same things which reason necessarily *does* enforce but is not *perceived* as enforcing. Or if many be grown unto that which the apostle did lament in some, of whom he writes, "Even what things they naturally know, in those very things, as beasts void of reason, they corrupted themselves."[227] Or if there is no such special circumstance, then the common sort are led by the sway of their sensual desires and, therefore, shun sin more because of the tangible evils which follow sin among men than because of any kind of judgement which reason pronounces against it.[228] This very thing is sufficient cause for why duties belonging to each type of virtue, although the law of reason teaches these duties to men, should nevertheless be also prescribed by human law—which law in this case we call, *mixed*, because the moral duty by which it binds is the same which reason necessarily requires at our hands, and from the law of reason it differs only in the manner of binding. For while men previously stood bound in conscience to do as the law of reason teaches, they are by virtue of human law now become constrainable and punishable if they outwardly transgress.

As for laws which are *merely* human, their scope is anything which reason merely recommends to be fit and convenient, so that until such time as a law has passed among men which

---

[227] *Jude* 1:10.

[228] Hoi polloi [i.e., the many] are more obedient to force than to a word, and to penalties than to toi kaloi [i.e., the beautiful, fair, noble, or virtuous].

—ARISTOTLE, *Nicomachean Ethics*, Book X, Chapter 9. Quote translated by Ret Miles.

An alternate, less literal translation is that of Peters' (1893):

For the generality of men are naturally apt to be swayed by fear rather than by reverence, and to refrain from evil rather because of the punishment that it brings than because of its own foulness.

—*The Nicomachean Ethics of Aristotle*, translated by F. H. Peters (Frank Hesketh Peters), M.A., 7th edition (Kegan Paul, Trench, Trübner & Co., Ltd., London, 1893)

> changes the recommendation of reason into a command, of itself reason's recommendation binds no man. One example may be this: by human law, after the owner's death, in some places lands are divided among all his children; in some other places all passes down to the eldest son.[229] Hypothetically, if the law of reason required that only one or the other of these two methods of inheriting property be done, they who, contrary to the law have taken an inheritance according to the other method, should be subject to "woe", that heavy judgement which denounces all who decree wicked, unjust, and unreasonable things.[230] In reality, though, whichever method of real property inheritance is used, there is no law of reason transgressed, because there is enough reason why either method may be expedient, and for either of them no other justification is necessary.

Whether *mixedly* or *merely* human, laws are made by governed societies. Some are those societies which are only civilly united, and some are those which are spiritually joined and make a body such as what we call, *the Church*. Of human laws for this latter kind of governed society we are to speak in the third book following.[231] Therefore, let it suffice for now to have touched upon the force with which Almighty God has graciously endowed our nature, and by that has enabled our nature to not only find out those laws which generally all men are forever bound to observe, but also those which are most suitable for their benefit who lead their lives in any state ordered by government.

Now, besides that law which simply concerns men as men, and that which belongs to them as they are men linked with others in some form

---

229 If we are using precise English Common Law terminology for real estate being transferred to heirs (and what is attached, like buildings and fencing), we would word the above clause as, "all devises to the eldest son", instead of saying, "passes down", "flows down", or "descends" (Hooker's term). (It should be noted, however, that the United Kingdom is moving away from "devise" to "bequeath" or "gift".) The paraphrase, above, uses, "passes down", for general readers who might not be familiar with legal language.

230 *Isaiah* 10:1.

231 i.e., *Of the Laws of Ecclesiastical Polity*, Book III: *Concerning Their Second Assertion, that In Scripture There Must Be of Necessity Contained a Form of Church Polity, the Laws whereof May in Nowise Be Altered.*

of governed society, there is a third kind of law which touches upon all such separate geopolitical bodies in as far as one of them has public commerce with another. And this third kind of law is *the law of nations.* Between men and beasts there is no possibility of sociable communion, because the well-spring of sociable communion is a natural delight which man has to transfuse from himself into others and to receive from others into himself mainly those things in which the excellency of speech most consists. Therefore, the highest instrument of human communion is speech, because by that we mutually impart to each other the concepts of our reasonable understanding.[232] And for that cause, seeing that beasts are not capable of speech—for as much as we can use no such conference with them, although to a degree they are above other creatures on Earth to whom nature has denied sense yet too low to be sociable companions of man to whom nature has given reason—it is said of Adam that among the beasts "He found not for himself any meet companion."[233] Civil society contents the nature of man more than any private kind of solitary living because in society this good of mutual participation is so much larger than otherwise. Regardless, we are not satisfied with this, but we covet to have some kind of society and fellowship even with all mankind, if possible—which thing Socrates, intending to signify, professed himself a citizen, not of this or that commonwealth, but of the world.[234] And an effect of that very natural

---

232 Now the reason why man is more of a political animal than bees or any other gregarious animals is evident. Nature, as we often say, makes nothing in vain, and man is the only animal whom she has endowed with the gift of speech...to set forth the expedient and inexpedient, and likewise the just and the unjust...

—Aristotle, *Politics*, Book I, Chapter 2, 1253a. See *The Politics of Aristotle*, translated by Benjamin Jowett (Clarendon Press, Oxford, 1885).

233 *Genesis* 2:20.

234 When Socrates was asked to name his city, he said, "The world;" for he regarded himself as an inhabitant and citizen of the whole world.

—Marcus Tullius Cicero, *Tusculan Disputations*, Book V, Chapter 37. See *Cicero's Tusculan Disputations*, translated by Andrew P. Peabody (Little, Brown, and Company, Boston, 1886).

...when he shall have attained in a great measure, the knowledge of that Being who superintends and governs them, and shall look on himself as not confined within the walls of one city, or as the member of any particular community, but as a citizen of the universe, considered as a single Commonwealth...

—Marcus Tullius Cicero, *Of Laws*, Book I, Marcus speaking. See *The Treatises of M. T. Cicero*, translated by C. D. Yonge (Henry G. Bohn, London, 1853).

desire in us, a manifestation of our wish for a sort of universal fellowship with all men, appears by a wonderful delight which men have, some of us to visit foreign countries, some of us to discover nations not heard of in former ages, all of us to know the affairs and dealings of other people, even to be in league of amity with them. And this is not only for traffic's sake, or to the end that when many are confederated each may make the others stronger, but also for such cause which moved the Queen of Saba to visit Salomon[235]—in a word, because nature presumes that however many men there are in the world, it is as if they are so many gods, or at least they should be as gods in their behavior towards men.[236]

Touching upon the laws which are necessary to govern human societies in this way:

> When man retained his original integrity, *the laws of reason* were sufficient to direct each particular person in all his affairs and duties. Now that man and his offspring are grown so corrupt and sinful, the laws of reason are no longer sufficient, but require the addition of other laws.
>
> When men lived together in public society and had a harmless disposition, *the laws of polity and government* would have served. Now, when men's iniquity is so hardly restrained

---

[235] i.e., Sheba and Solomon. *I Kings* 10:1, *II Chronicles* 9:1, *Matthew* 12: 42, and *Luke* 11:31.

[236] "Man is a god to man"...is often said of one who has brought sudden and unexpected salvation, or who has helped with some great benefit. For the ancients believed that nothing else was considered a god than to be of service to mortals.

—DESIDERIUS ERASMUS OF ROTTERDAM, *Adagia ("Adages")*, 1.1.69, "Homo Homini Deus". Quote translated by Ret Miles.

Again, let any one but consider the immense difference between men's lives in the most polished countries of Europe, and in any wild and barbarous region of the new Indies, he will think it so great, that man may be said to be a god unto man, not only on account of mutual aid and benefits, but from their comparative states—the result of the arts, and not of the soil or climate.

—Francis Bacon, *Novum Organum* (1620), Book I, Aphorism CXXIX 129. The quote, here, is excerpted from *Novum Organum*, by Lord Bacon, edited by Joseph Devey, M.A. (P. F. Collier, New York, 1902). "Novum Organum" means, "New Instrument", "New Method", or "New Logic". The title alludes to the *Organon*, Theophrastus' standard collection of Aristotle's six books on logic. Bacon was proposing the use of inductive logic based on observations, instead of Aristotle's system of logic based on syllogisms. Bacon's method is a forerunner of the modern scientific method.

> within any tolerable bounds, the laws of polity and government are no longer able to serve.
>
> In societies of a former and better quality, *the national laws of natural commerce*[237] *between societies* might have been other than now, when nations are so prone to offer violence, injury, and wrong.

Because of human corruption, there has grown in each of these three kinds of laws a distinction between *primary* and *secondary* laws—the one grounded upon integrity, the other built upon depraved nature:

> *Primary laws of nations* are such as concern embassies, the courteous entertainment of foreigners and strangers, accommodating traffic between societies, and the like.
>
> *Secondary laws of nations* are such as this present, unquiet world is most familiarly acquainted with: I mean *laws of arms*, which yet are much better known than kept.

But I omit, here, to search what is contained in the law of nations.

The strength and virtue of the law of nations is such that no particular nation can lawfully override that law by any of their own laws and ordinances, any more than a man, by his private resolutions, can lawfully override the civil law of the commonwealth or state in which he lives. For as civil law, being the act of a whole geopolitical body, therefore rules over each of the different parts of the same body, so that there is no reason for which any one commonwealth of itself should, to the prejudice of another, annihilate that upon which the whole world has agreed. For which cause, the Lacedemonians forbidding all access of strangers into their coasts are in that respect both by Josephus and Theodoret deservedly blamed as being enemies to that

---

[237] This is a paraphrase of the 1622 edition of Hooker's *Of the Laws of Ecclesiastical Polity*. Later editions have used the phrase, "mutual commerce", here, instead of "natural commerce". It is likely that "mutual commerce" more accurately conveys Hooker's intended point, although an economist might argue that it is a redundant phrase since commerce is necessarily mutual.

hospitality which for common humanity's sake all the nations on Earth should embrace.[238]

Now as there is great case of communion among nations and, consequently, of laws for the maintenance of communion among nations, so among Christian nations the like in regard even of Christianity has been always judged necessary.

And in this kind of correspondence among nations stands the force of general councils. For as one and the same divine law, of which in the next place we are to speak, is unto all Christian churches a rule for the highest things, by means of which they all in that respect make one Church, as having all only "one Lord, one faith, and one baptism",[239] so the urgent necessity of mutual communion for preservation of our unity in these things, as also for order in some other things convenient to be everywhere uniformly kept, makes it requisite that the Church of God

---

238 Moreover, the Lacedemonians continued in their way of expelling foreigners; and would not indeed give leave to their own people to travel abroad: as suspecting that those two things would introduce a dissolution of their own laws. And perhaps there may be some reason to blame the rigid severity of the Lacedemonians. For they bestowed the privilege of their city on no foreigners; nor indeed would give leave to them to stay among them. Whereas we, though we do not think fit to imitate others institutions, yet do we willingly admit of those that desire to partake of ours. Which, I think, I may reckon to be a plain indication of our humanity, and at the same time of our magnanimity also.

—FLAVIUS JOSEPHUS, *Against Apion*, Book II, Section 37, in *The Genuine Works of Flavius Josephus, the Jewish Historian. Translated from the Original Greek, according to Havercamp's accurate Edition. Containing Twenty Books of the Jewish Antiquities, with the Appendix or Life of Josephus, written by himself: Seven Books of the Jewish War: and Two Books against Apion. Illustrated with new Plans and Descriptions of the Tabernacle of Moses; and of the Temples of Solomon, Zorobabel, Herod, and Ezekiel; and with correct Maps of Judea and Jerusalem. Together with Proper Notes, Observations, Contents, Parallel Texts of Scripture, five compleat Indexes, and the true Chronology of the several Histories adjusted in the Margin. By William Whiston, M.A. Some time Professor of the Mathematicks in the University of Cambridge* (Cambridge University Press, London, 1737)

...lawgivers, such as Lycurgus, deservedly have been condemned by many writers for the unjust and cruel manner in which their laws treated strangers, not considering them worthy to associate with their citizens.

—THEODORET OF CYRUS, *On Curing Greek Maladies*, Book IX, paraphrase by Ret Miles

Lacedemonia (also called, "Lacedæmonia", "Lacedaemonia", or "Laconia"), is the name for the ancient state of which Sparta was the capital. The Spartans were also called, "Lacedemonians", etc., as were the people of that ancient region.

The word, "coasts", during Hooker's time, was used as a synonym for "borders".

239 *Ephesians* 4:5.

here on Earth have her laws of spiritual commerce between Christian nations, laws by virtue of which all churches may freely enjoy the use of those reverend religious and sacred consultations, which are called, *general councils*. A thing of which God's own blessed Spirit was the Author,[240] a thing practiced by the holy apostles, themselves, a thing always afterwards kept and observed throughout the world, a thing never otherwise than most highly esteemed of, until pride, ambition, and tyranny began by factious and vile endeavors to abuse that divine invention for the furtherance of wicked purposes. But as the just authority of civil courts and parliaments is not, therefore, to be abolished because sometimes there is cunning used to frame them according to the private intentions of men overpotent in the commonwealth, so the grievous abuse which has been of councils should rather cause men to study how so gracious a thing may again be reduced[241] to that first perfection than be held for ever in extreme disgrace in regard of the stain and blemishes since growing.

To speak of this matter as the cause requires would require a very long discourse. All I will presently say, is this:

> whether it is for the finding out of anything to which divine law binds us (but yet in such a way that men are not fully agreed),
>
> whether it is for the setting down of some uniform judgement to stand touching upon such things as are not necessarily wrong (yet are offensive and scandalous when there is open opposition about them),
>
> whether it is for the ending of strifes related to Christian doctrine (in which the one faction may seem to have probable cause of dissenting from the other),
>
> or whether it is concerning matters of polity, order, and government within the Church,

I do not doubt but that Christian men should much better frame themselves to those heavenly precepts which our Lord and Savior so

240 *Acts* 15:28.

241 i.e., restored.

earnestly gave as concerning peace and unity[242] if we all concurred in desire to have the use of ancient councils again renewed rather than continue these proceedings which either make all contentions endless or bring them to only one determination—and that of all others the worse, which is by sword.

Therefore, it follows that a new foundation being laid, we now proceed to what is next to be said—namely why God has, Himself, by Scripture made known such laws as serve for direction of men.

242 *John* 14:27.

CHAPTER ELEVEN

Why God Made Supernatural Laws Further Known by Scripture for Men's Direction

BESIDES THE NATURE which they have in themselves, all things—God only excepted—receive some perfection externally from other things, as has been shown, since everything in the whole world, great or small, relates to either knowledge or usefulness, and may somewhat add to our betterment. And whatever such betterment there is which our nature may acquire, the same we properly call, *our good.* Our *sovereign good or blessedness* is that in which all of our betterment consists to the highest degree—that which, once being attained, there can remain nothing further to be desired, and, therefore, with it our souls are fully content and satisfied in what they have. They rejoice and thirst for no more. When good things are desired, some are such that we do not covet them for themselves, but only because they serve as instruments to what we are seeking. Of this kind are riches. There is another kind of instrument, such as health, virtue, and knowledge, which, although we desire these for themselves, they are, nevertheless, not the last mark at which we aim but have their further end to which they lead; so, because we are not satisfied that these have attained what we ultimately desire, our desires still continue. These things are linked and chained, as it were, to each other: we labor to eat, we eat to live, we live to do good, and the good which we do is as seed sown for a future harvest.[243] But at length we must come to some pause. For if every thing was to be desired for some other thing without any limit, there could be no certain end proposed for our actions—we would go on to we know not where. Indeed, whatever we do would be in vain. Said another way, it would be impossible for anything at all to be done. If we were to remove the first efficient cause of our being, that would utterly annihilate our persons. Likewise, we cannot remove the last final cause of our work without stopping whatever our work is. Therefore, there must be something desired simply for itself and for no other reason. The nature of that which is simply desirable for itself is such that it is contradictory and repugnant to be desired as a means to anything else. The Ox and the Ass[244] desire their food only as food. Neither wants food for any other purpose. Why? Because of their imperfection, which cannot desire food for any other reason, while the excellence of that which is desired simply for itself is such that it does not in any way permit itself to serve a further purpose.

Now whatever man desires as a means to a further end, the same he desires in such measure as is proper to that end. But, what he covets as good, per se, towards that good his desire is ever infinite. So that, unless the last good of all which is desirable together for itself is also infinite, we do evil in making it our end,[245] even as they who placed their felicity in

---

[243] For he that soweth into his flesh, shall of the flesh reap corruption: But he that soweth into the spirit, shall of the spirit reap life everlasting.

—*Galatians* 6:8, Bishops' Bible, spelling updated

[244] See ARISTOTLE, *Nicomachean Ethics* (Book I, Chapter 7, and Book X, Chapter 7) and *Eudemian Ethics* (Book II, Chapter 10), and THOMAS AQUINAS, *Summa Contra Gentiles* (Book III, Chapter 24) and *Summa Theologiæ* (Prima Secundæ (I–II), Question 1, Article 5).

[245] But if happiness consists in activity in accordance with virtue, it is reasonable that it should be activity in accordance with the highest virtue; and this will be the virtue of the best part of us. Whether then this be the intellect, or whatever else it be that is thought to rule and lead us by nature, and to have cognizance of what is noble and divine, either as being itself also actually divine, or as being relatively the divinest part of us, it is the activity of this part of us in accordance with the virtue proper to it that will constitute perfect happiness…

—ARISTOTLE, *Nicomachean Ethics*, Book X, Chapter 7, Section 1. See *Aristotle in 23 Volumes*, Volume 19, translated by H. Rackham (Harris Rackham) (Harvard University Press, Cambridge, Massachusetts, 1934).

…for there will not be *eternal* movement, for that which is potentially may possibly not be. There must, then, be such a principle, whose very essence is actuality. … There

wealth, honor, pleasure, or anything here attained, because, we err in desiring anything as our final betterment which is not a betterment. Nothing may be infinitely desired but that good which, indeed, is infinite. For, the better, the more desirable. Therefore, the most desirable, in which there is an infinity of goodness (if anything desirable may be infinite), that must necessarily be the highest of all things which are desired. No good is infinite but only God. Therefore, He is our felicity and bliss. Moreover, desire tends toward union with that which is desired. If, then, in Him we are blessed, it is by the power of participation and union with Him. Again, it is not the possession of any good thing which can make them happy who have it unless they enjoy the thing which they possess. Therefore, we are happy when we fully enjoy God as an ultimate object in which the powers of our souls are satisfied even with everlasting delight—so that, though we be men, yet by being united to God we live, as it were, the life of God.

Therefore, happiness is that estate by which we attain, so far as possibly may be attained, the full possession of that which simply for itself is to be desired and contains in it after an eminent sort the satisfaction of our desires, the highest degree of all our perfection. We are incapable of such betterments in this life, for while we are in the world we are subject unto many imperfections,[246] grief of body, and defects of mind. Indeed, the best things we do are painful, and the exercise of them

is, then, something which is always moved with an unceasing motion, which is motion in a circle; and this is plain not in theory only but in fact. Therefore the first heaven must be eternal. There is therefore also something which moves it. And since that which moves and is moved is intermediate, there is something which moves without being moved, being eternal, substance, and actuality. And the object of desire and the object of thought move in this way; they move without being moved.

—ARISTOTLE, *Metaphysics*, Book XII, Chapters 6 and 7. See *The Works of Aristotle*, Volume VIII, *Metaphysica*, translated by William David Ross (Clarendon Press, Oxford, England, 1908).

246 O Asclepius, only the *name* of the good is in men, but the *deed* is nowhere in them... The not very bad, here is the good. But the good, here, is the least part of the bad. Therefore, it is impossible for the good, here, to be purified from evil... And I have gratitude to God, to Him who has thrown into my mind about the knowledge of the good, for it is impossible for it to be in the world, For the world is a "fullness" of evil, but God is the good, and the good is of God.

—MERCURIUS TRISMEGISTUS (HERMES TRISMEGISTUS), *Corpus Hermeticum*, Book VI, excerpts translated by Ret Miles. See, also, *Thrice Greatest Hermes*, translated by G. R. S. Meade (George Robert Stow Mead), Volume II (Theosophical Publication Society, London, 1906).

grievous, being continued without intermission. So, as in those very actions by which we are especially perfected in this life we are not able to persist, with very weariness we are forced, and that often, to interrupt them—which tediousness cannot fall into those operations which are in the state of bliss when our union with God is complete. Complete union with Him must be according to every power and faculty of our minds, apt to receive so glorious an ultimate object. We are capable of comprehending God both by understanding and will:

> by understanding, as He is that Sovereign Truth which comprehends the rich treasures of all wisdom;
>
> by will, as He is that Sea of Goodness, which, whoever tastes, shall thirst no more.

As the will does new work upon that object by desire—which is a motion, as it were, towards the as yet unobtained end—so, likewise, upon receiving the same in the future it shall also work by love. "Appetitus inhiantis fit amor fruentis," says Saint Augustine: "The longing disposition of them that thirst, is changed into the sweet affection of them that taste and are replenished."[247]

---

[247] Hooker might have been quoting from memory, rough notes, or a faulty text. The full quote of the clause is:

> ...idemque appetitus quo inhiatur rei cognoscendæ fit amor cognitæ dum tenet atque amplectitur placitam prolem, id est notitiam gignentique coniungit.
>
> —AURELIUS AUGUSTINUS, (AURELIUS AUGUSTIN, BISHOP OF HIPPO) (SAINT AUGUSTINE OF HIPPO), *De trinitate* ("*On the Trinity*"), Liber IX, Caput XII, Sectio 18

The quote can be translated as follows:

> ...and the same appetite [i.e., striving for], where one eagerly gawks at the cognition [knowing] of a thing, is made the love of what is recognized [known] while it holds and even embraces the pleasing outgrowth—that is, it conjoins [joins] notability [renown] and the generation of life.
>
> —AUGUSTINE OF HIPPO, *On the Trinity*, Book IX, Chapter XII, Paragraph 18, quote translated and annotated by Ret Miles
>
> ...and the same desire which led us to long for the knowing of the thing, becomes the love of the thing when known, while it holds and embraces its accepted offspring, that is, knowledge, and unites it to its begetter.
>
> —AUGUSTINE OF HIPPO, *On the Holy Trinity*, Book IX, Chapter XII, paragraph 18, translated by Arthur West Haddan and William G. T. Shedd, in *A Select Library of the Nicene and Post-Nicene Fathers of the Christian Church: Series I*, edited by Philip Schaff, Vol. III, *Doctrinal Treatises of St. Augustin* (Christian Literature Publishing Co., Buffalo, New York, 1887)

While we now love the thing which is good, but good especially for the sake of its benefit to us, we shall then love the thing that is good, only or principally for the goodness of its beauty. The soul, capable of being active, improved by love of that Infinite Good, shall, as it is receptive, be also improved with those supernatural passions of joy, peace, and delight—all of this endless and everlasting.[248] This perpetuity, in regard of which our blessedness is called, "a crown which withereth not",[249] neither depends upon the nature of the thing, itself, nor proceeds from any natural necessity which our souls should so exercise themselves forever in beholding and loving God, but from the will of God which both freely improves our nature in so high a degree and continues it so improved. Under man, no creature in the world is capable of felicity and bliss: firstly, because their highest improvement consists in that which is best for them, but not in that which is simply best, as ours does; secondly, because whatever external betterment to which they tend, it is not better than themselves, as ours is. Even in this respect, therefore, we have just cause with the prophet to admire the goodness of God, saying, "Lord, what is man that thou should exalt him above the works of thy hands, so far as to make thyself the inheritance of his rest, and the substance of his felicity?"[250]

---

[248] ...they...are as the angels of God in heaven.
—*Matthew* 22:30, Bishops' Bible, spelling updated

...the righteous [shall go] into life eternal.
—*Matthew* 25:46, Bishops' Bible, annotated and spelling updated

[249] *I Peter* 5:4. Hooker, who had a preference for a weightier style with more archaic language, has substituted the word, "withereth", for, "fadeth".

[250] 1 To the chief musician upon Gittith, a psalm of David. O God our Lord, how excellent is thy name in all the earth? for that thou hast set thy glory above the heavens.
2 Out of the mouth of very babes and sucklings thou hast laid the foundation of thy strength for thine adversaries' sake: that thou mightest still the enemy and the avenger.
3 For I will consider thy heavens, even the works of thy fingers: the moon and the stars which thou hast ordained.
4 What is man that thou art mindful of him? and the son of man that thou visitest him?
5 Thou hast made him something inferior to angels: thou hast crowned him with glory and worship.
6 Thou makest him to have dominion of the works of thy hands: and thou hast put all things in subjection under his feet,
7 All sheep and oxen, and also the beasts of the field:
8 the souls of the air, and the fish of the sea, and whatsoever swimmeth in the seas.
9 O God our Lord: how excellent great is thy name in all the earth?
—King David, *Psalm 8*, Bishops' Bible, spelling updated

Now if men did not naturally have this desire to be happy, how was it possible that all men should have it? All men have; therefore, this desire in man is natural. It is not in our power to not do the same. How then should it be in our power to do it indifferently or neglectfully?

Since this natural desire possesses an intensity which cannot be surpassed, is it probable that God would put such an infinite longing in the hearts of all men only to be satisfied by something finite? It is an axiom of nature that natural desire cannot be utterly frustrated. This desire of ours, being natural, would be frustrated if that which may satisfy the desire was something impossible for man to aspire to. Man seeks a triple betterment:

> firstly, a *sensual betterment*, consisting of those things which very life, itself, requires either as necessary supplements or as beauties and ornaments of the sensual life;
>
> then, an *intellectual betterment*, consisting of those things which none underneath man is either capable of or acquainted with;
>
> lastly, a *spiritual and divine betterment*, consisting of those things to which we, here, tend towards by supernatural means, but cannot, here, attain.

They who make *sensual betterment* the scope of their whole life are said by the apostle to have no God but only their belly—they are earthly-minded men.[251]

They who seek especially to excel in all such knowledge and virtue which most commend men, bend themselves to *intellectual betterment.* To this branch belongs the law of *moral and civil betterment.*

That there is something higher than either *sensual betterment* or *intellectual betterment*, no other proof is needed than the very process of man's desire, which being natural would be frustrated if there was not some further thing in which it might at length remain satisfied, which

---

[251] Whose end is damnation, whose God is their belly, and glory to their shame, which mind earthly things.

—*Philippians* 3:19, Bishops' Bible, spelling updated

in *sensual betterment* and *intellectual betterment* it cannot do. For man does not seem to remain satisfied either with the enjoyment of that by which his life is preserved or with performance of such actions which advance him most deservedly in esteem. Instead, he further covets—indeed, oftentimes manifestly pursues with great zeal and earnestness—that which is of no use for preserving life, that which exceeds the reach of sense. Indeed, he covets and earnestly pursues something above the capacity for reasoning, something divine and heavenly which, with hidden exultation, he surmises rather than conceives. He seeks what he does not know; yet, he very intensely desires it, which incites him to lay aside all other known delights and pleasures which give way to the search of this vague desire. If the soul of man served only to give him *being* in this life, then things belonging to this life would satisfy him, as we see they do other creatures—which creatures, enjoying what they live by, seek no further, but in this satisfaction show a kind of acknowledgement that there is no higher good which belongs to them in any way. *With us*, it is otherwise. For although one might currently possess the beauties, riches, honors, sciences, virtues, and betterments of all living, above and beyond all of this there would still be something sought and earnestly thirsted for. Therefore, even in this life, nature plainly claims and calls for a more *divine betterment* than either *sensual betterment* or *intellectual betterment.*

This *spiritual and divine betterment* is received by men in the nature of a reward.[252] Rewards always assume the performance of duties which are rewardable. Therefore, our works are our *natural* means to blessedness. Nor is it possible that nature should ever find any other way to salvation than only our works. But, examine the works which we do, and, since the first foundation of the world, what individual

---

[252] Rejoice and be glad: for great is your reward in Heaven.

—*Matthew* 5:12, Bishops' Bible, spelling updated

This reward, however, is the highest, so that we may enjoy it ourself, and all who enjoy it may, in turn, also enjoy it with us.

—AUGUSTINE OF HIPPO, *Of the Doctrine of Christ*, Book I, Section 76, quote translated by Ret Miles. See also, AUGUSTINE, *De doctrina Christiana*, translated by R. P. H. Green (Clarendon Press, Oxford, England 1995).

can say, "My ways are pure"? Seeing, then, that all flesh is guilty of that for which God has threatened to eternally punish, what possibility to be saved is there in our works? Therefore, there remains either no way to salvation, or, if there is any way to salvation, then it is surely a way which is *super*natural, a way which could never have entered into the heart of man even once to conceive of or imagine unless God, Himself, had not extraordinarily revealed it. Because of this, we call it, the *mystery*, or secret way of salvation. And, therefore, in this matter, Saint Ambrose justly appeals from man to God.

> Let God, Himself, that made me, let not man that knows not himself, be my instructor concerning the mystical way to Heaven.
>
> —AMBROSE, BISHOP OF MILAN (AURELIUS AMBROSIUS, or SAINT AMBROSE), *Epistola XVIII ad Valentinianum* ("*Letter 18 to Emperor Valentinian II*"), Section 7.[253]

To show that God, Himself, is the Teacher of the truth by which is made known the supernatural Way of salvation and the law for them to live in who shall be saved, Lactantius says:

> When men of excellent intelligence had wholly dedicated themselves to study, after abandoning all kinds of actions, both private and public, they spared no labor which might be spent in the search of truth, holding it a much more valuable thing to seek, and to discover the reason for all affairs, Divine as well as Human, than to stick fast in the toil of piling up riches and gathering together heaps of Honors. Nevertheless, they not only failed in their purpose, they did not even benefit from their efforts—because truth which is the secret of the most high God, Whose proper

[253] In 384 A.D., a conservative Pagan Roman senator and prefect, Symmachus, asked Emperor Valentinian II to restore an altar in the Senate to a popular goddess with the Roman soldiers, Victoria ("Victory", also known by her Ancient Greek name, Νικη, "Nike"), and to restore public funding for Pagan rituals. Ambrose wrote letters to the emperor in response, successfully arguing that the emperor, who was a Christian, should not grant the request. See also, *A Select Library of Early Church Fathers*, edited by Philip Schaff: *A Select Library of Nicene and Post-Nicene Fathers of the Christian Church, Second Series*, Volume X: *Ambrose: Select Works and Letters*, translated by H. de Romestin (Christian Literature Publishing Co., Buffalo, New York, 1887).

Although Symmachus, a Pagan, disagreed with Christians on this matter, he remained friends with Christian leaders, including Ambrose.

> handywork all things are, cannot be compared with the lesser intelligence and senses which are our own. For God and man should be very near neighbors, if man's cogitations were able to take a survey of the counsels and appointments of that everlasting Majesty. It being utterly impossible that the eye of man, by itself, could look into the bosom of Divine Reason, God did not tolerate man, who is desirous of the light of wisdom, to stray up and down any longer, and to wander in darkness with a useless expenditure of travel, with no passage by which to get out. At length, God opened man's eyes, and bestowed upon him the knowledge of the truth by way of a gift, so that man might both be clearly convinced of his folly and have plainly laid before him the path which leads to immortality, having mistakenly strayed out of the way.
>
> —LUCIUS CÆCILIUS FIRMIANUS LACTANTIUS, *The Divine Institutes*, Book I, Chapter 1.[254]

At first the natural path of everlasting life begins with that ability of doing good with which God imbued man in the day of man's Creation—absolute righteousness and integrity in all man's actions come from this obedience to the will of his Creator—and ends with the justice of God rewarding the worthiness of man's merits with the crown of eternal glory. Had Adam continued in his first estate, this would have been the way of life for him and all of his posterity. In which, I confess, notwithstanding the most intelligent of the school divines,[255] that if we speak of strict justice, God could in no way have

---

254 Lactantius, a Berber or Punic North African who was called the Christian Cicero by Renaissance scholars, was an ancient Christian apologist and advisor to Emperor Constantine I (Constantine the Great).

255 The "school divines", also called, "schoolmen" or "scholastics", were Christian priests and monks who were philosopher-theologians engaged in dialectical reasoning, influenced by Plato and Aristotle through exposure to mediæval Jewish and Muslim writers, and attempting to reconcile Christian theology with classical and ancient philosophy. By "most intelligent" (Hooker's term is "wittiest"), Hooker is referring to John Duns Scotus (or simply, Duns Scotus, meaning, "Duns the Scot"), one of the important scholastics of the Late Mediæval Era, along with Thomas Aquinas, Bonaventura da Bagnoregio, Alexander Hales, Albertus Magnus, and William of Ockham (Occam). In a note Hooker cites and quotes Duns Scotus:

> Speaking of strict justice, God is indebted to none of us for any reward, whatsoever, for returning a perfection [i.e., betterment] so intense, for the immoderate excess of that perfection [betterment] above those rewards. But let it be that, out

been bound to reward man's labors in so large and ample a measure as human happiness warrants, in as much as the dignity of human happiness so far exceeds the value of man's labors. But if it be that God, in His great generosity, had determined in lieu of man's labors to grant the same large and ample reward by the rule of whatever justice best suits Him—namely, the justice of One Who requires nothing sparingly, but all with pressed and heaped and even over-generous measure.[256] Yet even on this basis it could never necessarily follow that such justice should add to the attributes of that reward the property of eternally continuing, since possession of bliss, though for only a moment, would be an abundant reward. But, we do not now need to enter into a consideration of how gracious and bountiful our good God might still appear in so rewarding the sons of men, although they should exactly perform whatever duty to which their nature binds. In whatever way God proposed this reward, we that were to be rewarded must have done that which is required at our hands. We failing in the duty, it is naturally impossible that the reward should be sought. The light of nature is never able to find any way of obtaining the reward of bliss except by exactly performing the duties and works of righteousness.

Therefore, all flesh being excluded in this way from salvation and from life, behold how the wisdom of God has revealed a mystical and supernatural way, a way directing to the same end of life by a course

---

of His generosity, He has determined to confer a so much better deed as a reward, indeed with such justice as is proper for Him—namely, one who gives beyond what is owed in rewards. Nevertheless, it does not necessarily sequence [i.e., follow] from this that, per that justice, a perennial [i.e., eternal] perfection [betterment] is to be rendered as a reward; instead, an abundant [i.e., sufficient] recompense would occur in the blessedness [i.e., happiness] of a single moment.

—JOHN DUNS SCOTUS, *Commentary on the Sentences of Peter Lombard*, Book IV, Distinction 49, Question Six, I.2.c.α.390, p.212, translated by Ret Miles from Richard Hooker's quote. See, also, *Translation of the Ordinatio (aka the Oxford Work) of Blessed John Duns Scotus, using the Vatican Critical Edition of the text*, Book IV, by Peter L. P. Simpson (self-published, 2025): http://www.logicmuseum.com/wiki/Authors/Duns_Scotus/Ordinatio.

[256] Give, and it shall be given unto you: good measure, pressed down, and shaken together, and running over, shall men give into your bosoms. For with the same measure that ye mete withal, shall other men mete to you again.

—*Luke* 6:36, Bishops' Bible, spelling updated

which grounds itself upon the guiltiness of sin, and through sin the deserved consequence of condemnation and death. For in this way the first step is the tender compassion of God towards us who are drowned and swallowed up in misery. The next step is redemption from God by the precious death and merit of a mighty Savior, which has given witness of Himself, saying, "I am the Way",[257] the Way which leads us from misery to bliss. In Himself God had prepared this supernatural Way before all worlds. The Way of supernatural duty, which to us He has prescribed, our Savior in the *Gospel of Saint John* notes, calling it by an excellence, "The Work of God":

> This is the Work of God, that ye believe in him whom he has sent.[258]

Not that God requires nothing for happiness at the hands of men except only a naked belief—for hope and charity we may not exclude—that, without belief, all other things are as nothing, and that belief is the ground of those other divine virtues:

> *Faith.* The principal objective of faith is that eternal verity[259] which has discovered the treasures of hidden wisdom in Christ. Faith begins with a weak comprehension of things not seen, and ends with the intuitive vision of God in the world to come.
>
> *Hope.* The highest objective of hope is that everlasting goodness which in Christ quickens the dead.[260] Hope begins with

---

[257] *John* 14:6.

[258] *John* 6:29.

[259] i.e., truth.

[260] i.e., conquers death by resurrecting those who are dead into life.

> ...even he that raised up Christ from the dead, shall also quicken your mortal bodies, because that his spirit dwells in you.
>
> —*Romans* 8:11, Bishops' Bible, spelling updated
>
> For as the Father raiseth up the dead, and quickeneth them; even so the Son quickeneth whom he will.
>
> —*John* 5:21, Bishops' Bible, spelling updated
>
> And he commanded us to preach unto the people, and to testify that it is he which was ordained of God to be the Judge of quick and dead.
>
> —*Acts* 10:42, Bishops' Bible, spelling updated

> a trembling expectation of things far removed and as yet but only heard of, and ends with real and actual attainment of that which no tongue can express.
>
> *Charity*. The ultimate objective of charity is that incomprehensible beauty which shines in the countenance of Christ the Son of the living God. Charity begins with a weak inclination of heart towards Him unto Whom we are not able to approach, and ends with endless union, the mystery of which is higher than the reach of the thoughts of men.

Without faith, hope, and charity, there can be no salvation. Was there ever any mention made of these virtues other than only in that law which God, Himself, has revealed from Heaven? There is not in the Word a syllable muttered about these three with more certain truth than has been supernaturally received from the mouth of the eternal God.

Therefore, laws concerning these things are supernatural, both in the manner of delivering them, which is divine, and also in the things delivered, themselves, which are such as have not in nature any cause from

---

> I charge thee therefore before God, and the Lord Jesus Christ, who shall judge the quick and the dead at his appearing and his kingdom...
>
> —*II Timothy* 4:1, Bishops' Bible, spelling updated

The phrase, "the quick and the dead", meaning, "the living and the dead", is also used in some English-language translations of the *Apostles' Creed* and *Nicene Creed.*

Note that, in Hooker's time, the first heartbeat or other movement of a child felt in the womb by a pregnant mother was referred to as, the "quickening". According to English Common Law followed in England and other English-speaking countries and states who follow English Common Law, including all U.S. states and incorporated territories, except Louisiana (which follows the Civil Law system rooted in Spanish and French laws, including the Napoleonic Code), the quickening was the first point at which abortion laws were enforceable, and the Spanish and French laws in Louisiana and Canada (and the Spanish laws in Mexico, as well) also recognized the quickening standard.

With the advent of more modern diagnostic techniques and tools, the quickening was abandoned as the legal standard for the beginning of the enforceability of abortion laws. Examples:

An 1803 English statue abolished the quickening standard.

The Dominion of Canada outlawed abortion during all stages of gestation in 1869.

By 1910, all U.S. states (including Louisiana), territories, and protectorates had outlawed abortion throughout gestation, effectively abandoning the quickening as the standard.

Abortion at all stages of gestation was also already illegal in the U.S. Virgin Islands, purchased from Denmark in 1917.

which they flow, but were, by the voluntary appointment of God, ordained besides the course of nature, to rectify nature's vagueness as well.

CHAPTER TWELVE

Why So Many Natural Laws Are Set Down in Scripture

WHEN SUPERNATURAL DUTIES are necessarily required, natural duties are not rejected as needless. Therefore, the law of God is, although principally delivered for instruction in the one, yet also full with precepts of the other. The Scripture is even full with laws of nature. In so much that Gratian, in defining, *natural right*—by which is meant the right which exacts those general duties which concern men naturally even as they are men—he calls "natural right that which the books of the Law and the Gospel contain."[261] Neither is it in vain that the Scripture abounds with

---

261 The *Decretum* of GRATIAN, Part 1, Distinction 1, in *Corpus of Canon Law*, Part 2. (Lyon, 1584).

In the context of Gratian's original definition in Mediæval Latin, "jus" can refer to "law", "right", "justice". Gratian's "Jus Naturale" means, "Natural Law". While Hooker translates Gratian's "Jus Naturale" as, "Natural Right", he is intending a literal translation of, "jus", which is often translated as, "right", as in, "It is right for a man to do such and such", not in the sense of, "A man has a right to do or possess such and such."

So Hooker means "Natural Right" in the same sense as "Natural Law", the same sense in which Gratian meant it, and not in our more modern sense of "Natural Rights", a sense which largely began with *Mare Liberum* ("*The Free Sea*" or "*The Freedom of the Sea*", 1609) and *De Jure Belli ac Pacis* ("*On the Law* [or *Rights*] *of War and Peace*", 1625), both written by the Dutch lawyer, Hugo Grotius, after Hooker's death. These two works were taken from Grotius' larger work, *De Jure Prædæ* ("*On the Law of Prize*" or "*Of the Law of Plunder*"—or "Prey", "Predation", "Predatory Taking", or "Booty"), which, though not formally published until 1868, had been long-circulated among influential men, beginning after he wrote it in 1605–1606, and helped change the focus of political theorists and economists from natural law to natural rights.

A focus on natural rights can be increasingly seen in the writings of some key thought leaders over the next 250 years:

THOMAS HOBBES, *Leviathan* (1651).

RICHARD CUMBERLAND, *De Legibus Naturæ Disquisitio Philosophica*, "*A Philosophical Enquiry into the Laws of Nature*" (1672).

SAMUEL VON PUFENDORF, *De iure naturæ et gentium*, "*On the Law of Nature and of Nations*" (1672).

JOHN LOCKE, *Two Treatises on Government* (1689).

ALGERNON SIDNEY, *Discourses Concerning Government* (1660–1698).

JEAN-JACQUES BURLAMAQUI, *Principia Juris Naturalis et Publici*, "*The Principles of Natural and Politic Law*" or "*The Principles of Natural and Public Law*" (1747–1751).

CHARLES-LOUIS DE SECONDAT, BARON DE MONTESQUIEU, *De l'esprit des loix* or *De l'esprit des lois*, "*The Spirit of the Laws*" or "*The Spirit of Law*" (1748).

EMER DE VATTEL, *Le Droit des Gens; ou, Principes de la Loi Naturelle appliqués à la conduite et aux affaires des Nations et des Souverains*, "*The Law of Nations; or, Principles of the Law of Nature Applied to the Conduct and Affairs of Nations and Sovereigns*" (1758).

JEAN-JACQUES ROUSSEAU, *Du contrat social; ou, Principes du droit politique*, "*The Social Contract; or, Principles of Political Right*" (1762).

WILLIAM BLACKSTONE, *Commentaries on the Laws of England* (1765–1769).

The United States of America founding generation:

BENJAMIN FRANKLIN, *Plain Truth* (1747).

JOHN ADAMS, *A Dissertation on the Canon and Feudal Law* (1765).

SAM ADAMS, *Massachusetts Circular Letter* (1768).

JOSEPH WARREN, *Suffolk Resolves* (1774) and *Boston Massacre Oration* (1775).

1780 MASSACHUSETTS CONSTITUTIONAL CONVENTION, *Massachusetts Constitution of 1780*.

The Taunton Flag and the version of the Gadsen Flag on the Continental Navy ship, *Alfred*, both quoting Locke ("Life, Liberty, Property").

GEORGE MASON, *The Virginia Declaration of Rights* (1776).

SECOND CONTINENTAL CONGRESS, *Declaration of Independence* (1776), which quotes Burlamaqui and Locke.

THOMAS JEFFERSON, *Virginia Statute for Religious Freedom* (1777–1786).

1787 U.S. CONSTITUTIONAL CONVENTION, *U.S. Constitution* (1787) and its later Amendments, which quote Locke.

ALEXANDER HAMILTON, JOHN JAY, and JAMES MADISON, *The Federalist*, Nos. 2, 10, and 28 (1787–1788).

NOAH WEBSTER, *An Examination into the Leading Principles of the Federal Constitution* (1787).

JAMES WILSON, *Of the Natural Rights of Individuals* (1790–1792).

so great a store of laws in this kind. For they are either such as we of ourselves could not easily have found out, and then the benefit is not small to have them readily set down to our hands; or if they be so clear and manifest that no man imbued with reason can lightly be ignorant of them, yet the Spirit, as it were, borrowing them from the school of nature as serving to prove things less manifest, and to induce a persuasion of a truth which was, in itself, harder and darker, unless it should in such sort be cleared, the very applying of them unto particular cases is not without a most singular use and profit in many ways for men's instruction. Besides, be they plain of themselves or obscure, the evidence of God's own testimony added unto the natural assent of reason concerning the certainty of them does not a little comfort and confirm the same.

For in as much as our actions are conversant about things beset with many circumstances—which cause men of sundry wits to be also of sundry judgements concerning that which ought to be done—it cannot but seem requisite that the rule of divine law should help our imbecility in this, that

---

IMMANUEL KANT, *Grundlegung zur Metaphysik der Sitten*, "*Groundwork of the Metaphysics of Morals*" (1785).

ASSEMBLÉE NATIONALE CONSTITUANTE, "NATIONAL CONSTITUENT ASSEMBLY", *Déclaration des droits de l'Homme et du citoyen de 1789*, "*Declaration of the Rights of Man and of the Citizen of 1789*").

MARIE JEAN ANTOINE NICOLAS DE CARITAT, MARQUIS DE CONDORCET, or NICOLAS DE CONDORCET, *Sur l'admission des femmes au droit de cite*, "*On the Admission of Women to the Rights of Citizenship*" (1790).

MARY WOLLSTONECRAFT, *A Vindication of the Rights of Men, in a Letter to the Right Honourable Edmund Burke; Occasioned by His Reflections on the Revolution in France* (1790), and *A Vindication of the Rights of Woman: with Strictures on Political and Moral Subjects* (1792).

THOMAS PAINE, *Rights of Man* (1791).

MARY SHELLEY, *Frankenstein; or, The Modern Prometheus* (1818 and 1831).

FRÉDÉRIC BASTIAT, *La Loi*, "*The Law*" (1850), and *Harmonies Économiques*, "*Economic Harmonies*" or "*Harmonies of Political Economy*" (1850).

JOHN STUART MILL, *On Liberty* (1859).

The phrase, "books of the Law", in the context of Gratian's famous definition of "natural right", refers to the Christian Old Testament of the Bible (which is a different arrangement of the books of the Tanakh—i.e., the Hebrew Scriptures), and the phrase, "(books of) the Gospel", in that same definition, refers to the Christian New Testament of the Bible.

we might the more infallibly understand what is good and what is evil. The first principles of the law of nature are easy—it is hard to find men ignorant of them—but concerning the duty which nature's law requires at the hands of men in a number of particular things, the natural understanding, even of various whole nations, has been darkened so much that they have not discerned even gross iniquity to be sin.[262] Again, being so prone as we are to fawn over ourselves and to be, as much as possible, ignorant of our own deformities, without the painful awareness of which we are most wretched, we are all the more ignorant because not knowing our deformities we

---

262 In what manner are the Lacedæmonians not to be reprehended for their inhospitality and vile neglect of marriage? And the Eleans and Thebans, for their coitus with males, plainly impudent and against nature, which they reckoned to exercise usefully and purely? And when they had perpetrated these in all ways, they also mixed them with their own laws.

—FLAVIUS JOSEPHUS, *Against Apion*, Book II, Section 37, in *The Genuine Works of Flavius Josephus, the Jewish Historian. Translated from the Original Greek, according to Havercamp's accurate Edition. Containing Twenty Books of the Jewish Antiquities, with the Appendix or Life of Josephus, written by himself: Seven Books of the Jewish War: and Two Books against Apion. Illustrated with new Plans and Descriptions of the Tabernacle of Moses; and of the Temples of Solomon, Zorobabel, Herod, and Ezekiel; and with correct Maps of Judea and Jerusalem. Together with Proper Notes, Observations, Contents, Parallel Texts of Scripture, five compleat Indexes, and the true Chronology of the several Histories adjusted in the Margin. By William Whiston, M.A. Some time Professor of the Mathematicks in the University of Cambridge* (Cambridge University Press, London, 1737)

The [understanding of the] law of nature was so corrupted among the Germans that they did not repute "soldier's pay" [i.e., brigandage and rape] a sin.

—THOMAS AQUINAS, *Summa Theologiæ*, First Part of the Second Part, Question 94, Articles 4, 5, and 6. See *The Summa Theologiæ of St. Thomas Aquinas, Part I–II* (Questions 71–114), Literally translated by Fathers of the English Dominican Province, Second and Revised Edition, Volume VIII (Burns Oates & Washbourne Ltd, London, 1927).

Who does not know what is meet for the good of life, or ignores that which he otherwise does not in the least wish done to himself, he should not do to others? But truly where the natural law vanished, oppressed by the custom of delinquency, then it was required to be manifest in writing, where all will have heard the judgment of God (the law was manifested, so that by the Jews all men will have heard)—not that it has been inwardly obliterated [i.e., deeply forgotten], but because they lacked its maximum authority, they studied idolatry, the fear of God was not in the lands, fornication was at work, and there was avid lust for the property around a neighbor. Therefore, the law was given (donated) so that both what was known had authority, and what had begun as latent would be manifested.

—AUGUSTINE OF HIPPO (or PSEUDO-AUGUSTINE) *Book of Questions on the New and Old Testaments*, Question 4, quote translated by Ret Miles from Hooker's annotated quote in Latin

cannot desire as much as to have them taken away. How should our festered sores be cured, except that God has delivered a law as sharp as the two-edged sword, piercing the very closest and most unsearchable corners of the heart[263] which the law of nature can hardly—and human laws by no means—possibly reach into? By this we know that even secret lust is sin, and we are made afraid to offend, though it is but in a wandering cogitation.[264] Finally, of those things which are for direction of all of the necessary parts of our life, and not impossible to be discerned by the light of nature, itself, are there not many which few men's natural capacity, and some which no man's capacity, has been able to find out? They are, says Saint Augustine, but a few, and they, induced with great ripeness of wit and judgement, free from all such affairs as might trouble their meditations, instructed in the sharpest and the subtlest points of learning, who have been able—and that just barely—to find out but only the immortality of the soul.[265] At any time what man ever dreamed of the resurrection of the flesh having not heard it otherwise than from the school of nature? By which it appears how much we are bound to yield eternal thanks to our Creator, the Father of all mercy, for that He has delivered his law unto the world—a law in which so many things are laid open, clear and manifest—as a light which otherwise would have been buried in darkness, not without the risk of loss, or rather not just with the risk of loss, but with the *certain* loss of infinite thousands of souls most undoubtedly now saved.

Therefore, we see that:

> Our sovereign good is naturally desired.
>
> God, the Author of that natural desire, has appointed natural means by which to fulfill it.

---

263 For the word of God is quick, and mighty in operation, and sharper than any two-edged sword, and enters through, even unto the dividing asunder of the soul and the spirit, and of the joints and the marrow, and is a discerner of the thoughts and of the intents of the heart:
—*Hebrews* 4:12, Bishops' Bible, spelling updated

264 i.e., a stray thought.

265 In trying to find these by human argumentations, hardly a few, provided with great talent, abundant free time, and educated in the most subtle doctrines, have been able to succeed in an investigation of the immortality of the soul alone.
—AUGUSTINE OF HIPPO, *On the Trinity*, Book XIII, Chapter IX, Paragraph 12, quote translated and annotated by Ret Miles

Man, having utterly disabled his nature to those means, has had other means revealed from God, and has received from Heaven a law to teach him how that which is naturally desired must now be supernaturally attained.

Finally, because those later means do not entirely exclude the former means as unnecessary, therefore—together with such supernatural duties as could not possibly have otherwise been known to the world—the same law which teaches them also teaches them such natural duties as could not easily have been known by light of nature.

Chapter Thirteen

The Benefit of Written, Divine Laws

IN THE FIRST age of the world God gave laws to our fathers, and because of the number of their days their memories served instead of books. The many imperfections and defects of their memories being known to God, He often mercifully relieved these by reminding them of that which they should especially heed. In this respect we see how many times one thing has been reiterated to many of even the best and wisest among them. When, afterwards, the lives of men were shortened, the use of more durable means to preserve the laws of God from oblivion and corruption increased, not without a direction from God, Himself.

First, therefore, of Moses it is said that he "wrote all of the words of God",[266] not by his own private motion and device. For God takes this act to Himself: "I have written..."[267]

Furthermore, were not the prophets after Moses also commanded to do the same? How often is the express charge, "Scribe, write these things", given to the holy evangelist, Saint John?[268] Concerning the

---

[266] *Exodus* 24:4.

[267] And the Lord said unto Moses: Come up to me into the hill, and be there, and I will give thee tables of stone, and a law and commandments which I have written...

—*Exodus* 24:12, Bishops' Bible, spelling updated

I have written to them the great things of my law...

—*Hosea* 8:12, Bishops' Bible, spelling updated

[268] *Apocalypse* [*Revelation*] 1:11 and 14:13.

rest of our Lord's disciples, the words of Saint Augustine are, "Whatever He wanted us to read by these deeds and words, He commanded that these be written for them as if by His own hands."[269]

Finally, God's laws require obedience at our hands, regardless of how they are delivered. Even so, we do not deny that writing is merely the incidental delivery method of God's law, not the source of its authority or strength. Nevertheless, who does not see that we have cause to admire and magnify that it is His providence which has chosen writing as the principal way to deliver His laws?

We are not able to appreciate the value of the singular benefit which the world gains by receiving the laws of God committed to writing expressly by His own appointment. Therefore, when the question is whether we are to seek for any revealed law of God somewhere other than in the sacred Scripture, whether we now stand bound in the sight of God to yield the same obedience and reverence to the traditions urged by the Church of Rome which we yield to His written law—honoring and adoring both equally as divine—our answer is, "No." They who so earnestly plead for the authority of tradition—which is only by unwritten transmission,[270] and descends by way of former generations successively relating the tradition to the ages which follow—are not all so simple (and it would surely be a miracle if they were), and cannot be so ignorant, as to not know how maimed and deformed the authority of tradition becomes in the hands of unwritten transmission. Let them who are, indeed, of this mind consider just a little of the divine things which the Heathen have received by unwritten tradition. How miserable would the situation of the Church of God have been long before this, if she had received divine things by unwritten and oral tradition from her predecessors as had the Heathen from his predecessors?

---

[269] AURELIUS AUGUSTINUS (AUGUSTINE OF HIPPO), *On the Harmony of the Evangelists* (Latin: *De Consensu Evangelistarum*), Book I, Final Chapter, translated from Hooker's Latin quote by Ret Miles.

[270] i.e., orally.

By Scripture it has seemed meet, in the wisdom of God, to deliver to the world not only that which is personally expedient to be practiced by certain men, but also many of the

> deep and profound points of *doctrine*,[271] as being the main original upon which the precepts of duty depend;
>
> *prophesies*,[272] the clear performance of which might confirm the world in belief of things unseen;
>
> *histories*,[273] to serve as looking glasses[274] to behold the mercy, the truth, the righteousness of God towards all who faithfully serve, obey, and honor Him;
>
> indeed, entire *meditations of pieties*,[275] to serve as patterns and precedents in cases of similar nature;
>
> *things necessary for explanation, for application to particular occasions*,[276] which, from time to time, the providence of God has chosen to have the several books of his holy Ordinance written.

Even if it is true that, together with the necessary, principal laws of God, there are various other things written, of which we might happen to be ignorant and yet be saved—what, because of this shall we think them unnecessary? Shall we think of them much as riotous branches which we sometimes behold overgrowing the pleasantest vines? Surely no more than

---

[271] *doctrines*: such as laws, duties, articles of faith, the Beatitudes, and theological teachings (*foundational precepts*).

[272] *prophecies*: such as early prophecies in *Genesis*, and prophecies of Moses and other personages in the Old Testament, Major Prophets, Minor Prophets, Christ's prophecies, apostolic prophecies, and *Revelation* (*validation of God, His power, His Word, and His plan*).

[273] *histories*: such as the narrative and biographical accounts across all books of the Bible (*reflections of God's nature*).

[274] i.e., mirrors.

[275] *meditations of pieties*: such as *Psalms*, *Proverbs*, *Ecclesiastes*, the Lord's Prayer (which is also a doctrinal teaching), etc. (*patterns for devotions, prayers, and praise*).

[276] *things necessary for explanation, for application to particular occasions*: such as examples of sin or righteousness, directions for building the tabernacle and temple and other structures, advice given to individual church communities, warnings, temporary commands, etc. (*circumstantial guidance*).

we judge as superfluous our hands, our eyes, or any part whatever, which if our bodies did lack, we might still truly be a human being, regardless of any such defect. Therefore, as a complete man is neither destitute of any necessary part, and has some parts, the lack of which could not deprive him of his humanity—yet to have them provides unique benefits regarding the special uses for which they serve—likewise, all of those writings which include the law of God, all of those venerable books of Scripture, all of those sacred tomes and volumes of Holy Writ, they are with such absolute perfection written so that in them there neither lacks anything, the lack of which might deprive us of life, nor anything which abounds to the extent that it is superfluous, unfruitful, and altogether unnecessary that we would think it no loss or danger at all if we lacked it.

Chapter Fourteen

The Sufficiency of Scripture for Its Principal Intent

THEREFORE, ALTHOUGH THE Scripture of God is stored with an infinite variety of all kinds of topics, and although it abounds with all sorts of laws, yet the principal intent of Scripture is to deliver the laws of supernatural duties. In a very solemn manner it has often been disputed whether or not all things necessary to salvation are necessarily set down in the holy Scriptures.[277] If we define what is necessary to salvation as that by which the Way to salvation is made more plain, apparent, and easy to be known in any way, then there is no part of true philosophy, no art of arithmetic, no kind of science (rightly so called) but that the Scripture must contain it. If only those things are necessary, as surely as none else are, without the knowledge and practice of which it is not the will and pleasure of God to make any ordinary grant of salvation, it nevertheless may be, and often has been asked, how the books of holy Scripture contain all necessary things within them since the most important of necessary things is to know which books are those we are bound to think of as holy—a point confessedly impossible for the Scripture, itself, to teach. To which we may truthfully answer that there is not in the world any art or science which has, therefore, proposing to itself an end (as everyone does some end or the other), been thought defective if it has not simply

[277] JOHN DUNS SCOTUS, in *Ordinatio*, Book I, Prologue, Part 2, Question 1 (or Question 2, in some editions), affirms that "the supernatural knowledge necessary for a viator [a pilgrim on the way to Heaven] is sufficiently transmitted in Sacred Scripture".

delivered whatever is necessary to that end. But all kinds of knowledge have their specific bounds and limits. Each kind of knowledge also requires a knowledge of many necessary things learned in other sciences, and known beforehand. He that should take upon himself to teach men how to be eloquent in pleading causes must necessarily deliver to them whatever precepts are necessary to that end; otherwise, he does not do that task which he takes on. Seeing, then, that no man can eloquently plead unless he is first able to speak, it follows that the ability of speech is, in this case, a most necessary thing. Nevertheless, every man would think it ridiculous that he who undertakes to instruct an orator by writing should, therefore, be required to deliver *all* the precepts of grammar, because his profession is to deliver rules necessary to *eloquent* speech. Therefore, if the students who want to learn the rules of eloquence have already been taught the necessary foundation which comprises the basic skill of speaking, the teacher is then only required to provide precepts of eloquence. Similarly, although Scripture professes to contain in it all things which are necessary to salvation, that cannot simply mean *all* things which are necessary, but all things which are necessary *in some certain kind or form.* As all things which are necessary so that we may be saved, and either could not be known by the light of natural discourse or at least could not easily be known by that light but are known with a prior knowledge concerning certain principles which Scripture accepts as already believed by us, Scripture, therefore, instructs us in all the remaining necessary doctrines. One among these principles is the sacred authority of Scripture. Therefore, being persuaded by other means that these Scriptures are the Oracles of God, the Scriptures then teach us the rest and lay before us all of the duties which God requires at our hands as necessary to salvation.

Further, there have been similar doubts as to whether "containing in Scripture" means an express setting down in plain terms, or else *comprehending* in such a way that we may reasonably reach the necessary conclusions. Against the former of these two constructions various examples may be given. For our belief in the Trinity, the Co-eternity of the Son of God with his Father, the proceeding of the Spirit from the Father and the

Son, the duty of baptizing infants—these, with such other principal points, the necessity of which none denies, are nevertheless nowhere to be found in Scripture by express, literal mention. They are only deduced from Scripture by inference. Therefore, this kind of comprehension in Scripture being received, there is still no doubt as to how far we are to proceed by inference before the full and complete measure of necessary things are determined. For let us not think that, as long as the world endures, the wit of man shall be able to find the bottom of that which may be deduced from the Scripture—especially if "things contained by inference" do so far extend as to draw in whatever at any time may be from Scripture but probably and conjecturally surmised. But let *necessary* inference be made the standard so that we may boldly deny that their books have definitely demonstrated that Scripture contains all of those things which at this day are with so great necessity urged upon this Church under the name of reformed Church discipline. Let them, if they can, allege but one principal, theological point properly belonging to their cause and not common to them and us, and show the deduction of it from Scripture to be necessary.

It has been already shown how all things which are necessary to salvation in such a way as we have earlier maintained must necessarily be possible for men to know, and that many things are in this way necessary, the knowledge of which is impossible to attain by only the light of nature. Upon which it follows that either all flesh is excluded from possibility of salvation—which to think so would be most barbarous—or else that God has by supernatural means revealed the way of life as far as that suffices. Because of this, God has in so many times and ways spoken to the sons of men. Nor has He spoken only by speech, but He has also instructed and taught His Church by writing. The cause of writing has been such that things revealed to the world by Him might have a longer continuance and a greater certainty of assurance by how much that which is recorded has in both of those respects—permanence and certainty—preeminence above that which passes from hand to hand and has no pens but the tongues, no book but the ears of men to record it. The separate books of Scripture, each having had some distinct historical occasion and specific purpose which caused them to be written, the contents of which are according to the needs of that special end to which they are intended. This is why that every book of holy Scripture draws from all kinds of truth: natural,[278] historical,[279] foreign,[280] supernatural[281]—so much as the handled matter requires.

Now, as much as it has been alleged that there are sufficient reasons to conclude that all things necessary to salvation must be made known, and, therefore, that God, Himself, has revealed His will because men could not have otherwise known so much as is necessary, His ceasing to speak to the world since the publishing of the Gospel of Jesus Christ—and the delivery of that Gospel in writing—is a clear sign to us that the Way of salvation is now sufficiently revealed, and that we need no other means for our full instruction than by that which God has already furnished us.

The main drift of the whole New Testament is that which Saint John set down as the purpose of his own history:

> These things are written that ye might believe that Jesus is Christ, the Son of God, and that in believing ye might have life through his name.
> –*John* 20:31, updated spelling of Hooker's loose quoting

The drift of the Old Testament which the apostle mentions to Timothy:

> The holy Scriptures are able to make thee wise unto salvation.
> —*II Timothy* 3:15, updated spelling of Hooker's loose quoting

---

278 e.g.: For no man ever yet hated his own flesh: but nourishes and cherishes it, even as the Lord the Church.
—*Ephesians* 5:29, Bishops' Bible, spelling updated

279 e.g.: For as Jannes and Jambres withstood Moses, so do these also resist the truth: Men of corrupt minds, reprobate concerning the faith:
—*II Timothy* 3:8, Bishops' Bible, spelling updated

280 e.g.: One of themselves a prophet of their own, said: The Cretans always liars, evil beasts, slow bellies.
—*Titus* 1:12, Bishops' Bible, spelling updated

281 e.g.: For if God spared not the angels that sinned, but cast them down into hell, and delivered them into chains of darkness, to be kept unto judgement:
—*II Peter* 2:4, Bishops' Bible, spelling updated

So that the general end both of the Old and New Testaments is one. The difference between them consisting in this:

> the Old Testament makes wise by teaching salvation through Christ that should come;
>
> the New Testament makes wise by teaching that Christ, the Savior, is come, and that Jesus whom the Jews crucified, and whom God did raise again from the dead, is He.

Therefore, when the apostle affirms to *Timothy* that the Old Testament was able to make him wise to salvation, it was not his meaning that the Old Testament, alone, can do this to us which live since the publication of the New Testament. For he speaks with the prior knowledge that the doctrine of Christ is also known to Timothy. And, therefore, first it is said…

> Continue thou in those things which thou hast learned and are persuaded, knowing of whom thou hast been taught them.
>
> —*II Timothy* 3:14, updated spelling of Hooker's loose quoting

Again, he grants that those Scriptures were able to make him wise to salvation; but, he adds, "through the faith which is in Christ."[282] Therefore, without the doctrine of the New Testament teaching that Christ has wrought the redemption of the world—a redemption which the Old Testament foretold He should work—it is not the former alone which on our behalf can perform so much as the apostle avows, who assumes this knowledge when he magnifies that so highly. And as his words concerning the books of ancient Scripture do not take place but with foreknowledge and acceptance of the Gospel of Christ embraced, so our own words, when we extol the complete sufficiency of the whole entire body of the Scripture, must similarly be understood with this caution: the benefit of nature's light not be thought excluded as unnecessary because the necessity of a more divine light is magnified.

---

[282] *II Timothy* 3:15, updated spelling of Hooker's loose quoting.

Therefore, there is in Scripture no defect but that any man, whatever place or calling he holds in the Church of God, may have by the light of his natural understanding so bettered that, the one being relieved by the other, there can lack no part of necessary instruction to any good work which God, Himself, requires, be it natural or supernatural, belonging simply to men as men or to men as they are united in whatever kind of society. Therefore, it suffices that nature and Scripture serve in such a way that they both jointly, and not either of them separately, are so complete that for everlasting happiness we do not need the knowledge of anything more than that with which these two may easily furnish our minds in every respect[283] and, therefore, they who add traditions as a part of necessary, supernatural truth, have not the truth, but are in error. For they only plead that, whatever God reveals as necessary for all Christian men to do or believe, the same we ought to embrace, whether we have received it by writing or otherwise—which no man denies. What they who claim so great reverence to traditions should confirm is that those same traditions must be acknowledged divine and holy. For we do not reject traditions just because they are not in the Scripture, but because they are neither in Scripture nor can they, by any other reason, be sufficiently proven to be of God. What is of God, and may be evidently proven to be so, we do not deny but that it has in His kind, although unwritten, yet the selfsame force and

---

[283] Hooker's manuscript includes a quotation from pages 7 and 8 of a "Christian Letter" (i.e., a letter from his Puritan critics, here transposed to more-current, American English spelling):

> Although you exclude traditions as a part of supernatural truth, yet you infer that the light of nature teaches some natural knowledge which is necessary to salvation. ... What scripture approves such a saying,...that cases and matters of salvation are determinable by any other law than of holy Scripture.

Hooker's manuscript note also includes a memorandum to himself (here transposed to a more modern English spelling and usage):

> Remember here to show the use of the law of nature in handling matters of religion. Are there not cases of salvation in which a man may have controversy with infidels who do not believe the Scriptures? And even with them who believe Scripture, the law of nature is nevertheless not without force, that any man to whom it is alleged can cast it off as an impertinent thing.

authority with the written laws of God. It is acknowledged by our scholars "that the apostles did in every Church institute and ordain some rites and customs serving for the seemliness of Church discipline which rites and customs they have not committed unto writing."[284] Those rites and customs which are known to be apostolic, and which have the nature of changeable things, are to be no less regarded in the Church than other things of the same degree—that is to say, similarly capable of alteration, although set down in the apostles writings. For those rites and customs which are known to be apostolic, it is not the manner of delivering them to the Church, but the Author from Whom they proceed, which gives them their force and credit.

[284] We confess that the apostles ordained some rites and customs in individual churches for the sake of order and decorum, but did not write them down: for these rites were not to be perpetual, but were free, and which could be changed for accommodation and the circumstances of the times.

—WILLIAM WHITTAKER, *Controversies against Bellarmine* [i.e., the Jesuit priest and Cardinal Robert Bellarmine, a leading Roman Catholic counter-reformer of the time], Controversy 1, Question 6, Chapter 6 (Geneva, 1610). Given the date, this is a note added after Hooker's death, and included in the 1622 publication upon which this edition is based. Translation of this quote by Ret Miles.

Chapter Fifteen

Positive Laws in the Scripture

Laws being imposed by either…

> each man upon himself,
>
> a public society upon its individuals,
>
> all the nations of men upon every separate society,
>
> or the Lord, Himself, upon any or all of these,

…among these four kinds each contains both various natural and positive laws. Those who only take such laws for positive—as if these were solely made or inherited by men—and who also hold that all positive laws, and *only* positive laws, are mutable,[285] will certainly fall into a number of gross errors.

Natural laws always bind. *Positive laws* only bind after they have been expressly and intentionally im*posed.* There are positive laws in each of the four kinds mentioned, above.

> Examples of positive laws in the first kind include the promises which we have passed to men, and the vows we have made to God, for these are laws to which we tie ourselves. Until we have so tied ourselves, these do not bind us.
>
> Examples of positive laws in the second kind include the civil constitutions specific to each separate commonwealth.

---

[285] i.e., changeable, amendable, revisable, editable.

An example of positive laws in the third kind is the law of heraldry in war.

And an example of positive laws in the fourth kind is all of the *judicials*,[286] which God gave to the people of Israel to observe.

And although only positive laws are mutable, yet not all positive laws are mutable. Positive laws are either permanent or changeable, depending on the circumstances for which the laws were first made. Whether God or man is the maker of these, positive laws may be amended as [circumstances require.

Laws concerning supernatural duties are all][287] positive,[288] and either supernaturally concern men as men, or else as parts of a supernatural Society which we call, the Church. Supernatural duties for men as men are duties which necessarily belong to all yet could not be known unless God revealed them, Himself. These duties do not depend on any natural ground from which they may be deduced. Instead, these

---

[286] The term, *judicials*, refers to divine laws which God gave to the Ancient Israelites to govern their civil and political life: their judicial system, laws related to property, punishments of crimes, and so forth. These were other than the moral law, such as the Ten Commandments, and the ceremonial laws, such as the rules for sacrifices and other rituals. Although divinely instituted, these were positive laws because God instituted them to apply to a specific time and society. Being positive laws, these were mutable laws, unlike the moral law, which is universal across the ages and cultures.

[287] This bracketed text is a paraphrase of text missing from the 1622 edition, but included in *The Works of that Learned and Judicious Divine Mr. Richard Hooker with an Account of His Life and Death by Isaac Walton*, Volume I, arranged by the Rev. John Keble M.A., 7th edition revised by the Very Reverend R. W. Church and the Rev. F. Paget (Clarendon Press, Oxford, England, 1888).

[288] To prevent any misapplication of this principle, it may be useful to compare Butler's Analogy, p. ii. c. 1. § 2; where moral precepts and duties are contrasted with positive in a manner which may at first appear inconsistent with Hooker's language. But the appearance of discrepancy will perhaps be removed, if it is considered that Hooker opposes the term Positive to Natural, in regard of our ability or inability to obtain the knowledge of a law without express revelation: Butler on the other hand opposes Positive to Moral, in regard of our ability or inability to discern the reasonableness of a law made known to us by revelation or otherwise.

—a note at this location in *The Works of that Learned and Judicious Divine Mr. Richard Hooker with an Account of His Life and Death by Isaac Walton*, Volume I, arranged by the Rev. John Keble M.A., 7th edition revised by the Very Reverend R. W. Church and the Rev. F. Paget (Clarendon Press, Oxford, England, 1888)

are appointed by God to supply the defect of those natural ways to salvation which we are not now able to attain. The Church, being a *supernatural society*, differs from *natural societies* in this: that the persons to whom we associate ourselves in natural societies are men simply considered as men, while they to whom we are joined in the supernatural society, the Church, are God, angels, and holy men. Again, the Church, being both a society and a supernatural society, has, as a society, the same original foundation as other governed societies: the natural inclination toward social life, and consent to a bond of association which appoints order. However, to the Church, as a supernatural society, that part of the bond which uniquely belongs to the Church of God must be a supernatural law which God, Himself, has revealed concerning the kind of worship which His people shall render to Him. Therefore, the substance of the service of God, as far as it has anything in it more than the law of reason teaches, may not be invented by men as it is among the Heathens,[289] but must be received from God, Himself, as it always has been in the Church, excepting only when the Church has been forgetful of her duty.

Now to end with a general rule concerning all of the laws which God has tied men to: those divine laws which, whether naturally or supernaturally, belong either to men as men, to men as they live in a governed society, or to men as they are of that governed society which is the Church, without any further respect to any such variable accident, such as the circumstances to which men, societies of men, and the Church, itself, are subject in this world—indeed, all positive laws which belong to men—belong forever to men unless God, Himself, who made them, alters them. The reason is that the underlying subject or circumstance of laws, in general, is consistent. A law is instituted for the ordering of a specific circumstance. Such a law is not changeable without cause. Nor can there be reason for change when the circumstance for which the law was first instituted, remains, itself, forever unchanged.

---

289 ...the fear which they have unto me proceedeth of a commandment that is taught of men...

—*Isaiah* 29:13, Bishops' Bible, spelling updated

On the other hand, laws were made for men, societies, or churches because their circumstances are not permanent. They may later be entirely changed, requiring different regulations than before. No man with common sense will deny that the laws of God of this nature have a different constitution than the laws for consistent circumstances, because of those circumstances' consistency, and the mutability of laws made for impermanent circumstances. And this seems to have been the very cause why Saint John so peculiarly calls the doctrine which teaches salvation by Jesus Christ, "Evangelium æternum" ("An eternal Gospel").[290] There can be no reason why the Gospel should be taken away, and another proclaimed as long as the world continues. Conversely, the whole law of rites and ceremonies, although delivered with so great solemnity, is, nevertheless, completely repealed, since it only had a temporary cause for God's ordaining of it.

We may finally conclude this first general introduction to the nature and original birth, as of all other laws, so likewise of those which the sacred Scripture contains concerning the Author of which even Infidels have confessed that He can neither err nor deceive.[291] Things which are easy and obvious to all men using common sense need no higher advice because a man whose wisdom is admired in weighty affairs would disdain to have his counsel solemnly asked about a toy. So, to search the Scripture of God for the ordering of something trivial would be to diminish the revered authority and dignity of the Scripture no less than they do by whom Scriptures are, in ordinary conversations, very idly applied to vain and childish trifles. It is better to be superstitious than profane, to take our direction from Scripture, even in all things great or small, than to wade through matters of principal

---

[290] *Apocalypse* (*Revelation*) 14:6. The original Koine Greek phrase is, *αἰώνιον εὐαγγέλιον* ("aiōnion evangelion"), meaning, "perpetual good announcement [i.e., everlasting good news]". The term, "Gospel", is derived from Old English, "gōdspell", meaning, "good message", "good spiel", or "good story [or tale or account, etc.]".

[291] Thus, God attends simply and truthfully both in word and in deed, and He neither changes nor deceives others—in neither appearance nor words, neither pronouncements nor signs of pomp, neither consciously nor unconsciously.

—PLATO, *The Republic*, Book II, at the end, translated by Ret Miles from Hooker's quote

weight and moment without ever caring what the law of God has either for or against our designs. Concerning the custom of the Pagans, this much Strabo witnesses:

> Men who are civil lead their lives after one common law directing them what to do. For that otherwise a multitude should without harmony among themselves concur in the doing of one thing (for this is civilly to live), or that they should, in any way, manage community of life, it is not possible. Now Laws or Statutes are of two sorts. For they are either received from gods, or else from men. And our ancient Predecessors did Surely most honor and reverence that which was from the gods; for which cause consultation with oracles was a thing very usual and frequent in their times.[292]

Although Pagans believed so much in the voice of their gods, which in truth were not gods, shall we neglect the precious benefit of consulting those Oracles of the true and living God, of which so great a store is left to the Church, and to which there is so free, so plain, and so easy an access for all men?

"By Thy commandments," David confessed to God, "Thou has made me wiser than my enemies."[293]

Again, "I have had more understanding than all my teachers, because Thy testimonies are my meditations."[294]

What pains bestowed in the study of these books would men not have who travelled land and sea to gain the treasure of a few days' talk with men whose wisdom the world valued? What little some Heathens chanced to hear about such things as the sacred Scripture

---

[292] ...for, being members of states, they live under common mandates; for otherwise it would be impossible for the mass of people in any country to do one and the same thing in harmony with one another, which is precisely what life in a free state means, or in any other way to live a common life. And the mandates are twofold; for they come either from gods or from men; and the ancients, at least, held those from the gods in greater honour and veneration; and on this account men who consulted oracles were much in evidence at that time...

—*The Geography of Strabo*, Book XVI, Chapter 38, translated by H. L. Jones (Horace Leonard Jones) (Harvard University Press, Cambridge, Massachusetts, 1917)

[293] *Psalm* 119:98.

[294] *Psalm* 119:99.

plentifully contains, they affected in a wonderful way. Their speeches,[295] as often as they mentioned them, are strange in a such a way that they, themselves, could not utter those speeches as they did other things, but still acknowledged that their wits, which conquered difficulties everywhere else, were here profoundly over-matched.

Which—seeing that God has endowed us with

> *sense*, so that we might perceive what this present life needs,
>
> *reason*, so that what is necessary to know both now and in the future, yet which we cannot sense, should not remain obscure,
>
> and the heavenly support of *prophetic revelation*[296] of those hidden mysteries which reason could never have been able to discover or to have known of their necessity to our eternal good,

is why we use the precious gifts of God to the glory and honor of Him Who gave us these gifts, seeking by all means to know

> what is the *will* of our God,
>
> what is *righteous* before Him,
>
> and what is *holy*, *perfect*, and *good* in His sight,

that we may truly and faithfully do His will.

---

[295] See fragments of the *Orphei Carmina* ("*Orphic Poems*") in JUSTIN MARTYR, *ad Gentes* ("*To the Gentiles*"), Chapter 15); EUSEBIUS OF CÆSAREA, *Præparatio Evangelica* ("*Preparation for the Gospel*"), Book XIII, Chapter 12); and PROCLUS LYCIUS, *in Timæum* ("*On Timæus*"). These are all included in ORPHEUS, ET AL., *Orphica, Procli, Hymni, Musaci carmen de Hero et Leandro, Callimachi hymni et epigrammata ad Optimorum librorum fidem* (Karl Tauchnitz, Leipzig, 1829).

[296] For where reason is wanting, prophecy suffices.

—PHILO OF ALEXANDRIA, *On the Life of Moses*, Book II, Introduction, quote translated by Ret Miles

Chapter Sixteen

Conclusion

So far we have endeavored to reveal, in part, the nature and force of laws according to their different kinds:

> the law which God, with Himself, has eternally set down to follow in His own works;
>
> the law which He has made for his creatures to keep;
>
> the law of natural and necessary agents;
>
> the law which angels in Heaven obey;
>
> the law to which men, as men, find themselves bound by the light of reason;
>
> the law which men compose for multitudes and geopolitical societies of men to be guided by;
>
> the law which belongs to each nation;
>
> the law which concerns the fellowship of all;
>
> and lastly, the law which God, Himself, has supernaturally revealed.

Perhaps it might have been more popular and plausible to less-learned ears if this first book had been spent in extolling the force of laws in showing the great necessity of them when they are good, and in emphasizing the gravity of the offense of those who injuriously malign public laws. But with these kinds of things that way stirs the passions of men one way or the other rather than advancing their knowledge in any way so that they can resolve their doubts by properly examining the matter. Therefore, I have turned aside from that beaten path and have chosen a less-easy but more profitable way in regard of the end which we propose. Therefore, lest any man should marvel at that toward which all these things tend, the drift and purpose of all is this: to show that a law is properly that which reason defines to be good and which must be done, and to show in what manner as every good and perfect gift, so this very gift of good and complete laws is derived from the Father of lights[297] to teach men a reason why just and reasonable laws are of so great force and use in the world and, regarding the laws for which there presently is controversy, to inform their minds of some method to reduce the laws to their first, original causes so that, by this, it may be the better discerned in every particular ordinance whether or not the laws are reasonable, just, and righteous. Is there anything which can either be thoroughly understood or soundly judged until the very first causes and principles from which it originally springs are made manifest? Then, if all parts of knowledge have been thought by wise men to be most systematically explained and studied when they are drawn to their first original,[298] and seeing that our whole question concerns the quality of ecclesiastical laws let it not seem a superfluous labor that, as an introduction, all of these different kinds of laws have been considered. They all have their forcible operations in ecclesiastical laws to the extent that they all concur as principles, although not all in the same apparent and manifest manner. By

---

[297] Every good giving, and every perfect gift is from above, and cometh down from the father of lights, with whom is no variableness, neither shadow of turning.
—*James* 1:17, Bishops' Bible, spelling updated

[298] To know and to understand happens with all methods of inquiry having either principles, causes, or elements. For only then are we persuaded that we know each, whenever we recognize these first causes, these first principles, and so on to the elements.
—ARISTOTLE, *Physics*, Book I, Chapter 1, translated by Ret Miles. See also ARISTOTLE, *Physica*, translated by R. P. Hardie (Robert Purves Hardie) and R. K. Gaye (Russell Kerr Gaye), in *The Works of Aristotle Translated into English under the Editorship of W. D. Ross* (William David Ross), Volume II (Clarendon Press, Oxford, England, 1930).

means of which it comes to pass that the force which they have is not observed of many.

It is a great deal easier for men to be taught by law what they ought to do than to be instructed as to how to judge according to the law. Acting as one ought, according to the law, is something which generally applies to all. Judging according to the law is the kind of thing which only the wiser and more judicious can do. Indeed, the wiser who are always touching upon this point are the readiest to acknowledge that to soundly judge according to a law is the weightiest thing which any man can take upon himself.[299] But if we will judge according to the laws under which we live, then, first, let that eternal law always be before our eyes as being of principal force and moment to breed in religious minds a dutiful esteem of all laws, the use and benefit of which we see—because there can be no doubt but that apparently good laws are, as it were, things copied out of the very tables of that everlasting high Law, even as the book of that Law has said concerning itself, "By me, Kings reign, and [by me] Princes decree justice."[300] Not as if men did behold that book and then accordingly make their laws, but because it works *in* them, and discovers and, as it were, reads itself to the world *by* them, the laws which they make are righteous. Furthermore, if we nevertheless do not perceive the goodness of laws made, since things in themselves may have that which perhaps we do not discern, should not this breed a fear in our hearts as to how we speak or judge the worse part of those laws, the unadvised disgrace of which may be no little dishonor to Him towards Whom we profess all submission and awe? Surely there must first be a blatant iniquity in laws if we are to justify our insolent invectives against them. When we inveigh against the laws without just cause, it

---

299 To correctly discriminate [i.e., discern, determine, or judge] is the greatest.

—ARISTOTLE, *Nicomachean Ethics*, Book X, Chapter IX, Sections 1179a–1181b, quote translated by Ret Miles

This is often stated as the maxim: "To judge correctly is the main thing" or "most important thing." Hooker also quotes a Latin commentary which can be translated as, "He discerns the judgment of the quality of the laws."

300 *Proverbs* 8:15, Geneva Bible.

is mainly due to our ignorance of how inferior laws are derived from that supreme or highest law.

Natural agents are the first which receive impression from the eternal law. The law of the operations of natural agents might perhaps be thought less applicable when the question is about laws for human actions; but, in those very actions, that which most spiritually and supernaturally concerns men—the rules and axioms of natural operations—have their force. What can be more immediate to our salvation than our persuasion concerning the law of Christ[301] towards his Church? What greater assurance of love towards his Church than the knowledge of that mystical Union by which the Church is become as near to Christ as any one part of his flesh is to the other? Because the Church is His, in a way, He necessarily must protect it. What stronger proof can there be than if a manifest law requires that He must protect the Church, which law it is not possible for Christ to violate? And what other law does the apostle for this allege except what is both common to Christ with us, and to us with other natural things? "No man hates his own flesh, but doth love and cherish it."[302] Therefore, the axioms of that law by which natural agents are guided have their use in the moral actions of men—indeed, even in their spiritual actions—and, consequently, in all laws of any kind belonging to men.

Neither are the angels themselves so far severed from us in their kind and manner of working but that, between the law of their Heavenly operations and the actions of men in this our state of mortality, such correspondence there is as makes it expedient to know in some way the law of Heavenly operations for a better direction of our own actions. Could the angels acknowledge themselves to be "fellow servants"[303] with the sons of men if it were not for the fact that, both

---

[301] The context would seem to indicate that this is a typographical error for "love of Christ". However, in Hooker's list of errata, he makes no mention of this, and the word, "law", was retained in successive editions. Christ's bond with the Church is more than the emotion of "love", it is an unbreakable principle, a "law". Therefore, Hooker likely intended the word, "law".

[302] *Ephesians* 5:29, a paraphrase by Hooker.

[303] *Apocalypse* (*Revelation*) 19:10.

having one Lord, there must be some kind of law which is common to both? Their obedience, being better, is to our weaker obedience both a pattern and a spur. Or could the apostles, speaking of that which belongs to saints, as they are linked together in the bond of spiritual society,[304] so often make mention of how angels are delighted by things publicly done by the Church if we are not somehow to respect what the angels of Heaven do? Indeed, so far has the apostle, Saint Paul, proceeded as to signify that even of the outward orders of the Church, which only serve for comeliness, some regard is to be had of angels[305] who are like us the most when we are most like them in all parts of decent demeanor. So, we cannot judge the law of angels altogether irrelevant to the affairs of the Church of God.

Our largeness of speech is how men find out what things reason necessarily binds them to observe and what it guides them to choose in things which are left as arbitrary. The care we have exercised to declare the different nature of laws which each concern all men

> from such as belong to men either civilly or spiritually associated,
>
> or such as pertain to the fellowship which nations or Christian nations have among themselves,
>
> and, in the last place, such as concerning each and every one of those which God, Himself has revealed by his holy Word,

all serve only to make manifest that, as the actions of men are of many distinct kinds, so their laws must accordingly be distinguished. In men's operations there are some natural, some rational, some supernatural, some political, and, finally, some ecclesiastical—which, if we do not measure each by its own proper law, since the things, themselves, are so different, there will be confusion in our understanding and judgement of them.

This is shown by that first error on which our opponents in this controversy have grounded themselves. For as they rightly maintain

---

304 *I Peter* 1:12; *Ephesians* 3:10; *I Timothy* 5:21.
305 *I Corinthians* 11:10.

that God must be glorified in all things, and that the actions of men cannot tend to His glory unless they are in conformance with His law, so it is their error to think that the only law which God has appointed to men to that end is the sacred Scripture. By that which we naturally work—like when we breathe, sleep, or move—we set forth the glory of God as natural agents do,[306] although we have no express purpose to make that our end nor any advised determination in so doing to follow a law. But, for the most part, we do what we do without even thinking about it. In reasonable and moral actions another law takes place—a law by the observation of which we glorify God in such a way as no creature under man is able to.[307] Because other creatures do not have judgement to examine the quality of what is done by them, in what they do they can neither accuse nor approve themselves. Men do both, as the apostle teaches. Indeed, those men who have no written law of God to show what is good or evil carry written in their hearts the universal law of mankind—the law of reason, by which they judge by a rule which God has given to men for that purpose.[308] The law of reason somehow directs men how to honor God as their Creator. But how to glorify God in such a way as is required to the end that he may be an everlasting Savior, this we are taught by divine law, which both ascertains the truth and supplies to us the lack of that other law. So that in moral actions divine law exceedingly helps the law of reason to guide man's life; but, in supernatural action, it guides alone.

As we proceed further, let us place man in some public society with others, whether civil or spiritual—and in this case there is no remedy

---

[306] Praise ye him sun and moon: praise him all ye stars that give light
Praise ye him all ye heavens: and ye waters that be above the heavens
Even they should praise the name of God: for he commanded, and they were created
He hath set them sure for ever and ever: he hath given them a law which shall not be broken
Praise ye God from the earth: ye dragons and all deeps
Fire and hail, snow and vapors: stormy wind fulfilling his word
Mountains and all hills: fruitful trees and all Cedars
Beasts and all cattle: worms and feathered fowls

—*Psalm* 148:3–10, Bishops' Bible, spelling updated

[307] *Romans* 1:20–21.

[308] *Romans* 2:15.

other than that we must add yet a further law. For although even here the laws of nature and reason are likewise of necessary use, yet necessarily over and above them is human and positive law together with that law which is of commerce between grand societies, the law of nations and of Christian nations. For which cause the law of God has likewise said, "Let every soul be subject to the higher powers."[309] The public power of all societies is above every soul contained in the same societies. And the principal use of that power is to give laws to all who are under it—which laws in such case we must obey unless there is reason shown which may necessarily show that the law of reason or of God enjoins the contrary. Because, except our own private and but probable resolutions are by the law of public determinations overruled, we take away all possibility of sociable life in the world. We cannot have a plainer example of which than ourselves. How does it come to pass that we are at this present day so torn by mutual contentions, and that the Church is so much troubled about the polity of the Church? No doubt, if men had been willing to learn how many laws their actions in this life are subject to, and what the true force of each law is, all these controversies might have died the very day they were first brought forth.

It is both commonly said, and truly, that the best men, otherwise, are not always the best in regard of society. The reason for this is that the law of men's actions is one thing if men are regarded only as men, and another thing when men are considered as parts of a political body. There are many men for whom nothing is more commendable than when they are taken singly, and yet in society with others there are none less fit to perform the duties which are looked for at their hands.[310] Indeed, I am persuaded that of them with whom we strive in this current controversy there are those whose betters among men would hardly be found if they did not live among men but in some wilderness by themselves. The cause by which their disposition is so unsuited to the societies in which they

[309] *Romans* 13:1. Hooker's quote is almost verbatim from the Geneva and Bishops' Bibles.

[310] For while there are many men who can use virtue on their household's behalf, yet in those things on behalf of others they cannot.

—ARISTOTLE, *Nicomachean Ethics*, Book V, Chapter 3, quote translated by Ret Miles

live is that they discern not aright what place and force these several kinds of laws ought to have in all of their actions. Is there a question either concerning the rule of the Church in general, or about conformity between one church and another, or of ceremonies, offices,[311] powers, jurisdiction in our own church? Of all these things they judge by that rule to which they frame themselves with some show of probability, and what in that way seems convenient. The rule they think themselves bound to practice, the same they labor mightily to uphold by all means. Whatever to the contrary a law of man has determined, they give it no weight. Thus, they breed disturbance by following the law of private reason where the law of public reason should take place.

Therefore, for the better familiarizing of men's minds with the true distinction of laws and of their separate forces, according to the different kind and quality of our actions, perhaps it shall not be amiss to show in an example how they all take place. Look no further than that which there is not anything more familiar to us: our food. What things are food and what are not we naturally judge by sense.[312] Neither do we need any other law to be our director in that behalf than the selfsame which we have in common with beasts. But when we come to consider of food as a benefit which God in his bounteous goodness has provided for all living things,[313] the law of reason here requires by our hands the duty of thankfulness towards Him by whose hands we have it. And so that our appetite in the use of food does not lead us beyond that which is suitable, we owe in this case obedience to that law of reason which teaches moderation in meats and drinks. The same things divine law teaches also, as we have largely shown it does all parts of moral duty to which we all necessarily stand bound, in regard of the life to come.[314]

---

[311] i.e., duties or obligations.

[312] *Job* 34:3.

[313] *Psalm* 145:15–16.

[314] In response to an argument in the Puritans' Christian Letter (spelling here updated)…

> If from sound and sincere virtues (as you say) full joy and felicity ariseth, and that we all of necessity stand bound unto all parts of moral duty in regard of life to come, and God requireth more at the hands of men unto happiness, then such a naked belief, as Christ calleth the work of God: alas what shall we poor sinful wretches do, etc.

...Hooker's manuscript note states...

Repent, and believe.

Again, in response to an argument in the Puritans' letter...

Tell us...whether there be not other sufficient causes to induce a Christian to godliness and honesty of life, such as is the glory of God our Father; his great mercies in Christ; his love to us; example to others, but that we must do it to merit or to make perfect that which Christ hath done for us.

... Hooker's manuscript note states...

Your godfathers and godmothers have much to answer unto God for not seeing you better catechized.

And, again, in response to an argument in the Puritans' letter...

A thing necessary as you grant that by good works we should seek God's glory, show ourselves thankful for his mercies in Christ, answer his loving kindness towards us, and give other men good example. If then these things be necessary unto eternal life, and works necessarily to be done for these ends, how should works be but necessary unto the last end, seeing the next and nearest cannot be attained without them?

... Hooker's manuscript note states...

And is there neither heaven nor hell, neither reward nor punishment hereafter, to be respected here in the leading of our lives? When the apostle doth deter from sin, are his arguments only these? only these his reasons when he stirreth unto works of righteousness? See Eusebius Emisenus where he speaketh of Dorcas [i.e., Tabitha] **her garments made for the poor** [here translated from a subsequent editor's 1622 note].

"By prayers," he says, "and by almsgivings, sins are cleansed." By each thing, therefore, but chiefly by almsgiving, God's mercy is required. Therefore, it is required that each thing consent with each. That requests, this obtains. That in a way just praying for attention, this meriting grace. That knocks at the door, this opens it. That reveals desire, this procures the effect of desire. That supplicates, but this commends the supplicant. Thus, laudable Tabitha—who, it is said, is interpreted to be, Dorcas, in the *Acts of the Apostles*—closing the day of her life in good works, relinquishing the body as her soul flew away, when she had already renounced all duties of both operation work and life, widows ran weeping, and paupers gathered the tunics and outer garments which Dorcas made for them, showing them to heaven, they convened to God: the testimonies of their merits cried out. The dead worker, the voice of good works—what she had accomplished in this lifetime follows the soul into another life. They follow and are returned, and it returns from the location of death to the promised life. Therefore, here the garments are shown to paupers, there they work; here they still provide use, there they already contribute a reward. What miraculous and precious merits of generosity! Here, they were still warming the cold shoulders of users, yet there they were cooling the soul of the generous. Therefore, dearest, our souls, liable to death, let us also raise by pious works. Without doubt they will give eternal life, and often they also restore temporal life.

—"De Initio Quadragesimæ" ("On the Beginning of Lent"), *Bibliotheca Patrum* ("*Library of Church Fathers*"), Volume DLI (Cologne, 1618)

But of certain kinds of food which the Jews at one time had, and of which we, ourselves, likewise have a mystical, religious, and supernatural use—they of their Paschal lamb and oblations,[315] we of our bread and wine in the Eucharist[316]—for which use, none but divine law could institute.

Now as we live in civil society, the state of the Commonwealth[317] in which we live both may and does require certain laws concerning

---

A note in a much-later edition states that it is uncertain who authored the sermon, "On the Beginning of Lent", and that it evidently is *not* EUSEBIUS OF EMESA. It might be SALVIAN, EUCHERIUS OF LYONS, or another Father of the Gallic Church in the Fourth or Fifth Century. See WILLIAM CAVE, *Scriptorum Ecclesiasticorum Historia Literaria* ("*A Literary History of Ecclesiastical Writers*") Volume I, page 157, and Book VI of HOOKER, *Of the Laws of Ecclesiastical Polity* (not published until 1648), available in *The Works of that Learned and Judicious Divine Mr. Richard Hooker with an Account of His Life and Death by Isaac Walton*, Volume I, edited by John Keble, Seventh Edition revised by R.W. Church (Richard William Church) and F. Paget (Francis Paget) (Clarendon Press, Oxford, England, 1888).

On this whole subject Hooker's notes say to look at SAINT AUGUSTINE, *De Fide et Operibus* ("*On Faith and Works*"), of which the following is an excerpt.

> For this is to evangelize Christ—not only to say what are to be believed about Christ, but also what are to be observed by him who approaches to the bond of the body of Christ. Truly, rather, to say all which are to be believed about Christ—not solely Whose Son He is, from where [born] according to divinity, from where begotten according to the flesh, what endured and why, what the power is of His resurrection, [and] what gift the Spirit promised and has given to the faithful, but also what kinds of members [i.e., parts or limbs of the body] for whom there is a Head [Who] seeks, institutes, chooses, liberates, and also conducts to eternal life and honor. When these things are said, sometimes more briefly and more concisely, sometimes more broadly and abundantly, Christ is evangelized. And yet, not solely that of faith, but also that which is pertinent to the mores of the faithful, is not omitted.
>
> —AUGUSTINE OF HIPPO, *De Fide et Operibus* ("*On Faith and Works*"), Volume VI, Chapter IX, page 172, Section F (The Benedictine Monks of the Congregation of Saint Maur, Paris, 1679–1700: this is also known as the Benedictine edition or the Maurist edition). See also Chapters X – XIV.

[315] i.e., the Passover meal.

[316] i.e., the Communion meal or Lord's Supper.

[317] Although capitalized, Hooker is using the term, "Commonwealth", as a generic name for a geopolitical state. Having died a generation before the creation of the English Commonwealth after the English Civil War and the execution of King Charles, Hooker could neither have known of nor have been referring to that Commonwealth.

food.[318] These are laws which we would not need to respect as rules of action if we were not members of the Commonwealth where those laws are in force. Since we are, these laws must be respected and obeyed.

Indeed, the same food is also a subject in which at times ecclesiastical laws have place; so that unless we will be authors of confusion in the Church, our private discretion, which otherwise might guide us a contrary way, must here submit itself to be that way guided which the public judgement of the Church has thought better. In which case that of Zonaras[319] concerning fasts may be remembered: "Fastings are good, but let good things be done in good and convenient manner. He that transgresseth in his fasting the orders of the holy Fathers, the positive laws of the Church of Christ, must be plainly told that good

---

[318] As examples, the 1888 Keble edition notes here the following English laws, passed during the reign of Queen Elizabeth I.

> **5 Eliz. c. 5. § 14, 15 (Maintenance of the Navy Act 1562).** To grow the English fishing fleet, sections 14 and 15 required all English subjects to eat fish and abstain from meat on Wednesdays, Fridays, and Saturdays. To make sure that no one mistook this economic protectionist law as a Roman Catholic or otherwise religious law, the law made it a crime to say that eating the fish was for "the service of God". While this seems to be an example of an unjust government interference in the economy, bear in mind that the main purpose of the mandate was to help make England more militarily secure by strengthening naval assets (and potential assets) during the threat from Spain and its armada.
>
> **27 Eliz. c. 11 (The First Continuance, 1584).** Among other provisions, this act continued the mandate to eat fish, as described, above, which would have otherwise expired.
>
> **35 Eliz. c. 7. § 22 (The Second Continuance & Amendment, 1592).** This continued the mandate to eat fish, with certain amended provisions.

To Hooker's point, these laws are examples of how government can and must make laws for the common weal (i.e., the commonwealth or common good—what the Romans called, "salus", and the Preamble to the Constitution of the United States of America calls, "the general Welfare") which are not found in revealed law (i.e., Biblical Scripture) and are not discoverable by the law of reason (i.e., logic).

[319] Joannes Zonaras was a Twelfth-Century Byzantine historian and lawyer who specialized in canon law (i.e., the laws which regulate the affairs and public interactions of the church congregations and bureaucracy with a Christian denomination).

things do lose the grace of their goodness when they are not performed in a good way."[320]

And as men's private fancies must here give place to the higher judgement of that Church which is in authority a mother over them, so the very actions of whole churches have, in regard of commerce and fellowship with other churches, been subject to laws concerning food, the contrary to which laws had been otherwise thought more convenient for them to observe—such as the order of abstinence from eating meat from animals which were strangled, and the order of abstinence from eating blood (orders grounded upon that fellowship which the churches of the gentiles had with the Jews).[321]

Thus, we see how, under various considerations, even one and the same thing is conveyed through many laws, and that to measure by any one kind of law all the actions of men would be to confound the admirable order in which God has disposed all laws—each as in nature, so in degree—distinct from each other.

So that we may briefly end here, of Law it can be no less acknowledged than that her seat is the bosom of God, her voice the harmony of the world, all things in Heaven and Earth do her homage, the very least as feeling her care, and the greatest as not exempted from her power; both[322] angels and men and creatures of whatever condition, though each in different way and manner, yet all with uniform consent, admiring her as the mother of their peace and joy.

---

[320] i.e., the good is not good when done in a bad way. Put another way, the ends do not justify the means.

Hooker's quote is of an excerpt from the commentary of JOANNES ZONARAS on the 66th Apostolic Canon. An 1888 edition of *Of the Laws of Ecclesiastical Polity* notes that the passage from Zonaras is cited in WILLIAM BEVERIDGE, *Synodicon*, Volume I, page 43. (The influential, Seventeenth-Century, Anglican bishop, William Beveridge, was a scholar of canon law. His *Synodicon* is a still-cited, massive collection of church council proceedings and canon law.)

[321] *Acts* 15:5–21 (especially verse 20).

[322] Hooker's first edition stated, "but". Beginning with the 1604 edition, this was revised to, "both".

Without order there is no living in public society, because the want thereof is the mother of confusion, whereupon division of necessity followeth, and out of division, inevitable destruction. The Apostle therefore giving instruction to public societies, requireth that all things be orderly done. Order can have no place in things, unless it be settled amongst the persons that shall by office be conversant about them. And if things or persons be ordered, this doth imply that they are distinguished by degrees. For order is a gradual disposition.

—RICHARD HOOKER, *Of the Laws of Ecclesiastical Polity*, Book VIII, in *The Works of That Learned and Judicious Divine, Mr. Richard Hooker: With An Account of His Life and Death by Isaac Walton*, in Three Volumes, Volume III, Arranged by Rev. John Keble M.A., Seventh Edition revised by the Very Reverend R. W. Church and the Reverend F. Paget (Clarendon Press, Oxford, England, 1888), Chapter 2

Appendix

The Intellectual and Moral Background: A Guide to Hooker's Influences and Sources for Concerning Laws, and Their Several Kinds in General

To counter the Puritans' argument that Scripture must determine every detail of life, Richard Hooker reached back to ideas associated with Aristotle, the early Christian "Church Fathers", and Thomas Aquinas, as well as the Bible and the Apocrypha, in his argument that God governs the world through different kinds of law, not just the Bible.

Classical Influence: The Authority of Reason, and the Contribution of Archetypes

Classically educated, Hooker drew from **Plato** the concepts of forms[323] and political societies, with society and government being natural and necessary for human perfection, not just a remedy for sin.

---

[323] To understand forms, it might be helpful to read these dialogs of Plato in this order:

Forms as ideals, standards, and values	Theory of forms	Refinement of the theory
Euthyphro	*Meno*	*Parmenides*
Apology of Socrates	*Phædo*	*Theætetus*
Crito	*Symposium*	*Sophist*
Laches	*Republic*	*Statesman*
Lysis	*Phædrus*	*Philebus*
Charmides		*Ion*
Protagoras		*Timæus*
		Critias
		Laws
		Epinomis (by Pseudo-Plato)

In relation to *Concerning Laws, and Their Several Kinds in General*, the main classical influence on Hooker, besides the **Bible** and the **Apocrypha**, was **Aristotle**. However, given Plato's foundational role in much of Western philosophy, any treatise within that tradition, apart from guidance or laws given in the Bible—is ultimately a commentary on Plato.

Aristotle's *Politics* was foundational for Hooker's understanding of the natural origins of geopolitical societies, the need for government, the structure of law, and the idea that man is naturally a social and political animal—all concepts which Hooker used while defending the episcopalism of the Church of England. In considering and discussing the purpose of human existence and societies, as well as practical reason, Hooker drew upon Aristotle's *Nicomachean Ethics*. And in his discussion of the nature of change Hooker used ideas from Aristotle's *Physics*, while to support his argument for the existence of a universal, eternal law established by God Hooker cited Aristotle's argument in *Metaphysics* that God is the primary cause and principle of all things in creation (also called the *unmoved mover*, the *prime mover*, or *first cause*).

Hooker referred to Aristotle's *Rhetoric* to support his view on natural justice, specifically regarding the common idea of justice which all men naturally have. Aristotle's κοινὸς νόμος ("coinòs nómos", meaning, "common custom"—i.e., the general, universal, or natural law, the law of reason) in *Rhetoric*, Book I, Chapter Thirteen, corresponds to Hooker's "the general and perpetual voice of men" in Chapter Eight of *Concerning Laws*, and Aristotle's ἴδιος νόμος ("ídios nómos", meaning, "private custom"—i.e., a particular or positive law), also in *Rhetoric*, Book I, Chapter Thirteen, corresponds to Hooker's human or positive law in Chapter Ten of *Concerning Laws*. Hooker also contrasts the general and the particular in the following passage from his Chapter Ten:

> Where the generality, "Virtue is rewardable, and vice is punishable", is natural, the particular determination of the reward or punishment belongs to those who make the laws. Theft is naturally punishable, but the form of that punishment is positive, and it is lawful only if deliberative men include that punishment in the law.
>
> In laws, that which is *natural* universally binds, and that which is *positive* does not universally bind.

Hooker cites Aristotle's *On the Soul* when explaining that a rule to determine what is good is also the rule to determine what is evil.

Other Aristotelian concepts used by Hooker in *Concerning Laws* include teleology, the study of how everything has a natural purpose, and active and passive intellect, which are distinctions used to define reason. Hooker also drew from Aristotle (as well as from Plato) the idea that human beings are rational creatures capable of discovering truth by reasoning, apart from divine revelation.

Hooker draws upon an insight of Aristotle's successor, **Theophrastus**, from his book, *Metaphysics*: "Seeking logos of everything, they are taking logos away." Hooker words this as (paraphrased):

> They which seek a reason for all things do utterly overthrow reason.

When integrating classical reason with Christian doctrine, Hooker often alluded to the ideas of **Cicero**, especially the concept of "consensus gentium" ("agreement of all people"), which Hooker used to support arguments for natural law and collective reasoning.

And balancing ideas of **Seneca the Younger** with scripture and tradition, Hooker developed his own interpretations of ethics and ecclesiology.

Some of Hooker's other classical influences include the Ancient Greeks, **Hesiod** and **Homer** (each directly or indirectly influencing Hooker's use of characterizations from ancient myths), **Anaxagoras** (through fragments of his work preserved in the Sixth Century A.D. by Simplicius of Cilicia), **Sophocles**' play, *Antigone*, **Alcinous**' work, *The Handbook of Platonism*, the ***Corpus Hermeticum*** ascribed to Hermes Trismegistus, and **Hierocles of Alexandria**, a Fifth-Century A.D. Neoplatonist philosopher who discerned by reason that God works according to law. Classical Roman influences include **Virgil**'s epic, *Æneid*, and **Ancient Roman laws** (given as examples of legal principles). Classical Era Jewish influences include **Philo of Alexandria** (Philo Judæus) and **Flavius Josephus** (Yosef ben Mattityahu). All of these are cited by Hooker or his editors, as is *On the Consolation of Philosophy* by Anicius Manlius Severinus **Bœthius** (Saint Bœthius, 480 – 524 A.D.), the Christian martyr and philosopher who, while a classical author, is arguably a forerunner of the mediæval Roman Catholic Scholastics.

PATRISTIC INFLUENCE: THE CONSENSUS OF HISTORY AND THE AUTHORITY OF TRADITION

The adjective, "patristic", refers to the "patres", the early Church fathers. These men, who lived from the closing of the New Testament (ca. 100 A.D.) to the death of Isidore of Seville in the Western Europe (ca. 636 A.D.) or John of Damascus in the Near East (ca. 749 A.D.), were the intellectual and spiritual leaders of early Christianity who developed much of the theological vocabulary of Christianity (such as "the Trinity", "the Incarnation", and "original sin"), defended the Christian faith against Paganism and heresies, adhered to core Christian dogma (in most cases), were pious, and were recognized as authoritative by Christian clerics and scholars.

In *Concerning Laws*, Hooker does not use the early Church fathers to debate specific rituals (although he does do that in a later book); instead, he uses their ideas to validate natural law, the authority of reason, the authority of tradition, and the psychology of human desire in order to show that the Elizabethan Settlements are in continuity with the ancient Church.

In regards to the question of Church tradition being an authority, albeit a lesser authority than Scriptures, the early Church fathers argued for *universality* and *apostolicity*. If a practice was observed by all of the church congregations ("universality") founded by the apostles ("apostolicity"), then, according to the early Church fathers, the practice is valid. Hooker applied to his own time this patristic principle that the consensus of the faithful matters. Drawing upon the patristic reliance on universality and apostolicity, he argued that, if the early Church fathers thought a consensus which had lasted three centuries was authoritative, how much more authoritative is a consensus lasting fifteen centuries?

Hooker relies on this and other concepts discussed by the early Church fathers:

> Hooker cites an early Church father in Cappadocia, **Basil of Cæsarea** (Saint Basil the Great, 330 – 379 A.D.), to support

his argument that even angels and natural agents operate according to a law created by God, reinforcing the idea of the universality of law, the idea that *law* is universal for even angels and non-rational natural agents, not just something written in a book for humans.

Hooker relies on **Augustine of Hippo** (Saint Augustine, 354 – 430 A.D.) in arguments related to the following concepts.

- Augustine often argued that "custom has the force of law" when Scripture is silent. By his time, the church had existed for around three centuries, so he could and did appeal to "ancient custom". Augustine spoke of the "authority of the whole Church" as a valid guide for practice where Scripture is silent. Although Hooker does not quote or cite this specific phrase of Augustine's in *Concerning Laws*, his position is clearly informed by it.
- Teleology is the philosophical study or explanation of the intrinsic purposes of objects and actions instead of the causes or the extrinsic purposes,[324] or the theological doctrine of design and purpose in the material cosmos. From a teleological perspective, human desire for happiness serves a purpose. Hooker opens Chapter Five with the Augustinian premise (from *Confessions* and *City of God*) that all human action is driven by a longing for goodness and ultimate happiness, which can only be found in God. In Chapter Eleven Hooker culminates his Augustinian exploration of the human longing for God.

[324] An intrinsic purpose is a natural, inherent purpose, while an extrinsic purpose results from why a human or other agent designs or uses some object or performs some action. Examples of intrinsic purposes are a seed's purpose is to become a plant, a heart's function is to pump blood, Examples of extrinsic purposes include the time-telling function of a clock, the light-giving function of a desk lamp, the marking and writing functions of a pencil, the warming and possibly cooking functions of a campfire, and the soil-turning and -loosening of plowing (for crop residue and weed burying for decomposing into nutrients, aeration, better water absorption, and the disruption of habitats for pest control).

- Hooker's distinction between eternal law and natural law is influenced by *Contra Faustum* (also called, *Reply to Faustus the Manichæan*), in which Augustine defines the eternal law as the divine reason or the will of God.
- In Chapters Fourteen and Sixteen Hooker makes an Augustinian argument that, while Scripture is the supreme authority for salvation, the visible Church has authority to make laws for order, based upon the custom of faithful Christians. In Chapter Fourteen Hooker explains that Scripture is intended for "things necessary for salvation". This leaves room for other laws. In Chapter Sixteen Hooker defends the right of the Church to create human laws for the sake of "public order and comeliness".

Vincent of Lérins (died ca. 445 A.D.), a monk famous for the Vincentian Canon (a list of early Church fathers), formulated the definition of tradition most favored by Hooker, that tradition is the truth which has been believed "everywhere, always, and by all" ("ubique, semper, et ab omnibus"). Although he does not provide this exact quote in *Concerning Laws*, in Chapter Eight Hooker adapts this principle of universality to natural law, arguing that if all societies in all times share a common moral conviction (e.g., that God exists or parents must be honored), it must be a voice of nature which has been planted by God. When Hooker argues that universal consent is natural law ("The general and perpetual voice of men is as the sentence of God himself."), he is effectively taking Vincent's theological rule for the Church that universal consent is orthodoxy, and applying it to the whole human race.

Believed in Hooker's time to be Dionysius the Areopagite, a Christian convert mentioned in *Acts* 17, **Pseudo-Dionysius** (ca. Fifth – Sixth Centuries A.D.) was actually a Fifth-Century Syrian monk. His concept of a celestial hierarchy of angels (what we might refer to as a chain of command) was used by Hooker in his discussion or the law of angels, and the concept of a cosmic order in which the universe is ordered. This hierarchy, in which lower orders of angels obey higher orders, is essential to Hooker's argument that law is the force which binds the cosmos together.

Hooker's other patristic influences, although only cited in later books of *Of the Laws of Ecclesiastical Polity*, not in *Concerning Laws*, include **Lactantius** (240 – ca. 325), **Tertullian** (Saint Tertullian in the Church of England, ca. 155 – ca. 220–240 A.D.), **Origen of Alexandria** (ca. 185 – ca. 254 A.D.), **Cyprian of Carthage** (Saint Cyprian, ca. 200 – 258 A.D.), **Jerome of Strydon** (Saint Jerome, ca. 340–347 – 420 A.D., the translator of the Latin Vulgate version of the Bible), **Gregory of Nyssa** (Saint Gregory, c. 332 – c. 395 A.D.), and **Theodoret of Cyrus** (Saint Theodoret in the Eastern Orthodox Church, ca. 393–397 to ca. 457–458 A.D.).

Scholastic and Related Influences: The Categorization of Laws, and the Synthesis of Reason and Revelation

While classical philosophers provided Hooker the tools of reason and archetypes, and early Church fathers provided the spirit of Hooker's argument, mediæval Scholastics provided structure. The "scholastic" method of the mediæval Roman Catholic Church involved rigorous dialectic and precise definitions to synthesize Christian theology with Aristotelian philosophy. Hooker used this synthesis to defend the English Church against the Puritans and demonstrate that its ecclesiastical laws were reasonable and consistent with the laws of God.

To define law, Hooker used a structure modeled on that in *Summa Theologica* by **Thomas Aquinas** (1225 – 1274 A.D.):

eternal law:	God's mind and perfect, unchangeable reason
natural law:	the law of reason (the participation, discovered by reason, of the eternal law in rational agents)
divine law:	revealed law in Scripture
human law:	specific and changeable applications of natural law to society

And Hooker adopts Aquinas' definition that law is "an ordinance of reason for the common good, made by him who has care of the community." Hooker expands this to include God's own internal reason (eternal law). While he does not exactly quote Aquinas' principle, he uses different aspects of the principle:

> The rule of voluntary agents on earth is the sentence which reason gives concerning the goodness of those things which they are to do.
> —Chapter Two

> ...even presuming that man's depravity is little better than a wild beast, they nonetheless provide laws...so that his actions will not hinder the common good...
> —Chapter Ten

> The lawful power of making laws to command whole geopolitical societies of men belongs so properly to the whole society... Therefore, laws are not laws unless public approval has made them so.
> —Chapter Ten

> ...a law is properly that which reason defines to be good and which must be done...
> —Chapter Sixteen

Toward the end of Chapter Fourteen Hooker also relies on the Thomistic principle that grace perfects nature instead of destroying it.

> Therefore, there is in Scripture no defect but that any man, whatever place or calling he holds in the Church of God, may have by the light of his natural understanding so bettered that, the one being relieved by the other, there can lack no part of necessary instruction to any good work which God, Himself, requires, be it natural or supernatural, belonging simply to men as men or to men as they are united in whatever kind of society. Therefore, it suffices that nature and Scripture serve in such a way that they both jointly, and not either of them separately, are so complete that for everlasting happiness we do not need the knowledge of anything more than that with which these two may easily furnish our minds in every respect...

This allowed Hooker to refute the Puritan claim that human reason was so utterly corrupted by sin as to be useless, and instead argue that reason is a valid God-given tool which cooperates with Scripture.

In Chapter Two of *Concerning Laws* Richard Hooker generally favors *intellectualism*, associated with Thomas Aquinas, the doctrine that God's intellect precedes and is superior to His will, instead of *voluntarism*, associated with **John Duns Scotus** (ca. 1266 – 1308), the doctrine that God's will precedes and is superior to His intellect. Hooker argues that God's will is not arbitrary but is guided by His reason.

> They err, therefore, who think that, of the will of God to do this or that, there is no reason besides His will.

Aquinas' and Hooker's doctrine of intellectualism holds that God commands things because they are good—His will follows His reason. Scotus' doctrine of voluntarism (also associated with William of Ockham, and later the Calvinists) holds that things are good simply because God commands them—His will is supreme and arbitrary.

Even so, in Chapter Fourteen Hooker favorably cites Scotus as an authority to demonstrate that even the Scholastics believed that, while Scripture is sufficient for salvation, it is neither sufficient nor intended for every purpose. In support of the proposition that "all things necessary to salvation are necessarily set down in the holy Scriptures", Hooker cites the Book I Prologue of Scotus' *Ordinatio*:

> ...the supernatural knowledge necessary for a viator is sufficiently transmitted in Sacred Scripture...

Hooker cites this to establish a middle ground against Puritans.

affirming sufficiency:	Hooker agrees with Scotus that Scripture contains everything needed for supernatural salvation (the viator's journey—the journey of a pilgrim to Heaven).
limiting scope:	By defining the scope as "necessary for a viator" (necessary for the viator's/pilgrim's salvation), Hooker implicitly argues that Scripture is not intended as a rulebook for matters not directly related to salvation (like civil government or church rituals), which are left to reason and human law.

Hooker's use of this citation regarding the supernatural salvation of a viator (pilgrim) on the way to Heaven underscores that Scripture is the map for the journey or pilgrimage to Heaven, not necessarily the manual for building the temporal church structure.

Cardinal Cajetan (Tommaso de Vio, 1469–1534), an Italian who was the Master General of the entire Dominican Order, and the leading Thomist philosopher of the Renaissance, is perhaps best known to Protestants as the papal legate who examined Martin Luther at the Diet of Augsburg in 1518. Although he lived during the Renaissance, he wrote in the tradition of the mediæval Scholastics, and his philosophy and theology are in line with those of Thomas Aquinas. Indeed, in the Sixteenth-Century standard editions of Aquinas' *Summa Theologica*, Cajetan's extensive commentaries were often printed alongside the text. Hooker respected him for his intellectual rigor on the nature of law, and quoted him in Chapter Three of *Concerning Laws* to explain the inescapable nature of the eternal law: while men may rebel against the *precepts* of the eternal law, they cannot escape the *order* of the eternal law, for when they deviate from duty they immediately fall under the law's punishment. (Actions have consequences.)

Moses Maimonides (1138–1204) of Cairo, Egypt (where he was the Sultan's physician) was a mediæval Sephardic Jewish physician and a preeminent philosopher and Torah scholar. He is often simply referred to as, "Maimonides", and by Scholastics (who treated him as a representative Jewish voice) as, "Rabbi Moses" or "Moses Ægyptius" ("Moses the Egyptian"). He is also known as הנשר הגדול ("HaNesher HaGadol", "The Great Eagle") in the Jewish tradition (in recognition of his intellect and authority) and "Rambam" in Jewish scholarship, which is short for, "Rabbi Moshe ben Maimon" ("Rabbi Moses, son of Maimon"). Though a Jewish philosopher, his major philosophical work, *The Guide for the Perplexed*, influenced Thomas Aquinas and later Scholastics in their efforts to reconcile Aristotelian philosophy with revealed religion.

In Chapter Two of *Concerning Laws* Hooker cites Maimonides in support of the doctrine of intellectualism. Hooker argues that just because we do not always understand the reason for a divine law, we should not assume God commanded it without a purpose. In his 1593 edition, to support the doctrine of intellectualism and his assertion that...

> They err, therefore, who think that, of the will of God to do this or that, there is no reason besides His will.

...Hooker provided a translated citation from Maimonides, here paraphrased:

> As the theologians of the doctrine of divine will say who believe there is no reason, but only the will of God revealed to us... However, the truth is that all precepts of the law have a cause and are directed towards some end and use.

By citing a Jewish philosopher along with Pagan philosophers and Christian theologians, Hooker reinforces the universality of the law of reason and demonstrates that the wisest minds across different traditions agree that God is a rational Lawgiver, not an arbitrary tyrant—contrary to the Puritan insistence on arbitrary divine will.

LEGAL AND HUMANIST INFLUENCE: CONSTITUTIONAL AND LITERARY FOUNDATION

Living and preaching at the Temple Church, Hooker was deeply immersed in the English legal tradition. He drew heavily upon ancient jurists to argue that the power of the monarch is not absolute but is derived from and limited by the law. In Chapter Ten Hooker anchors his argument for the consent of the governed and the limitations of royal power in the works of **Henry de Bracton** (ca. 1210 – 1268 A.D.), *De Legibus et Consuetudinibus Angliæ* and the late-Thirteenth Century summary known as *Britton*. It is likely Hooker accessed these through the standard legal textbook of his own time, WILLIAM STAUNFORD, *The Pleas of the Crown* (1557). By citing Bracton, Hooker unites the law of reason with English Common Law, arguing that the English monarch's power is derived from the governed society.

As a Christian humanist Hooker shared a conviction with **Desiderius Erasmus** (1466 – 1536 A.D.) that wisdom could be found in Pagan antiquity as well as the Church fathers. Hooker frequently utilizes classical proverbs and maxims to illustrate moral points in *Concerning Laws*. Scholars suggest that Hooker often accessed these classical sayings not through the original texts, but through Erasmus' massive compendium, *Adagia* ("*Adages*"), a standard reference work for scholars in the Sixteenth Century, highlighting Hooker's participation in the broader European movement of reconciling classical education with Christian theology.

REFORMED PROTESTANT AND CONTEMPORARY INFLUENCE

While Richard Hooker opposed a presbyterian form of church government, he maintained a high respect for the intellect of **John Calvin** (1509 – 1564 A.D.), a French theologian who was a leading figure of the Protestant Reformation. In his preface to *Of the Laws of Ecclesiastical Polity*, Hooker referred to Calvin as "incomparably the wisest man that ever the French church did enjoy."

However, Calvin and his followers insisted that the Bible provides a specific, immutable form of government for the Church. Hooker disagreed, and in *Concerning Laws* he counters by distinguishing between the Way of salvation in Scripture and the external polity of the Church left to the law of reason and the discretion of the Church.

John Jewel (1522 – 1571 A.D.), Bishop of Salisbury and the author of the *Apologia Ecclesiæ Anglicanæ* ("*Apology of the Church of England*"), was Hooker's early mentor and patron, funding his education at Oxford and serving as a mentor. Hooker called Jewel, "the worthiest Divine that Christendom hath bred for the space of some hundreds of years."

Jewel provided the first systematic theological defense of the Church of England, arguing that England had returned to the purity of the early Church fathers. Hooker continued this legacy but pivoted the defense: while Jewel defended the English Church's doctrine against Roman Catholic critics, Hooker defended the English Church's laws and reason against the radical Protestant Reformers.

Hooker's later patron, the Archbishop of Canterbury, **John Whitgift** (1530 – 1604 A.D.), engaged in a long pamphlet war with the Puritan, Thomas Cartwright, regarding church polity and clerical vestments. While Whitgift fought the Puritans with intense disputes and authoritative opinion, he recognized that the English Church needed a philosophical defense and encouraged Hooker's work.

Hooker's philosophical distinction between "things necessary to salvation" (Chapter Fourteen) and "laws...made for men, societies, or churches because their circumstances are not permanent" and which "may later be entirely changed" (Chapter Fifteen) provided the intellectual bedrock for Whitgift's ecclesiastical policies.

CONCLUSION:
THE SYNTHESIS OF LAW AND REASON

Richard Hooker's contribution in *Concerning Laws* lies not in inventing new doctrines, but in his synthesis of the old. By using classical archetypes, the consensus of the early Church fathers, the intellectual rigor of the mediæval Scholastics, the constitutional principles of English law, and the insights of Christian Reformers, Hooker constructed a defense of the Church of England and the Elizabethan Settlements which was both rational and faithful. Against the Puritan insistence on Sola Scriptura for every aspect of life, Hooker restored the dignity of human reason as a gift from God. He demonstrated that to use reason in matters of ecclesiastical polity (church government) is not to abandon Scripture, but to obey the eternal law of God.

Finally, a practical result of Hooker's synthesis of concepts from Aristotle and Aquinas is a moral system of natural law which is rigid in principle but flexible in application.

BIBLIOGRAPHY

Adams, John. "A Dissertation on the Canon and the Feudal Law". *The Works of John Adams, Second President of the United States*. Edited by Charles Francis Adams. Volume 3. Boston: Little, Brown and Company, 1851.

Adams, Samuel. "Massachusetts Circular Letter" (February 11, 1768). *The Writings of Samuel Adams*. Edited by Harry Alonzo Cushing. Volume 1. New York: G. P. Putnam's Sons, 1904.

Alcinous. *Alcinoi in Platonicam philosophiam introductio*. Edited by John Fell. Oxford, England: Typis Lichfieldianis, 1667.

——. *The Handbook of Platonism*. Translated by John Dillon. Oxford: Clarendon Press, 1993.

Anonymous. *The Book of Filial Duty*. Translated by Ivan Chên. London: John Murray, 1908.

Aquinas, Saint Thomas. *Commentary on the Metaphysics of Aristotle*. Translated by John P. Rowan. Library of Living Catholic Thought. 2 volumes. Chicago: Henry Regnery Company, 1961.

——. *Summa Theologiae*. Translated by Fr. Laurence Shapcote, O.P., Volumes 13–22 of the *Latin/English Edition of the Works of St. Thomas Aquinas*. Edited and revised by The Aquinas Institute. Green Bay, Wisconsin: Aquinas Institute, Inc., 2012.

——. *The Summa Theologica*. Translated by the Fathers of the English Dominican Province. 22 volumes. London: R. & T. Washbourne, 1911–1925.

Aristotle. *Aristotle in 23 Volumes*. Edited and translated by H. Rackham. Cambridge, Massachusetts: Harvard University Press, 1934.

——. *Aristotle's Metaphysics*. Translated by W. D. Ross. 2 volumes. Oxford, England: Clarendon Press, 1924.

——. *The "Art" of Rhetoric.* Translated by J. H. Freese. Loeb Classical Library. Cambridge, Massachusetts: Harvard University Press, 1926.

——. *The Complete Works of Aristotle.* The Revised Oxford Translation. Edited by Jonathan Barnes. 2 volumes. Princeton: Princeton University Press, 1984.

——. *The Nicomachean Ethics of Aristotle.* Translated by F. H. Peters. 7th edition. London: Kegan Paul, Trench, Trübner & Co., Ltd., 1898.

——. *The Politics of Aristotle.* Translated by Benjamin Jowett. 2 volumes. Oxford, England: Clarendon Press, 1885.

——. *The Works of Aristotle.* Translated into English under the editorship of J. A. Smith and W. D. Ross. 12 volumes. Oxford, England: Clarendon Press, 1908–1952.

Augustine, Saint. *The City of God against the Pagans.* Edited and translated by R. W. Dyson. Cambridge, England: Cambridge University Press, 1998.

——. *Confessions.* Translated by Henry Chadwick. Oxford, England: Oxford University Press, 2009.

——. *De doctrina Christiana.* Translated by R. P. H. Green. Oxford, England: Clarendon Press, 1995.

——. *The Trinity.* Second Edition. Translated by Edmund Hill, O.P. Hyde Park, New York: New City Press, 2012.

——. *The Works of Aurelius Augustine, Bishop of Hippo. A New Translation.* Edited by Marcus Dods. 15 volumes. Edinburgh: T. & T. Clark, 1871–1876.

Bacon, Francis. *Novum Organum.* Edited by Joseph Devey. New York: P. F. Collier, 1902.

Basil of Caesarea, Saint. "The Treatise de Spiritu Sancto". Translated by Blomfield Jackson. A Select Library of the Nicene and Post-Nicene Fathers of the Christian Church. Second Series, Volume 8: *Basil: Letters and Select Works.* Edited by Philip Schaff and Henry Wace. Edinburgh: T. & T. Clark, 1894.

Bastiat, Frédéric. *Essays on Political Economy.* Translated by Patrick James Stirling. London: Provost & Co., 1874.

——. *Harmonies of Political Economy.* Translated by Patrick James Stirling. Edinburgh: Oliver and Boyd, 1880.

——. *The Law.* Translated by Dean Russell. Irvington-on-Hudson, New York: Foundation for Economic Education, 1950.

Baxter, Richard. *A Christian directory, or, A summ of practical theologie and cases of conscience directing Christians how to use their knowledge and faith, how to improve all helps and means, and to perform all duties, how to overcome temptations, and to escape or mortifie every sin.* London: Nevill Simmons, 1673.

Beveridge, William. *Synodikon sive Pandectae Canonum SS. Apostolorum, et Conciliorum ab Ecclesia Graeca receptorum.* 2 volumes. Oxford, England: Sheldonian Theatre, 1672.

Beza, Theodore. "An admonition to the Parliament". *Early English Books Online.* University of Michigan Library Digital Collections. https://name.umdl.umich.edu/A00718.0001.001 (accessed January 5, 2026).

Blackstone, William. *Commentaries on the Laws of England.* 4 volumes. Oxford, England: Clarendon Press, 1765–1769.

Boethius, Anicius Manlius Severinus. *On the Consolation of Philosophy.* Translated from the Latin by W. V. Cooper. London: J. M. Dent and Company, 1902.

Boswell, James. *Life of Samuel Johnson, LL.D.: Comprehending an Account of His Studies and Numerous Works, in Chronological Order; a Series of His Epistolary Correspondence and Conversations with Many Eminent Persons; and Various Original Pieces of His Composition, Never before Published; the Whole Exhibiting a View of Literature and Literary Men in Great-Britain, for Near Half a Century, during Which He Flourished; in Two Volumes.* London: Charles Dilly, 1791.

Bracton, Henry de. *De Legibus et Consuetudinibus Angliae.* Edited by George E. Woodbine. Translated by Samuel E. Thorne. 4 volumes. Cambridge, Massachusetts: Belknap Press of Harvard University Press, 1968–1977.

Burlamaqui, Jean-Jacques. *The Principles of Natural and Politic Law.* Translated by Thomas Nugent. 2 volumes. London: J. Nourse, 1763.

Burke, Edmund. *An Appeal from the New to the Old Whigs, in Consequence of Some Late Discussions in Parliament, Relative to the* Reflections on the French Revolution. Third Edition. London: J. Dodsley, 1791.

Cajetan, Cardinal (Tommaso de Vio). "Commentaria in Summam Theologicam". *Sancti Thomae Aquinatis Opera Omnia* (Leonine Edition). Volume 7. Rome: Ex Typographia Polyglotta, 1892.

The Catholic Church. *Breviarium Romanum, ex decreto Sacrosancti Concilii Tridentini restitutum, Pii V. Pont. Max. jussu editum.* Rome: Apud Paulum Manutium, 1568.

Cave, William. *Scriptorum Ecclesiasticorum Historia Literaria.* 2 volumes. Oxford, England: Sheldonian Theatre, 1740–1743.

The Church of England. *The booke of common prayer, and administration of the sacramentes and other rites and ceremonies in the Churche of England.* London: 1562.

——. *The Thirty-Nine Articles.* Church of England, 1562, adopted 1571.

——. *The Two Books of Homilies Appointed to Be Read in Churches.* Oxford, England: University Press, 1859.

Cicero, Marcus Tullius. *Cicero, De Officiis.* Translated by Walter Miller. London: William Heinemann, 1913.

——. *Cicero's Tusculan Disputations.* Translated by Andrew P. Peabody. Boston: Little, Brown, and Company, 1886.

——. *Ethical Writings of Cicero: De Officiis, De Sennectute, De Amicitia, and Scipio's Dream.* Translated by Andrew Preston Peabody. Boston: Little, Brown, and Company, 1887.

——. *The Treatises of M. T. Cicero.* Translated by C. D. Yonge and Francis Barham. Bohn's Classical Library. London: Henry G. Bohn, 1853.

Clement of Alexandria. "The Miscellanies; or Stromata", Book 1. Translated by William Wilson. *Ante-Nicene Christian Library: Translations of the Writings of the Fathers down to A.D. 325*, Volume 4: *Clement of Alexandria*, Volume 1. Edited by Alexander Roberts and James Donaldson. Edinburgh: T. & T. Clark, 1867.

——. "The Miscellanies; or Stromata", Books 2–8. Translated by William Wilson. *Ante-Nicene Christian Library: Translations of the Writings of the Fathers down to A.D. 325*, Volume 12: *Clement of Alexandria*, Volume 2. Edited by Alexander Roberts and James Donaldson. Edinburgh: T. & T. Clark, 1867.

——. "The Miscellanies; or Stromata", Books 2–8. Translated by William Wilson. *Ante-Nicene Christian Library: Translations of the Writings of the Fathers down to A.D. 325*, Volume 12: *Clement of Alexandria*, Volume 2. Edited by Alexander Roberts and James Donaldson. Edinburgh: T. & T. Clark, 1869.

Coleridge, Samuel Taylor. *I. On the Constitution of the Church and State according to the Idea of Each. II. Lay Sermons. I. The Statesman's Manual. II. "Blessed Are Ye That Sow beside All Waters".* Edited from the Author's Corrected Copies with Notes by Henry Nelson Coleridge. London: William Pickering, 1830.

Condorcet, Marquis de (Marie Jean Antoine Nicolas de Caritat). "On the Admission of Women to the Rights of Citizenship" (1790). In *Condorcet: Selected Writings*. Edited by Keith Michael Baker. Indianapolis: Bobbs-Merrill, 1976.

Confucius. *The Analects of Confucius*. Translated by William Edward Soothill. Yokohama: William Edward Soothill, 1910.

Cumberland, Richard. *A Treatise of the Laws of Nature*. Translated by John Maxwell. London: R. Phillips, 1727.

Cyprian of Carthage. *Sancti Caecilii Cypriani opera recognita & illustrata* ["*The Works of St. Cyprian, Recognized and Illustrated*"]. Edited by John Fell. Oxford, England: Sheldonian Theatre, 1682. Reprinted as Editio Tertia, Amsterdam: Joannes Ludovicus de Lorme, 1700.

d'Entrèves, Alessandro Passerin. *The Medieval contribution to political thought: Thomas Aquinas, Marsilius of Padua, Richard Hooker*. London: Oxford University Press, 1939.

——. *Riccardo Hooker: Contributo alla teoria e alla storia del diritto naturale*. Torino: Presso l'Istituto Giuridico della R. Università, 1932.

Dharmatrâta. *Udanavarga: A Collection of Verses from the Buddhist Canon; Being the Northern Buddhist Version of Dhammapada*. Translated from the Tibetan of the *Bkah-hgyur* by W. Woodville Rockhill. London: Trübner & Co., 1883.

Donne, John. The Variorum Edition of the *Poetry of John Donne*. Volume 7, Part 1, *The Holy Sonnets*. Gary R. Stringer, General Editor. Bloomington: Indiana University Press, 2005.

Duns Scotus, John. *The Ordinatio*. Translated by Peter Simpson. Based on the Vatican Critical Edition. Self-published, 2014. Available via the Logic Museum. https://www.logicmuseum.com/wiki/Authors/Duns_Scotus/Ordinatio (accessed January 8, 2026).

Eadmer Of Canterbury. *Eadmer's History of Recent Events in England*. Translated by Geoffrey Bosanquet. Chester Springs, Pennsylvania: Dufour Editions, Inc., 1964.

Erasmus, Desiderius. *Adages*. Translated by Margaret Mann Phillips, R. A. B. Mynors, et al. Volumes 31–36 of *Collected Works of Erasmus*. Toronto: University of Toronto Press, 1982–2006.

Federici, Michael. "Reassessing Russell Kirk: Three Critical Views". *The Imaginative Conservative*, April 27, 2014. Houston: Free Enterprise Institute, 2008.

France, National Constituent Assembly. "Declaration of the Rights of Man and of the Citizen, 1789". *The French Revolution and Human Rights: A Brief Documentary History*. Edited by Lynn Hunt. Boston: Bedford/St. Martin's, 1996.

Franklin, Benjamin. *Plain Truth: or, Serious Considerations on the Present State of the City of Philadelphia, and Province of Pennsylvania*. 1747.

Gladstone, William Ewart. "Early Religious Opinions, 1828–41", July 26, 1894. *The Prime Minister's Papers: W. E. Gladstone*. I: *Autobiographica*. Edited by John Brooke and Mary Sorensen. London: Her Majesty's Stationery Office, 1971.

Gratian. *Corpus Juris Canonici*. 2 volumes. Rome: In Aedibus Populi Romani, 1582.

Grotius, Hugo. *Commentary on the Law of Prize and Booty*. Translated by Gwladys L. Williams. Washington, District of Columbia: Carnegie Endowment for International Peace, 1950. Edited by Martine Julia van Ittersum. Indianapolis: Liberty Fund, 2006.

——. *The Free Sea, trans. Richard Hakluyt, with William Welwod's Critique and Grotius' Reply*. Edited by David Armitage. Indianapolis: Liberty Fund, 2004.

——. *The Rights of War and Peace*. Translated by Jean Barbeyrac. London: W. Innys and R. Manby, et al., 1738. Edited by Richard Tuck. 3 volumes. Indianapolis: Liberty Fund, 2005.

Hamilton, Alexander, James Madison, and John Jay. *The Federalist: A Collection of Essays, Written in Favour of the New Constitution*. 2 volumes. New York: J. and A. McLean, 1788.

Heraclitus of Ephesus. "Fragments". *Poēsis Philosophica. Poesis philosophica, vel saltem, reliquiae poesis philosophicae, Empedoclis, Parmenidis, Xenophanis, Cleanthis, Timonis, Epicharmi. Adiuncta sunt Orphei illius carmina qui a suis appellatus fuit ho theologos. Item, Heracliti et Democriti loci quidam, & eorum epistolae*. Edited by Henri Estienne (Henricus Stephanus). Geneva: Henri Estienne, 1573.

Hermes Trismegistus. *Thrice Greatest Hermes: Studies in Hellenistic Theosophy and Gnosis, Being a Translation of the Extant Sermons and Fragments of the Trismegistic Literature, with Prolegomena, Commentaries, and Notes*. Translated by G. R. S. Mead. 3 volumes. London: Theosophical Publishing Society, 1906.

Hesiod. *The Homeric Hymns and Homerica with an English Translation by Hugh G. Evelyn-White*. Cambridge, Massachusetts: Harvard University Press, 1914.

——. *Theogony*. Translated by Richard S. Caldwell. Newburyport, Massachusetts: Focus Information Group, Inc., 1987.

Hilary of Poitiers, Saint. "On the Trinity". Translated by E. W. Watson and L. Pullan. *A Select Library of the Nicene and Post-Nicene Fathers of the Christian Church*, Series 2, Volume 9: *St. Hilary of Poitiers, John of Damascus*. Edited by Philip Schaff and Henry Wace. New York: Christian Literature Company, 1899.

Hobbes, Thomas. "Leviathan, or The Matter, Form, and Power of a Commonwealth, Ecclesiastical and Civil". *The English Works of Thomas Hobbes of Malmesbury*. Edited by William Molesworth. Volume 3. London: John Bohn, 1839.

Hooker, Richard. *Folger Library Edition of The Works of Richard Hooker*. Edited by W. Speed Hill. Cambridge, Massachusetts: Belknap Press, 1977–1998.

——. *Of the Lawes of Ecclesiasticall Politie*. London: William Stansbye, 1622.

——. *The Works of that Learned and Judicious Divine Mr. Richard Hooker with an Account of His Life and Death by Isaac Walton*. Arranged by John Keble. Seventh edition revised by R. W. Church and F. Paget. Oxford, England: Clarendon Press, 1888.

Jefferson, Thomas. *The Virginia Statute for Religious Freedom* (1786).

Jewel, John. *Apologia Ecclesiæ Anglicanæ*. London: Reginald Wolfe, 1562.

——. *An Apologie or Answere in Defence of the Church of England*. Translated by Anne Bacon. London: Reginald Wolfe, 1564.

Johnson, Samuel. *A Dictionary of the English Language: in which The Words are deduced from their Originals, and Illustrated in their Different Significations by Examples from the best Writers. To which are prefixed, A History of the Language, and An English Grammar.* The Second Edition. London: Knapton et al., 1755.

Josephus, Flavius. *The Genuine Works of Flavius Josephus, the Jewish Historian*. Translated by William Whiston. 2 vols. London: Cambridge University Press, 1737.

Justinian I. *The Civil Law*. Translated by S. P. Scott. 17 volumes. Cincinnati: The Central Trust Company, 1932.

Kant, Immanuel. *Fundamental Principles of the Metaphysic of Morals*. Translated by Thomas Kingsmill Abbott. London: Longmans, Green, and Co., 1895.

Kirk, Russell. *The Conservative Mind: From Burke to Santayana*. Chicago: Henry Regnery Company, 1953.

——. *Enemies of the Permanent Things: Observations of Abnormality in Literature and Politics*. New Rochelle, New York: Arlington House, 1969.

——. *The Roots of American Order*. La Salle, Illinois: Open Court, 1974.

Knippenberg, Joseph M. "C. S. Lewis in a Secular Core: The Abolition of Man and a More Natural Science". *Public Discourse*, August 5, 2018. Princeton: Witherspoon Institute, 2018.

Lactantius (Lucius Caecilius Firmianus Lactantius). "The Divine Institutes". Translated by William Fletcher. *The Ante-Nicene Fathers*. Edited by Alexander Roberts, James Donaldson, and A. Cleveland Coxe. Volume 7. Buffalo: Christian Literature Publishing Co., 1886.

Laërtius, Diogenes. *The Lives and Opinions of Eminent Philosophers*. Translated by R. D. Hicks. New York: G. P. Putnam's Sons, 1925.

Lewis, C. S. *The Abolition of Man or Reflections on Education with Special Reference to the Teaching of English in the Upper Forms of Schools*. New York: HarperOne, 2017.

——. *The Discarded Image: An Introduction to Medieval and Renaissance Literature*. Cambridge, England: Cambridge University Press, 1964.

——. *English Literature in the Sixteenth Century, Excluding Drama*. Oxford, England: Clarendon Press, 1954.

——. "The Poison of Subjectivism". *Christian Reflections*. Grand Rapids: Wm. B. Eerdmans Publishing Co., 1967.

Littlejohn, W. Bradford. "The Founders' Founder". *The University Bookman*, April 21, 2014. Mecosta, Michigan: The Russell Kirk Center, 2014.

Locke, John. *Two Treatises of Government*. Third Edition. Edited by Peter Laslett. Cambridge, England: Cambridge University Press, 1988.

Maimonides, Moses (Moses ben Maimon). *Guide for the Perplexed*. Translated from the Original Arabic Text by M. Friedländer, Ph.D. Second Edition. London: George Routledge & Sons, 1904.

——. *Mishneh Torah*. Translated by Eliyahu Touger. Jerusalem: Moznaim Publications, ca. 1988 – ca. 2007.

Manu. *Manusmriti*. Translated by Georg Bühler. Oxford, England: Oxford University Press, 1886.

Mason, George. "First Draft of the Virginia Declaration of Rights" and "Final Draft of the Virginia Declaration of Rights". *The Papers of George Mason, 1725–1792*, Volume 1. edited by Robert A. Rutland. Chapel Hill: The University of North Carolina Press, 1970.

Massachusetts Constitutional Convention. *A constitution or frame of government, agreed upon by the delegates of the people of the State of Massachusetts-Bay*. Boston, State of Massachusetts-Bay: Printed by Benjamin Edes & Sons, 1780.

Mill, John Stuart. *On Liberty*. London: John W. Parker and Son, 1859.

Montesquieu, Baron de (Charles-Louis de Secondat). *The Spirit of Laws*. Translated by Thomas Nugent. 2 volumes. London: J. Nourse and P. Vaillant, 1750.

Orpheus, et al. *Orphica, Procli Hymni, Musaei carmen de Hero et Leandro, Callimachi hymni et epigrammata*. Leipzig: Karl Tauchnitz, 1829.

Paine, Thomas. *Rights of Man: Being an Answer to Mr. Burke's Attack on the French Revolution*. London: J. S. Jordan, 1791.

Philo of Alexandria. "Allegorical Interpretation". Translated by C. D. Yonge. *The Works of Philo Judaeus, the Contemporary of Josephus*. Vol. 1. London: Henry G. Bohn, 1854.

Plato. *The Dialogues of Plato*. Translated by Benjamin Jowett. Third Edition. 5 volumes. Oxford, England: Clarendon Press, 1892.

——. *Plato: Complete Works*. Edited by John M. Cooper. Indianapolis: Hackett Publishing Company, 1997.

——. *Plato in Twelve Volumes, with an English Translation*. Translated by H. N. Fowler, et al. 12 volumes. London: William Heinemann Ltd., 1913.

——. *The Republic of Plato: An Ideal Commonwealth*. Translated by Benjamin Jowett. New York: The Colonial Press, 1901.

Pope, Alexander. *The Dunciad. An Heroic Poem. In Three Books*. The Third Edition. London: A. Dodd, 1728.

——. *An Essay on Man. Moral Essays and Satires*. London: Cassell & Company, Limited, 1891.

Pseudo-Dionysius. *Pseudo-Dionysius: The Complete Works*. Translated by Colm Luibheid. Classics of Western Spirituality. New York: Paulist Press, 1987.

——. *Dionysius the Areopagite: On the Divine Names and the Mystical Theology*. Translated by C. E. Rolt. London: Society for Promoting Christian Knowledge, 1920.

Pufendorf, Samuel von. *Of the Law of Nature and Nations*. Translated by Basil Kennett. London: J. Walthoe, et al., 1729.

Pusey, E. B., et al., editors. *A Library of Fathers of the Holy Catholic Church, Anterior to the Division of the East and West.* 48 volumes. Oxford, England: John Henry Parker, 1838–1885.

Rousseau, Jean-Jacques. *The Social Contract and Discourses.* Translated with Introduction by G. D. H. Cole. London: J. M. Dent & Sons Ltd., 1913.

Sallust. "Conspiracy of Catiline". *Sallust, Florus, and Velleius Paterculus.* Translated by John Selby Watson. New York: Harper & Brothers. 1899.

Schaff, Philip, editor. *A Select Library of the Nicene and Post-Nicene Fathers of the Christian Church.* Series 1. 14 volumes. Buffalo: Christian Literature Publishing Co., 1886–1890.

Second Continental Congress. "The Declaration of Independence". *The Annals of America.* Volume 2, 1755–1783. Chicago: Encyclopædia Britannica, Inc., 1976.

Shelley, Mary. *Frankenstein: 1818 text.* Edited by Marilyn Butler. Oxford, England: Oxford University Press, 2009.

——. *Frankenstein.* Edited by M. K. Joseph. Oxford, England: Oxford University Press, 2008. (1831 text, which is more critical of the title character.)

Sidney, Algernon. *Discourses Concerning Government.* Edited by Thomas G. West. Indianapolis: Liberty Fund, 1996.

Sisson, C. J. *The Judicious Marriage of Mr. Hooker and the Birth of The Laws of Ecclesiastical Polity.* Cambridge, England: Cambridge University Press, 1940.

Sophocles. "Antigone". Translated by F. Storr. *Sophocles with an English Translation.* 2 volumes. Loeb Classical Library. London: William Heinemann, 1912.

Spenser, Edmund. *The Faerie Queene.* London: William Ponsonbie, 1590.

——. "Fæirie Queene". *The Complete Works in Verse and Prose of Edmund Spenser.* Edited by Alexander B. Grosart. London: Grosart, 1882.

——. "Mutabilitie Cantos". (See *Spenser's Faerie Queene, a Poem in Six Books; with the Fragment Mutabilitie*, below.)

——. *The Poetical Works of Edmund Spenser.* Edited by J.C. Smith and Ernest de Sélincourt. London: Oxford University Press, 1912.

——. *Spenser's Faerie Queene, a Poem in Six Books; with the Fragment Mutabilitie.* Edited by Thomas J. Wise. Pictured by Walter Crane. 6 volumes. London: George Allen, 1895–1897.

Staunford, William. *Les Plees del Coron.* London: Richard Tottel, 1557.

Strabo. *The Geography of Strabo*. Translated by H. L. Jones. Cambridge, Massachusetts: Harvard University Press, 1917.

Swift, Jonathan. *A Tale of a Tub and The History of Martin*. Edited by Henry Morley. London: George Routledge and Sons, 1889.

Tertullian (Quintus Septimius Florens Tertullianus). *Tertullian, Volume 1, Apologetic and Practical Treatises.* Translated by the C. Dodgson. Oxford, England: John Henry Parker, 1842.

Theodoret of Cyrus. *A Cure of Pagan Maladies*. Translated by T. Halton. Ancient Christian Writers 67. New York: The Newman Press, 2013.

——. *Thérapeutique des maladies helléniques.* Translated by P. Canivet. 2 vols. Paris: Éditions du Cerf, 1958. [Latin text and French translation.]

Theophrastus of Eresus. *Metaphysics*. Translated by W. D. Ross and F. H. Fobes. Oxford, England: Clarendon Press, 1929.

U.S. Constitution. *The Constitution of the United States*. 1787.

Vattel, Emer de. *The Law of Nations; or, Principles of the Law of Nature, Applied to the Conduct and Affairs of Nations and Sovereigns*. London: G. G. and J. Robinson, 1797.

Virgil. *The Æneid of Virgil.* Translated by Theodore C. Williams. Boston: Houghton Mifflin Company, 1910.

Voak, Nigel. *Richard Hooker and Reformed Theology: A Study of Reason, Will, and Grace*. Oxford, England: Oxford University Press, 2003.

Voegelin, Eric. *The New Science of Politics, An Introduction*. Chicago: The University of Chicago Press, 1952.

Warren, Joseph. "Boston Massacre Oration" (March 6, 1775). *Orations Delivered at the Request of the Inhabitants of the Town of Boston*. Boston: Peter Edes, 1785.

——. "The Suffolk Resolves". *Journals of the Continental Congress, 1774–1789*. Volume 1. Washington, D.C.: Government Printing Office, 1904.

Webster, Noah. *An American dictionary of the English language*. New York: S. Converse, 1828.

——. *An Examination into the Leading Principles of the Federal Constitution.* Philadelphia: Prichard & Hall, 1787.

Whittaker, William. *Controversies against Bellarmine*. Geneva, 1610.

Wilson, James. "Of the General Principles of Law and Obligation". *Collected Works of James Wilson*. Edited by Mark David Hall and Kermit L. Hall. Indianapolis: Liberty Fund, 2007.

Wollstonecraft, Mary. *A Vindication of the Rights of Men*. London: J. Johnson, 1790.

——. *A Vindication of the Rights of Woman*. London: J. Johnson, 1792.

WEBSITES:

Bible Gateway, part of HarperCollins Christian Publishing, has several searchable online versions of the Bible (in multiple languages) and study tools. Of the Bible websites listed here, this site has the most versions.

https://www.biblegateway.com

Blue Letter Bible, a website with several Bible translations, word-study tools, and other references, and a useful search engine. Although not as many versions are offered as the Bible Gateway site, for the several versions offered, and for general Bible study, this is the most useful site.

https://www.blueletterbible.org

Christian Classics Ethereal Library, is a website with several classics of Christian literature, including Richard Hooker's *A Learned Discourse of Justification, Works, and how the Foundation of Faith is Overthrown.*

https://www.ccel.org

Early English Books Online Collections, a sometimes difficult to navigate University of Michigan Library website including works such as the 1572 *An admonition to the Parliament.*

https://quod.lib.umich.edu/e/eebogroup/

Internet Archive, texts and other files which have been archived for free use.

https://archive.org

The Library of Economics and Liberty (Econlib), a free collection of books and other resources for students, teachers, researchers, and the general public.

https://www.econlib.org

λογος, Logos Virtual Library, a free online collection of public domain philosophical, theological, and literary texts.

https://www.logoslibrary.org

Online Library of Liberty (OLL), a free "extensive digital library of scholarly works focused on individual liberty and free markets."

https://oll.libertyfund.org

Perseus Digital Library, classical texts and translations available online, with word-study tools and other aids.

https://www.perseus.tufts.edu

Textus Receptus Bibles, a website with online transcriptions of Ancient Greek Textus Receptus (Latin for, "Received Text") Biblical manuscripts, which are a series of Byzantine Greek Biblical texts. The website also has several online English-language Bibles with New Testaments translated from the Textus Receptus, and Old Testaments translated from the Ancient Hebrew and Aramaic Masoretic text. Among the included versions are the 1534 Tyndale Bible, the 1535 Coverdale Bible, the 1537 Matthew's Bible, the 1539 Great Bible, the 1560 and 1599 Geneva Bible, the 1568 Bishops' Bible, and the 1611 King James Version (also called the Authorized Version). Some historical non-Textus Receptus Bibles (such as the Wycliffe Bible) and manuscripts are also available. Although more specialized than the Bible Gateway or Blue Letter Bible sites, this site is the only one of the three offering certain Sixteenth Century versions.

https://www.textusreceptusbibles.com

Index

About the Author

Richard Hooker (1554–1600) was an English priest and theologian. Known as "the Judicious Hooker" for his moderate and reasoned approach, his work defended the Elizabethan Settlement from Puritan critics, and established the theological backbone of Anglicanism. His political thought heavily influenced John Locke and the development of English constitutionalism.

About the Editor

Ret Miles, a retired logistician and former teacher who enjoyed a successful career in international trade and a longtime involvement in local and state politics, is now an independent scholar and the founder of Pilos Press. He is also a musician, photographer, and fly fisherman. He lives in Rogers, Arkansas.

www.ingramcontent.com/pod-product-compliance
Lightning Source LLC
LaVergne TN
LVHW100525110826
845146LV00002B/781

* 9 7 9 8 2 3 4 0 6 7 4 9 4 *